E-LEARNING AND KNOWLEDGE SHARING

E-LEARNING AND KNOWLEDGE SHARING
TOOLS AND APPLICATIONS

Alexis Ma
Fu Wang

Kruger Brentt
Publishers
2023

Kruger Brentt Publishers UK. LTD.
Company Number 9728962

Regd. Office: 68 St Margarets Road, Edgware, Middlesex HA8 9UU

ISBN: 9781787150744

Disclaimer:

Every possible effort has been made to ensure that the information contained in this book is accurate at the time of going to press, and the publisher and author cannot accept responsibility for any errors or omissions, however caused. No responsibility for loss or damage occasioned to any person acting, or refraining from action, as a result of the material in this publication can be accepted by the editor, the publisher or the author. The Publisher is not associated with any product or vendor mentioned in the book. The contents of this work are intended to further general scientific research, understanding and discussion only. Readers should consult with a specialist where appropriate.

Every effort has been made to trace the owners of copyright material used in this book, if any. The author and the publisher will be grateful for any omission brought to their notice for acknowledgement in the future editions of the book.

For information on all our publications visit our website at http://krugerbrentt.com/

PREFACE

Knowledge sharing encompasses both making information available to those who actively seek it within your organization and directly communicating the appropriate knowledge to a user who could potentially apply it for the benefit of your business. Team leaders should regularly encourage, and possibly incentivize, knowledge sharing to make it part of a culture of learning within their organization. To facilitate the dissemination of knowledge and support learning system, an organisation must have a system capable of accommodating all the needs of the organisation in terms of knowledge dissemination with high-cost efficiency and ease of access by its employees. The main purpose of the knowledge-management system is to increase the competencies of employees in the organisation as part of human-resource management. The rapid development of Information Technology (IT) has created a new culture for everyone around the world. The integration of Information Technology into the world of business has made a huge impact. By leveraging the power of Information Technology,enterprise knowledge-management systems can be used more efficiently and consistently.

One of the products of Information-Technology integration into the business world is electronic learning, or fondly known as e-learning. Today, e-learning begins to pull the attention of many parties,be they academia, professionals, corporates, or industries. E-learning is a form of conventional learning that is poured into digital format and presented through Information Technology. In the world of business and industry, e-learning is valued to assist processes in improving employee competencies or human resources. E-learning is a powerful tool that has been increasingly used to power the knowledge-management system. With the advent of e-learning, the process of accessing recorded information can be done from a place even far away from a workplace. Hence, e-learning not only serves as a facilitator but also makes it easier for the employees of a company to continue learning from their or others' past experiences that have been recorded, documented, and stored in a repository. With the right e-learning system in place, an organisation or a company can quickly increase its efficiency in replicating knowledge that has been successfully acquired and learned to one side across the whole body of the organisation or company. This rapid replication is crucial to ensure that the company does not repeat the same mistake(s) over and over again in learning what is necessary and that knowledge information is not isolated to only individual parts of the organisation or company.

The present book contains ten chapters covering all related disciplines. These chapters include introduction to knowledge sharing, knowledge sharing methods, knowledge management, collective intelligence and transfer of learning, information and communications technology and e-learning, e-learning theory, online teaching and learning, online teaching techniques, online learning in educational technology and infrastructure support for online programs and the impact of e-learning during covid-19 pandemic.

It shows how to build the enabling environment and develop the skills needed to capture and share knowledge gained from operational experiences to improve performance and scale up successes.

This book will be of interest to researchers' academics, practitioners, and students in the fields of human resource management, leadership,and practitioners working in organization science and business administration. Also, consultants and organizations at large will find the book useful as it will provide them with insights into how other organizations manage and facilitate knowledge sharing and how potential failures can be prevented.

We are grateful to all those persons as well as various books, manuals, periodicals, magazines, journals etc. that helped in the preparation of this book. In spite of the best efforts, it is possible that some errors may have occurred into the compilation and editing of the book. Further queries, constructive suggestions and criticisms for the improvement of the book are always welcome and shall be thankfully acknowledged.

Alexis Ma

Fu Wang

CONTENTS

CHAPTER 1
KNOWLEDGE SHARING: AN INTRODUCTION

1.1 INTRODUCTION

Knowledge sharing is an activity through which knowledge is exchanged among people, friends, peers, families, communities, or within or between organizations. It bridges the individual and organizational knowledge, improving the absorptive and innovation capacity and thus leading to sustained competitive advantage of companies as well as individuals. Knowledge sharing is part of the Knowledge management process.

Apart from traditional face-to-face knowledge sharing, social media is a good tool because it is convenient, efficient, and widely used. Organizations have recognized that knowledge constitutes a valuable intangible asset for creating and sustaining competitive advantages. However, technology constitutes only one of the many factors that affect the sharing of knowledge in organizations, such as organizational culture, trust, and incentives. The sharing of knowledge constitutes a major challenge in the field of knowledge management because some employees tend to resist sharing their knowledge with the rest of the organization.

In the digital world, websites and mobile applications enable knowledge or talent sharing between individuals and/or within teams. The individuals can easily reach the people who want to learn and share their talent to get rewarded.

1.2 KNOWLEDGE SHARING

Deb works in accounting for a large office supply company with many locations and warehouses across the United States. She has been there for 20 years and just announced that she is leaving the company at the end of this year. Now management is scrambling trying to figure out what knowledge Deb has that might need to be passed along to a new employee.

One of the tasks that only Deb knows is the payroll system. Yikes! Without Deb's knowledge, it will be far more complicated to get everyone paid on time. What the company needs to follow is a knowledge-sharing system to transfer Deb's understanding to future workers.

Knowledge sharing is the act of exchanging information or understanding between individuals, teams, communities, or organizations. Knowledge may be explicit. Sharing knowledge is an intentional process that not only bolsters an individual's understanding but helps create or enhance an archive of accessible knowledge for others.

The concept of knowledge sharing is important because it helps individuals and businesses be more agile and adaptable in the face of change and helps ensure continued growth and survival.

Think about it this way: If you're the only person at work who understands the company's filing system, and something happens to you (for example, you become ill, lose your job, or relocate), who will have knowledge of the filing system? The answer is no one, unless you've engaged in the process of knowledge sharing to pass along what you know.

Knowledge sharing can be achieved in a number of ways, from writing a book or manual to delivering a presentation to having an informal chat during lunch or offering mentoring or job shadowing opportunities.

Knowledge sharing refers to the process of exchanging information between people, teams, or organizations. This knowledge may be explicit, which comes from documents or procedures, or tacit, meaning it was developed from experience. Sharing knowledge has benefits for the sharer as well as the recipient. It can create understanding, a feeling of importance, and even help employees grow their leadership skills.

Benefits for businesses that encourage knowledge sharing include becoming more agile and adaptable. Employees engaging in knowledge sharing can develop more effective and streamlined procedures and processes. It can also help cultivate a more loyal and productive workforce.

Knowledge sharing is related to knowledge transfer. But knowledge transfer is specifically about how to work out a plan to get critical know-how from employees who are leaving to those who are staying. Organizations should always have a plan for keeping tacit knowledge within their company.

1.2.1 Why is Knowledge Sharing Important in the Workplace?

The global pandemic caused waves of disruption to organizations, economies and the world. To meet the challenges, organizations will need to adjust, and it's not all about developing remote or hybrid workplaces.

Companies will need to focus more on internal development and mobility. According to the LinkedIn report, internal hiring has increased by 19 percent since 2019. Moreover, employees who are given an opportunity for internal mobility stay twice as long as those who aren't promoted. When you make a new hire, it's wise to provide knowledge sharing opportunities to equip them for internal job opportunities. Allowing your new hire the chance to share their knowledge and learn from others creates connection as well as a skilled workforce.

Your younger workers are hyper-focused on learning and growth opportunities. Gen Z employees watch 50 percent more learning content than your other employees. Seventy-six of them believe learning is the key to success. To prepare future leaders in your organization, give them a chance to learn from more experienced employees and senior leadership.

Knowledge sharing also improves your remote teams' performance and wellbeing. Many employees who work from home struggle with collaboration and communication with team members. It's one of the top problems identified in Buffer's State of Remote Work report. Twenty percent of those surveyed identified collaboration as a significant issue for remote work. You can overcome collaboration and communication challenges by encouraging more knowledge sharing among employees and remote teams.

1.2.2 Breaking Down Silos and Democratizing Tacit Know-How

Research has found that knowledge sharing benefits everyone, from your employees to your executives.

One of the key benefits of encouraging knowledge sharing is democratizing learning. By getting subject matter experts together with other employees, you can increase the collective knowledge of the organization. And the collective knowledge will be of best practices and the right way to do things. This is a great way for organizations to get everyone on the same page. And this will reflect in your employees' attitudes at work and towards your company

One study found that 94 percent of employees have said they'll stay at a company longer if there is a learning opportunity. This rings particularly true for younger employees, with 27 percent of Gen Z or Millennials saying they would leave a job if there were no opportunities to learn.

1.2.3 Which Employees Need to Participate in Knowledge Sharing?

Before embarking on knowledge sharing opportunities for your employees, you need to be clear on what they have to gain. It all begins with understanding who will be involved.

- New hires need knowledge sharing to ramp up in their new role. One-on-one mentorships and peer mentoring are two great ways to help your new hire fit in, learn the ropes, and build connections. Knowledge sharing is key for a great onboarding experience.
- Future leaders don't often get the training they need to be great leaders. Knowledge sharing and mentorship can set them up for success. They'll learn vital skills and

tips to help them meet the challenges they'll face. It is also a crucial ingredient to any succession plan.

- Remote workers face challenges around feeling a part of a team and having informal learning opportunities. Connecting with other team members or leaders through knowledge sharing activities can fill this gap. An MIT article encourages organizations to institute water cooler calls "that can reveal experiences and ideas that otherwise would have remained unexpressed — and keep team members connected on a personal level."

1.3 BENEFITS OF KNOWLEDGE SHARING

Employers and employees have a lot to gain from knowledge sharing. Here are some of the main advantages of encouraging it in your organization.

1.3.1 Increase Employee Engagement

Research has shown that employees love to learn. Offering access to learning opportunities is one of the top ways to increase employee engagement. This is particularly true for younger workers who demonstrate a commitment to learning.

1.3.2 Aids Employee Learning and Development

Employees who connect through social learning activities are more successful in retaining what's learned. Essentially, we learn better when we're together. And information that is retained is there to be used. In other words, when your employees are able to remember what they've learned and use it, you'll get a more efficient and effective workplace. Yet, many organizations still insist on using solitary study methods like coursework, quizzes, surveys, etc. Social learning is the key that can unlock a more skilled workforce.

1.3.3 Builds a Learning Culture

Learning cultures make employee development a priority. They demonstrate their commitment to employee growth and learning by providing growth opportunities through mentoring, training classes, and knowledge sharing. Organizations that build a learning culture encourage employees to spend time on development and knowledge sharing activities. That's because they understand the more employees learn, the more productive and effective they are.

1.3.4 Retain Critical Tacit Knowledge

Tacit knowledge is information that is learned through experience and not through printed documentation, such as policies or procedures. However, it is no less valuable to an organization. It can even be used to redefine processes or procedures in some cases. Yet, unless knowledge sharing opportunities are present in an organization, tacit knowledge can be lost when those with that critical information leave the company.

1.4 EXAMPLES OF WORKPLACES THAT ENCOURAGE KNOWLEDGE SHARING

Workplaces that encourage knowledge sharing have done so in different ways, and each has unlocked employee development that has been a boon to their businesses. Here are just two examples of organizations that have encouraged knowledge sharing successfully.

Cooley is a global law firm with 1,500 lawyers, and because their legal work is complicated, they need to have the most talented minds in play. They leverage knowledge sharing by pairing up new lawyers with more experienced ones. Doing this has made their onboarding faster and more effective, bringing new hires up to speed quickly. The experience allows mentors to provide insight that helps younger lawyers learn what they need to do at a much faster rate than on-the-job learning or formal training program. It's one of the reasons why 95 percent of their employees say it is a great place to work.

Cruise Automation, a self-driving car manufacturer, needs to share niche engineering knowledge about autonomous vehicles. To democratize this knowledge and encourage all engineers to come up with innovative ideas, they pair up their engineering team for monthly meetings to discuss ideas. They've found that this knowledge sharing opportunity also prepares employees for internal promotion. Participants of their program noted it allowed employees of all levels and skills to learn from each other.

1.4.1 Knowledge Sharing as Flow or Transfer

Although knowledge is commonly treated as an object, Dave Snowden has argued it is more appropriate to teach it as both a flow and a thing. Knowledge as a flow can be related to the concept of tacit knowledge. While the difficulty of sharing knowledge is in transferring knowledge from one entity to another, it may prove profitable for organizations to acknowledge the difficulties of knowledge transfer and adopt new knowledge management strategies accordingly.

1.4.2 Knowledge Sharing Levels

Knowledge can be shared in different ways and levels. The following segmentation sheds light on the essence of sharing.

Explicit Knowledge

Explicit knowledge sharing occurs when explicit knowledge is made available to be shared between entities. Explicit knowledge sharing can happen successfully when the following criteria are met:

- **Articulation:** the knowledge provider can describe the information.
- **Awareness:** the recipient must be aware that knowledge is available.
- **Access:** the knowledge recipient can access the knowledge provider.

- **Guidance:** the body of knowledge must be defined and differentiated into different topics or domains so as to avoid information overload, and to provide easy access to appropriate material. Knowledge managers are often considered key figures in the creation of an effective knowledge sharing system.
- **Completeness:** the holistic approach to knowledge sharing in the form of both centrally managed and self-published knowledge.

Tacit Knowledge

Tacit knowledge sharing occurs through different types of socialization. Although tacit knowledge is difficult to identify and codify, relevant factors that influence tacit knowledge sharing include:

- Informal networks such as daily interactions between people within a defined environment (work, school, home, etc.). These networks span hierarchies and functions.
- The provision of space where people can engage in unstructured or unmonitored discussions, thereby fostering informal networks.
- Unstructured, less-structured or experimental work practices that encourage creative problem solving, and the development of social networks.
- An organizational culture which is based on trust. This encourages employees to share their knowledge.
- Employees' strong organizational commitment and loyalty to their employers supports tacit knowledge sharing.

Embedded Knowledge

Embedded knowledge sharing occurs when knowledge is shared through clearly delineated products, processes, routines, etc. This knowledge can be shared in different ways, such as:

- Scenario planning and debriefing: providing a structured space to create possible scenarios, followed by a discussion of what happened, and how it could have been different.
- Management training.
- Knowledge transfer: deliberately integrating systems, processes, routines, etc., to combine and share relevant knowledge.

1.5 CONNECTION TO ADJACENT DISCIPLINES

1.5.1 Information Technology Systems

Information technology (IT) systems are common tools that help facilitate knowledge sharing and knowledge management. The main role of IT systems is to help people share knowledge through common platforms and electronic storage to help make access simpler, encouraging economic reuse of knowledge. IT systems can provide codification, personalization, electronic repositories for information and can help people locate each other to communicate directly. With appropriate training and education, IT systems can make it easier for organizations to acquire, store or disseminate knowledge. For instance, the implementation of discussion forums for enabling meaningful conversation, knowledge acquisition and peer engagement can pave the way for a knowledge-sharing culture as opposed to a knowledge-hoarding culture.

1.5.2 Economic Theory

In economic theory, knowledge sharing has been studied in the field of industrial organization and in the field of contract theory. In industrial organization, Bhattacharya, Glazer, and Sappington (1992) have emphasized the importance of knowledge sharing in research joint ventures in a context of imperfect competition. In the theory of incomplete contracts, Rosenkranz and Schmitz (1999, 2003) have used the Grossman-Hart-Moore property rights approach to study how knowledge sharing is affected by the underlying ownership structure.

1.6 IMPORTANCE TO ORGANIZATIONS

Knowledge is transferred in organizations whether it is a managed process or not since everyday knowledge transfer is a key part of organizational life. However, finding the best expert to share their knowledge in a specific matter could be hard, especially in larger organizations. Therefore, a structured strategy for knowledge transfer is required for the organization to thrive. Larger companies have a higher tendency to invest more on knowledge management processes, although competitive benefits are gained regardless of organization size.

In an organizational context, tacit knowledge refers to a kind of knowledge that human beings develop by the experience they gain over years. At present the employees' experience and knowledge can be seen as the most important and most valuable source that organizations have to protect. Knowledge constitutes a valuable, intangible asset for creating and sustaining competitive advantages within organizations. Several factors affect knowledge sharing in organizations, such as organizational culture, trust, incentives, and technology. In an organization, five distinct conditions of the organizational culture have a positive effect on knowledge-sharing: communication and coordination between groups, trust, top management support, the reward system, and openness. Concerning the communication and coordination between groups condition, the organizations that are centralized with a bureaucratic management style can hinder the creation of new knowledge whereas a flexible decentralized organizational structure encourages knowledge-sharing. Also, internationalization is crucial for compliance or conformity. Dalkir (2005) says that internationalization is believing that the "behavior dictated by the norm truly the right and proper way to behave". If the norm is to communicate and collaborate between teams, it will be much easier for members of the group to internalize these values and act accordingly. Knowledge sharing activities are commonly supported by knowledge management systems, a form of Information Technology (IT) that facilitates and organizes information within a company or organization.

1.6.1 Challenges

Knowledge sharing can sometimes constitute a major challenge in the field of knowledge management.

The difficulty of knowledge sharing resides in the transference of knowledge from one entity to another. Some employees and team leaders tend to resist sharing their knowledge because of the notion that knowledge is property; ownership, therefore, it becomes very important. Leaders and supervisors tend to hoard information in order to demonstrate power and supremacy over their employees.

In order to counteract this, individuals must be reassured that they will receive some type of incentive for what they create. Supervisors and managers have a key role in this – they need to create a work culture which encourages employees to share their knowledge. However, Dalkir (2005) demonstrated that individuals are most commonly rewarded for what they know, not what they share. Negative consequences, such as isolation and resistance to ideas, occur when knowledge sharing is impeded.

Sometimes the problem is that a part of an employee's knowledge can be subconscious and therefore it may be difficult to share information. To promote knowledge sharing and remove knowledge sharing obstacles, the organizational culture of an entity should encourage discovery and innovation. Members who trust each other are willing to exchange knowledge and at the same time want to embrace knowledge from other members as well. National culture is also one of the common barriers of knowledge sharing because culture has a huge effect on how people are tend to share knowledge between each other. In some cultures, people share everything, in other cultures people share when asked, and in some cultures, people don't share even if it would help to achieve common goals.

The political scientist Hélène Hatzfeld has pointed out that people who have knowledge can be reluctant to share that knowledge when they are not confident in their own expertise, so to facilitate knowledge sharing, structures can be designed to elevate everyone to the status of a potential expert and make them more comfortable contributing; one example of such a system, to which Hatzfeld attributes mixed success in this regard, is Wikipedia.

Pinho et al. (2012) have made comprehensive literature review of knowledge management barriers and facilitators. Barriers are considered to be obstacles that hinder knowledge acquisition, creation, sharing and transfer in and between organizations based on individual, socio-organizational or technological reasons. Respectively facilitators are seen as enabling factors that improve, stimulate or promote the flow of knowledge. According to Maier et al. (2002) understanding of the process supporting knowledge management enables further consideration of the obstacles and facilitating factors.

1.7 TYPICAL STEPS IN KNOWLEDGE MANAGEMENT PROCESSES

- **Discovery:** The process of knowledge management begins with discovery. Knowledge discovery is the process of extracting information from data that can be useful to your organization's strategy, operations, communication, and relationship development. Using data mining to identify patterns, trends, or correlations within large sets of transactional or customer relationship data is an example of discovery.
- **Capture:** Knowledge capture is acquiring the knowledge your organization already possesses—within individual employees, teams, documents, or processes—as well as external knowledge, so it can be documented, communicated, and shared to the benefit of your business. Conducting an audit of your existing documentation and encouraging content creation in knowledge areas where you have gaps are key to capturing knowledge.
- **Organization:** Knowledge organization means describing, classifying, categorizing, and indexing information so it can be easily retrieved, navigated, reused, and shared among employees, teams, and other critical users. The right knowledge management system can help you sort and segment knowledge so information is readily accessible by the people who need it most.
- **Assessment:** In order for knowledge to drive beneficial business decisions, spark collaboration and innovation, and improve internal and external processes, you must ensure that knowledge is verified and validated. That means integrating processes that ensure any information your organization intends to apply is accurate, complete, consistent, and up to date. Automatic validation features within your knowledge management system, as well as regular reviews by your internal experts, are critical.
- **Sharing**: Knowledge sharing encompasses both making knowledge available to those who actively seek it within your organization and directly communicating appropriate knowledge to a user who could potentially apply it for the benefit of your business. Team leaders should regularly encourage, and possibly incentivize, knowledge sharing.
- **Reuse/application**: Knowledge reuse or application is when an individual or team can take captured knowledge and apply that knowledge to enhance efficiency, improve business operations, complete a strategic task, communicate more effectively with colleagues or customers, etc. A documented lesson learned

from one employee's complex customer interaction may streamline the process for a colleague in a similar situation, for example.

- **Creation:** Knowledge creation is when individuals or teams within your organization add what they've learned—through practice, process navigation, internal and external interactions, independent research, and other experiences—to the organization's collective knowledge. That individual knowledge can then be shared, reused, and applied, as well as expanded upon by future knowledge seekers. Establishing content creation guidelines and regularly communicating the value of – and praising/rewarding the completion of—new relevant content can help you establish a culture of knowledge creation among your teams.

1.7.1 Explicit Knowledge and Knowledge Sharing

Successful explicit knowledge sharing is determined by the following criteria:

- **Articulation:** The ability of the user to define what he needs.
- **Awareness:** Awareness of the knowledge available. The provider is encouraged to make use of directories, maps, corporate yellow pages, etc.
- **Access:** Access to the knowledge.
- **Guidance:** Knowledge managers are often considered key in the build-up of a knowledge sharing system. They must help define the areas of expertise of the members of the firm, guide their contributions, assist users, and be responsible for the language used in publications and other communication material. This is so as to avoid an information/knowledge overload.
- **Completeness:** Access to both centrally managed and self-published knowledge. The former is often more scrutinized but takes longer to publish and is not as hands-on (and potentially relevant). Self-published information on the other hand runs the risk of not being as reliable.

IT systems have proved extremely useful in aiding or performing many of these functions.

1.7.2 Explicit Knowledge Sharing and IT

IT is useful in most stages of the knowledge sharing process, and it is used for content management as well as data and text mining (looking for hidden knowledge, relationships, etc. within data and documents).

Content management systems are used to update, distribute, tag, and otherwise manage content. They may include a wide range of functions, including web content management and document management systems. They may be used to:

- Import and create documents and multimedia material.
- Identify key users and their roles.

- Assign roles and responsibilities to different instances of content categories or types.
- Define workflow tasks. Content managers can be alerted when changes in content are made.
- Track and manage multiple versions of content.
- Publish content to a repository to support access. Increasingly, the repository is a part of the system, incorporating search and retrieval.

Document management systems use numerous advanced indexing, searching, and retrieval mechanisms to facilitate explicit knowledge sharing.

To take advantage of all of these functions, it is a foregone conclusion that the system was chosen and implemented appropriately. This aspect is discussed in the section on knowledge management systems.

All in all, IT is a very useful tool in the management of explicit knowledge and information. This is not to say that humans no longer play a part. They certainly do, and knowledge and content managers are instrumental in ensuring that the knowledge is relevant, up to date, and presented correctly.

1.7.3 Can Explicit Knowledge Sharing Systems Yield Competitive Advantage?

For the actual storage and retrieval, there is very little disagreement on the value of IT as a means of sharing, sorting, and accessing explicit knowledge. Where one does find disagreement is on the value placed on this function. KM and organizational learning theorists have sometimes downplayed the value of explicit knowledge and focused largely on tacit knowledge. However, it has also been argued that in a world where we have an overflow of explicit knowledge and information, the ability to manage it, and thus to provide continuous streams of relevant knowledge and information, can be a source of competitive advantage in itself. The latter view appears to be gaining support, although one important point should be considered: explicit knowledge management systems are quite transparent and therefore fairly easy to replicate. This means that they cannot be the source of sustained long term competitive advantage.

All this being said, in most cases, implementing a solid system that enables explicit knowledge sharing is crucial for the following reasons:

- Not doing so would almost certainly become a source of competitive disadvantage.
- They may well provide a short term advantage, which may be extended through continuous improvements and new technologies.
- With proper care, such systems will also play a limited role in the sharing of tacit knowledge, as will be discussed in the next section.

1.7.4 Tacit Knowledge Sharing

- Sharing tacit knowledge requires socialization. This can take many different forms. Davenport & Prusak (2000) outline a few relevant factors:
- Informal networks, which involve the day to day interaction between people within work environments are considered very important
- Unlike the formalized structure of the firm, these networks span functions and hierarchies. They are therefore difficult to identify and monitor.
- Management should support these networks by providing the means for communication. Japanese firms have created talk rooms where employees can engage in unstructured, unmonitored discussions. A specific location is useful but not mandatory - this process also occurs in cafeterias etc. Management must simply provide the means for employees to foster informal networks and "trade" tacit knowledge.
- Management must also understand the value of chaos. This refers to the value of unstructured work practices that encourage experimentation and social interaction. Within a more chaotic environment, individuals are given the freedom to solve problems creatively and, in so doing, must tap into and evolve their social networks. This is closely linked to the notion of theory in use vs espoused theory. The value of less structured work environments is also well known within innovation management.

Codification of tacit knowledge is difficult and sometimes outright impossible. There will often be a resulting knowledge loss (Bukowitz and Williams 1999, Davenport & Prusak 2000). Often, it is much more reasonable to simply externalize the sources of tacit knowledge rather than the knowledge itself (Davenport & Prusak 2000). This means that often it is better for experts to externalize what they know rather than how they know it. The main role of KM then becomes making sure that experts can be found so that tacit knowledge can be passed on through practice, mentoring, and networking (socialization), and that the firm supports and encourages the networking that is necessary for these functions to occur.

To share tacit knowledge requires a culture conducive to this type of sharing. Furthermore, knowledge managers (generalists that understand the types of knowledge that exist in the communities) must be used to locate and translate knowledge elements, thus facilitating their integration into other communities. This endeavor is very much about people and managing organizational culture change.

1.7.5 Tacit Knowledge Sharing and IT

It is important for tacit sharing of knowledge to be people focused. However, increasingly, IT systems are becoming useful in this area as well. They can support interaction between people that are not in the same location and some tools are designed to capture unstructured thoughts and ideas. The important factor to remember is that tacit knowledge cannot always be made explicit. Therefore, IT systems should not attempt or pretend that they can carry out this process, but instead act as an important support to existing practices.

IT can be useful as a forum for externalization of tacit knowledge. For example, groupware systems that support brainstorming can help in the codification process. Online discussion databases and forums can also be sources of externalized knowledge, although the richness of this knowledge should be questioned.

While IT is crucial for information management, it is important not to confuse information with knowledge. Using IT to move tacit knowledge is difficult since knowledge represents the shared understanding and the sense making that is deeply rooted in the social practice of the community. The focus for the successful sharing of tacit knowledge must be on social interaction, problem solving, mentoring, and teaching, and IT systems must be used to support these processes intelligently.

IT's contribution to OL therefore depends on its fit to the social context of the communities. Technology must not be seen as the superior solution and should not be used to structure organizational practice. There is also the danger that IT may limit the participation of some members of the community. It may make it more difficult for individuals to become accepted members of the community by limiting socialization channels. The challenge is to extend the reach of communication without sacrificing reciprocity in regards to knowledge sharing or socialization.

During KM's boom at the turn of the century, IT-driven KM initiatives turned out to be a major pitfal. Today you still see a divide between technologically-centric views and people-oriented approaches. Increasingly however, IT is being recognised for its ability to provide support to sound KM initiatives, within knowledge sharing, creation, etc. In different capacities, IT should be regarded as a critical tool (though not as the initiative itself).

The role of IT for tacit knowledge sharing can thus be summarized as follows:

- **As an expert finder:** To located the source of the tacit knowledge through systems like corporate yellow pages.
- **As providing support in the socialization of tacit knowledge:** If IT systems support varied, formal and informal forms of communication then they can help tacit knowledge sharing by supporting teams, projects, communities, etc. Functions like being able to attach notes to documents, or video conferencing can support work environments over long distances to some degree. It is important not to replace existing socialization functions with IT; instead socialization should be ehanced and extended between people who would otherwise be unable to participate.

- **As providing some support in the externalization of tacit knowledge:** Through groupware applications that support the codification process, discussion forums etc. However, not only is this aspect limited, but externalization itself is only rarely feasible.

1.7.6 Embedded Knowledge Sharing

As a reminder, embedded knowledge refers to knowledge locked in products, processes, routines, etc.

Embedded knowledge can be shared when the knowledge from one product or process is incorporated into another. Management must understand what knowledge is locked within those sources, and they must transfer the relevant parts into a different system. To do this, Gamble and Blackwell advocate the use of:

- **Scenario planning:** The practice of creating a set of scenarios and hypothesizing how they might unfold by drawing upon the perspectives of experts, the firm's knowledge asserts, and so on.
- **After action reviews:** "is a structured review or de-brief process for analyzing what happened, why it happened, and how it can be done better".

1.7.7 Management Training

Embedded knowledge could theoretically be transferred as is, simply by testing the effects of procedures or design features transferred from one area to another. However, often it will have to be made explicit, or partially explicit, at least to the responsible managers. This way they can hypothesize the effects that embedded knowledge has in a given situation and use simulation and experimentation to implement it in a new area.

Beyond the knowledge mapping functions described in the subsection on organization and assessment, IT's use is usually more indirect. It can be used as support in the design of simulations, experiments, and product design, and it can also provide modeling tools used in reverse engineering of products. However, these tools are not typically considered as being knowledge management systems and are thus beyond the scope of this website.

One direct role of IT systems is as an embedded knowledge repository where procedures, guidelines, etc are stored and retrieved. If implemented properly, with the IT system complementing rather than disrupting existing processes and culture, then it can support practices and routines, and eventually become an embedded knowledge artifact in its own right.

1.8 CONCEPTS OF E-LEARNING

E-learning comprises all forms of electronically supported learning and teaching. The information and communication systems, whether networked learning or not, serve as specific media to implement the learning process. The term will still most likely be utilized to reference out-of-classroom and in-classroom educational experiences via technology, even as advances continue in regard to devices and curriculum.

E-learning is essentially the computer and network-enabled transfer of skills and knowledge. E-learning applications and processes include Web-based learning, computer-based learning, virtual education opportunities and digital collaboration. Content is delivered via the Internet, intranet/extranet, audio or video tape, satellite TV, and CD-ROM. It can be self-paced or instructor-led and includes media in the form of text, image, animation, streaming video and audio.

Abbreviations like CBT (Computer-Based Training), IBT (Internet-Based Training) or WBT (Web-Based Training) have been used as synonyms to e-learning. Today one can still find these terms being used, along with variations of e-learning such as elearning, Elearning, and eLearning. The terms will be utilized throughout this chapter to indicate their validity under the broader terminology of E-learning.

1.8.1 Market

The worldwide e-learning industry is estimated to be worth over $48 billion according to conservative estimates. Developments in internet and multimedia technologies are the basic enabler of e-learning, with consulting, content, technologies, services and support being identified as the five key sectors of the e-learning industry.

1.8.2 Higher Education

By 2006, 3.5 million students were participating in on-line learning at institutions of higher education in the United States. According to the Sloan Foundation reports, there has been an increase of around 12–14 percent per year on average in enrollments for fully online learning over the five years 2004–2009 in the US post-secondary system, compared with an average of approximately 2 per cent increase per year in enrollments overall. Allen and Seaman (2009) claim that almost a quarter of all students in post-secondary education were taking fully online courses in 2008, and a report by Ambient Insight Research suggests that in 2009, 44 percent of post-secondary students in the USA were taking some or all of their courses online, and projected that this figure would rise to 81 percent by 2014. Thus it can be seen that e-learning is moving rapidly from the margins to being a predominant form of post-secondary education, at least in the USA.

Many higher education, for-profit institutions, now offer on-line classes. By contrast, only about half of private, non-profit schools offer them. The Sloan report, based on a poll of academic leaders, indicated that students generally appear to be at least as satisfied with their on-line classes as they are with traditional ones. Private institutions may become more involved with on-line presentations as the cost of instituting such a system decreases. Properly trained staff must also be hired to work with students on-line. These staff members need to understand the content area, and also be highly trained in the use of the computer and Internet. Online education is rapidly increasing, and online doctoral programs have even developed at leading research universities.

1.8.3 K–12 Learning

E-learning is also utilized by public K–12 schools in the United States. Some E-Learning environments take place in a traditional classroom, others allow students to attend classes from home or other locations. There are several states that are utilizing cyber and virtual school platforms for E-learning across the country that continued to increase. Virtual school enables students to log intosynchronous learning or asynchronous learning courses anywhere there is an internet connection. Technology kits are usually provided that include computers, printers, and reimbursement for home internet use. Students are to use technology for school use only and must meet weekly work submission requirements. Teachers employed by K–12 online public cyber schools must be certified teachers in the state they are teaching in. Cyber schools allow for students to maintain their own pacing and progress, course selection, and provides the flexibility for students to create their own schedule.

E-learning is increasingly being utilized by students who may not want to go to traditional brick and mortar schools due to severe allergies or other medical issues, fear of school violence and school bullying and students whose parents would like to homeschool but do not feel qualified. Cyber schools create a safe haven for students to receive a quality education while almost completely avoiding these common problems. Cyber charter schools also often are not limited by location, income level or class size in the way brick and mortar charter schools are.

The more established cyber charter schools offer students a full range of supplemental programs which not only enhance the curriculum choices that are offered, but they also provide support for students so that they can become as successful as possible in an on line environment. Some of these supplemental programs include: Student Assistance Program for students who may be struggling with other areas in their life and not just academics. Open tutoring for those students that require extra support, Guidance Counseling, Title 1 Reading, Gifted Education Services, Special Education Services, Field Trips to enhance socialization in a cyber environment, Study Island to help students improve their math and reading skills to prepare them for state testing, and Early College Scholarships. Students are also assigned to a supervisor shortly after enrollment. This supervisor is the main point of contact initially, and acts in a an advisory capacity to support students throughout their on line education. They monitor student progress and act as liaisons for students, families, staff, and administration to provide continuous communication and guidance.

1.8.4 Corporate

E-Learning has now been adopted and used by various companies to inform & educate both their employees and customers. Companies with large and spread out distribution chains use it to educate their sales staff as to the latest product developments without the need of organizing physical courses. Compliance has also been a big field of growth with banks using it to keep their staff's CPD's level up.

1.8.5 History

In the early 1960s, Stanford University psychology professors Patrick Suppes and Richard C. Atkinson experimented with using computers to teach math and reading to young children in elementary schools in East Palo Alto, California. Stanford's Education Program for Gifted Youth is descended from those early experiments. In 1963, Bernard Luskin installed the first computer in a community college for instruction, working with Stanford and others, developed computer assisted instruction. Luskin completed his landmark UCLA dissertation working with the Rand Corporation in analyzing obstatcles to computer assisted instuction in 1970.

Early e-learning systems, based on Computer-Based Learning/Training often attempted to replicate autocratic teaching styles whereby the role of the e-learning system was assumed to be for transferring knowledge, as opposed to systems developed later based onComputer Supported Collaborative Learning (CSCL), which encouraged the shared development of knowledge.

As early as 1993, William D. Graziadei described an online computer-delivered lecture, tutorial and assessment project using electronic mail.

In 1997 Graziadei, W.D., et al., published an article entitled "Building Asynchronous and Synchronous Teaching-Learning Environments: Exploring a Course/Classroom Management System Solution". They described a process at the State University of New York (SUNY) of evaluating products and developing an overall strategy for technology-based course development and management in teaching-learning. The product(s) had to be easy to use and maintain, portable, replicable, scalable, and immediately affordable, and they had to have a high probability of success with long-term cost-effectiveness. Today many technologies can be, and are, used in e-learning, from blogs to collaborative software, ePortfolios, and virtual classrooms. Most eLearning situations use combinations of these techniques.

1.8.6 E-Learning 2.0

The term E-Learning 2.0 is a neologism for CSCL systems that came about during the emergence of Web 2.0 From an E-Learning 2.0 perspective, conventional e-learning systems were based on instructional packets, which were delivered to students using assignments. Assignments were evaluated by the teacher. In contrast, the new e-learning places increased emphasis on social learningand use of social software such as blogs, wikis, podcasts and virtual worlds such as Second Life. This phenomenon has also been referred to as Long Tail Learning.

E-Learning 2.0, by contrast to e-learning systems not based on CSCL, assumes that knowledge issocially constructed. Learning takes place through conversations about content and grounded interaction about problems and actions. Advocates of social learning claim that one of the best ways to learn something is to teach it to others.

However, it should be noted that many early online courses, such as those developed by Murray Turoff and Starr Roxanne Hiltz in the 1970s and 80s at the New Jersey Institute of Technology, courses at the University of Guelph in Canada, the British Open University, and the online distance courses at the University of British Columbia (where Web CT, now incorporated into Blackboard Inc. was first developed), have always made heavy use of online discussion between students. Also, from the start, practitioners such as Harasim (1995) have put heavy emphasis on the use of learning networks for knowledge construction, long before the term e-learning, let alone e-learning 2.0, was even considered.

There is also an increased use of virtual classrooms as an online learning platform and classroom for a diverse set of education providers such as Minnesota State Colleges and Universities and Sachem School District.

In addition to virtual classroom environments, social networks have become an important part of E-learning 2.0. Social networks have been used to foster online learning communities around subjects as diverse as test preparation and language education. Mobile Assisted Language Learning (MALL) is a term used to describe using handheld computers or cell phones to assist in language learning. Some feel, however, that schools have not caught up with the social networking trends. Few traditional educators promote social networking unless they are communicating with their own colleagues.

1.8.7 Approaches to E-Learning Services

E-learning services have evolved since computers were first used in education. There is a trend to move towards blended learning services, where computer-based activities are integrated with practical or classroom-based situations.

Bates and Poole (2003) and the OECD (2005) suggest that different types or forms of e-learning can be considered as a continuum, from no e-learning, i.e. no use of computers and/or the Internet for teaching and learning, through classroom aids, such as making classroom lecture Powerpoint slides available to students through a course web site or learning management system, to laptop programs, where students are required to bring laptops to class and use them as part of a face-to-face class, to hybrid learning, where classroom time is reduced but not eliminated, with more time devoted to online learning, through to fully online learning, which is a form of distance education. This classification is somewhat similar to that of the Sloan Commission reports on the status of e-learning, which refer to web enhanced, web supplemented and web dependent to reflect increasing intensity of technology use. In the Bates and Poole continuum, 'blended learning' can cover classroom aids, laptops and hybrid learning, while 'distributed learning' can incorporate either hybrid or fully online learning.

It can be seen then that e-learning can describe a wide range of applications, and it is often by no means clear even in peer reviewed research publications which form of e-learning is being discussed. However, Bates and Poole argue that when instructors say they are using e-learning, this most often refers to the use of technology as classroom aids, although over time, there has been a gradual increase in fully online learning (see Market above).

Two popular tools for E-learning are Blackboard Inc. and Moodle:

Blackboard Inc. has over 20 million users daily. Offering six different platforms: Blackboard Learn, Blackboard Collaborate, Blackboard Mobile, Blackboard Connect, Blackboard Transact, and Blackboard Analytics; Blackboard's tools allow educators to decide whether their program will be blended or fully online, asynchronous or synchronous. Blackboard can be used for K-12 education, Higher Education, Business, and Government collaboration.

Moodle is an Open Source Course Management System. It is free to download and provides blended learning opportunities as well as platforms for distance learning courses. The Moodle website has many tutorials for creating a program or becoming a Moodle student.

1.8.8 Computer-Based Learning

Computer-based learning, sometimes abbreviated to CBL, refers to the use of computers as a key component of the educational environment. While this can refer to the use of computers in a classroom, the term more broadly refers to a structured environment in which computers are used for teaching purposes.

Cassandra B. Whyte researched about the ever increasing role that computers would play in higher education. This evolution, to include computer-supported collaborative learning, in addition to data management, has been realized. The type of computers has changed over the years from cumbersome, slow devices taking up much space in the classroom, home, and office to laptops and handheld devices that are more portable in form and size and this minimalization of technology devices will continue.

1.8.9 Computer-Based Training

Computer-Based Trainings (CBTs) are self-paced learning activities accessible via a computer or handheld device. CBTs typically present content in a linear fashion, much like reading an online book or manual. For this reason they are often used to teach static processes, such as using software or completing mathematical equations. The term Computer-Based Training is often used interchangeably with Web-Based Training (WBT) with the primary difference being the delivery method. Where CBTs are typically delivered via CD-ROM, WBTs are delivered via the Internet using a web browser. Assessing learning in a CBT usually comes in form of multiple choice questions, or other assessments that can be easily scored by a computer such as drag-and-drop, radio button, simulation or other interactive means. Assessments are easily scored and recorded via online software, providing immediate end-user feedback and completion status. Users are often able to print completion records in the form of certificates.

CBTs provide learning stimulus beyond traditional learning methodology from textbook, manual, or classroom-based instruction. For example, CBTs offer user-friendly solutions for satisfying continuing education requirements. Instead of limiting students to attending courses or reading printed manuals, students are able to acquire knowledge and skills through methods that are much more conducive to individual learning preferences. For example, CBTs offer visual learning benefits through animation or video, not typically offered by any other means.

CBTs can be a good alternative to printed learning materials since rich media, including videos or animations, can easily be embedded to enhance the learning. Another advantage to CBTs is that they can be easily distributed to a wide audience at a relatively low cost once the initial development is completed.

However, CBTs pose some learning challenges as well. Typically the creation of effective CBTs requires enormous resources. The software for developing CBTs (such as Flash or Adobe Director) is often more complex than a subject matter expert or teacher is able to use. In addition, the lack of human interaction can limit both the type of content that can be presented as well as the type of assessment that can be performed. Many learning organizations are beginning to use smaller CBT/WBT activities as part of a broader online learning program which may include online discussion or other interactive elements.

1.8.10 Computer-Supported Collaborative Learning (CSCL)

Computer-Supported Collaborative Learning (CSCL) is one of the most promising innovations to improve teaching and learning with the help of modern information and communication technology. Most recent developments in CSCL have been called E-Learning 2.0, but the concept of collaborative or group learning whereby instructional methods are designed to encourage or require students to work together on learning tasks has existed much longer. It is widely agreed to distinguish collaborative learning from the traditional 'direct transfer' model in which the instructor is assumed to be the distributor of knowledge and skills, which is often given the neologism E-Learning 1.0, even though this direct transfer method most accurately reflects Computer-Based Learning systems (CBL).

Blogs, wikis, and Google Docs are commonly used CSCL mediums within the teaching community. The ability to share information in an environment that is becoming easier for the lay person, has caused a major increase of use in the average classroom. One of the main reasons for its usage states that it is "a breeding ground for creative and engaging educational endeavors."

Using Web 2.0 social tools in the classroom allows for students and teachers to work collaboratively, discuss ideas, and promote information. According to Sendall (2008), blogs, wikis, and social networking skills are found to be significantly useful in the classroom. After initial instruction on using the tools, students also reported an increase in knowledge and comfort level for using Web 2.0 tools. The collaborative tools additionally prepare students with technology skills necessary in today's workforce.

Locus of Control remains an important consideration in successful engagement of E-learners. According to the work of Cassandra B. Whyte, the continuing attention to aspects of motivation and success in regard to E-learning should be kept in context and concert with other educational efforts. Information about motivational tendencies can help educators, psychologists, and technologists develop insights to help students perform better academically.

1.8.11 Technology-Enhanced Learning (TEL)

Technology enhanced learning (TEL) has the goal to provide socio-technical innovations (also improving efficiency and cost effectiveness) for e-learning practices, regarding individuals and organizations, independent of time, place and pace. The field of TEL therefore applies to the support of any learning activity through technology.

1.8.12 Technology Issues

Along with the terms learning technology, instructional technology, the term Educational Technology is generally used to refer to the use of technology in learning in a much broader sense than the computer-based training or Computer Aided Instruction of the 1980s. It is also broader than the terms Online Learning or Online Education which generally refer to purely web-based learning. In cases where mobile technologies are used, the term M-learning has become more common. E-learning, however, also has implications beyond just the technology and refers to the actual learning that takes place using these systems.

E-learning is naturally suited to distance learning and flexible learning, but can also be used in conjunction with face-to-face teaching, in which case the term Blended learning is commonly used. E-Learning pioneer Bernard Luskin argues that the "E" must be understood to have broad meaning if e-Learning is to be effective. Luskin says that the "e" should be interpreted to mean exciting, energetic, enthusiastic, emotional, extended, excellent, and educational in addition to "electronic" that is a traditional national interpretation. This broader interpretation allows for 21st century applications and brings learning and media psychology into the equation.

In higher education especially, the increasing tendency is to create a Virtual Learning Environment (VLE) (which is sometimes combined with a Management Information System (MIS) to create a Managed Learning Environment) in which all aspects of a course are handled through a consistent user interface standard throughout the institution. A growing number of physical universities, as well as newer online-only colleges, have begun to offer a select set of academic degree and certificate programs via the Internet at a wide range of levels and in a wide range of disciplines. While some programs require students to attend some campus classes or orientations, many are delivered completely online. In addition, several universities offer online student support services, such as online advising and registration, e-counseling, online textbook purchase, student governments and student newspapers.

E-Learning can also refer to educational web sites such as those offering learning scenarios, worksheets and interactive exercises for children. The term is also used extensively in the business sector where it generally refers to cost-effective online training.

The recent trend in the E-Learning sector is screencasting. There are many screencasting tools available but the latest buzz is all about the web based screencasting tools which allow the users to create screencasts directly from their browser and make the video available online so that the viewers can stream the video directly. The advantage of such tools is that it gives the presenter the ability to show his ideas and flow of thoughts rather than simply explain them, which may be more confusing when delivered via simple text instructions. With the combination of video and audio, the expert can mimic the one on one experience of the classroom and deliver clear, complete instructions. From the learner's point of view this provides the ability to pause and rewind and gives the learner the advantage of moving at their own pace, something a classroom cannot always offer.

Research on the use of video in lessons is preliminary, but early results show an increased retention and better results when video is used in a lesson. Creating a systematic video development method holds promise for creating video models that positively impact student learning.

1.8.13 Communication Technologies Used in E-Learning

Communication technologies are generally categorized as asynchronous or synchronous. Asynchronous activities use technologies such as blogs, wikis, and discussion boards. The idea here is that participants may engage in the exchange of ideas or information without the dependency of other participants involvement at the same time. Electronic mail (Email) is also asynchronous in that mail can be sent or received without having both the participants' involvement at the same time. Asynchronous learning also gives students the ability to work at their own pace. This is particularly beneficial for students who have health problems. They have the opportunity to complete their work in a low stress environment.

Synchronous activities involve the exchange of ideas and information with one or more participants during the same period of time. A face to face discussion is an example of synchronous communications. In an "E" learning environment, an example of synchronous communications would be a skype conversation or a chat room where everyone is online and working collaborativelly at the same time.Synchronous activities occur with all participants joining in at once, as with an online chat session or a virtual classroom or meeting.

Virtual classrooms and meetings can often use a mix of communication technologies. Participants in a virtual classroom use icons called emoticons to communicate feelings and responses to questions or statements. Students are able to 'write on the board' and even share their desktop, when given rights by the teacher. Other communication technologies available in a virtual classroom include text notes, microphone rights, and breakout sessions. Breakout sessions allow the participants to work collaboratively in a small group setting to accomplish a task as well as allow the teacher to have private conversations with his or her students.

The virtual classroom also provides the opportunity for students to receive direct instruction from a qualified teacher in an interactive environment. Students have direct and immediate access to their instructor for instant feedback and direction. The virtual classroom also provides a structured schedule of classes, which can be helpful for students who may find the freedom of asynchronous learning to be overwhelming. The virtual classroom also provides a social learning environment that closely replicates the traditional "brick and mortar" classroom. Most virtual classroom applications provide a recording feature. Each class is recorded and stored on a server, which allows for instant playback of any class over the course of the school year. This can be extremely useful for students to review material and concepts for an upcoming exam. This also provides students with the opportunity to watch any class that they may have missed, so that they never have to fall behind. It also gives parents the ability to monitor any classroom to insure that they are satisfied with the education their child is receiving.

In asynchronous online courses, students proceed at their own pace. If they need to listen to a lecture a second time, or think about a question for awhile, they may do so without fearing that they will hold back the rest of the class. Through online courses, students can earn their diplomas more quickly, or repeat failed courses without the embarrassment of being in a class with younger students. Students also have access to an incredible variety of enrichment courses in online learning, and can participate in college courses, internships, sports, or work and still graduate with their class.

In many models, the writing community and the communication channels relate with the E-learning and the M-learning communities. Both the communities provide a general overview of the basic learning models and the activities required for the participants to join the learning sessions across the virtual classroom or even across standard classrooms enabled by technology. Many activities, essential for the learners in these environments, require frequent chat sessions in the form of virtual classrooms and/or blog meetings.

1.9 LEARNING MANAGEMENT SYSTEM AND LEARNING CONTENT MANAGEMENT SYSTEM

A Learning Management System (LMS) is software used for delivering, tracking and managing training/education. LMSs range from systems for managing training/educational records to software for distributing courses over the Internet and offering features for online collaboration.

A Learning Content Management System (LCMS) is software for author content (courses, reusable content objects). An LCMS may be solely dedicated to producing and publishing content that is hosted on an LMS, or it can host the content itself. The Aviation Industry Computer-Based Training Committee (AICC) specification provides support for content that is hosted separately from the LMS.

A LMS allows for teachers and administrators to track attendance, time on task, and student progress. LMS also allows for not only teachers and administrators to track these variables but parents and students as well. Parents can log on to the LMS to track grades. Students log on to the LMS to submit homework and to access the course syllabus and lessons.

Some systems have tools to deliver and manage instructor-led synchronous and asynchronous online training based on learning objectmethodology. These systems are called learning content management systems or LCMSs. LCMSs provide tools for authoring and reusing or re-purposing content as well as virtual spaces for student interaction (such as discussion forums, live chat rooms and live web-conferences). Despite this distinction, the term LMS is often used to refer to both an LMS and an LCMS, although the LCMS is a further development of the LMS. Due to this conformity issue, the acronym CLCIMS(Computer Learning Content Information Management System) is now widely used to create a uniform phonetic way of referencing any learning system software based on advanced learning technology methodology.

In essence, an LMS is software for planning, delivering, and managing learning events within an organization, including online, virtual classroom, and instructor-led courses. For example, an LMS can simplify global certification efforts, enable entities to align learning initiatives with strategic goals, and provide a means of enterprise-level skills management. The focus of an LMS is to manage students, keeping track of their progress and performance across all types of training activities. It performs administrative tasks, such as reporting to instructors, HR and other ERP systems but isn't used to create course content.

By contrast, an LCMS is software for managing learning content across an organization's various training development areas. It provides developers, authors, instructional designers, and subject matter experts the means to create and re-use e-learning content and reduce duplicated development efforts. In the remote AICC hosting approach, an LCMS may host the content in a central repository and allow multiple LMSs to access it.

Primary business problems an LCMS solves are:

- Centralized management of an organization's learning content for efficient searching and retrieval,
- Productivity gains around rapid and condensed development timelines,
- Productivity gains around assembly, maintenance and publishing / branding / delivery of learning content.

Criticism of LMS is that it is not content centric. In this sense, the technology is used for organizational control rather than theempowerment of the learner. The platform is usually poor in its content, and is part of a hierarchical bureaucratic (Max Weber) rather than socially oriented system. A/R/D/T is a term referring to its implementation in complex organizations sometimes replacing regularweb sites

Rather than developing entire courses and adapting them to multiple audiences, an LCMS provides the ability for single course instances to be modified and republished for various audiences maintaining versions and history. The objects stored in the centralized repository can be made available to course developers and content experts throughout an organization for potential reuse and repurpose. This eliminates duplicate development efforts and allows for the rapid assembly of customized content.

To look at this another way, an LMS is learner-centric. It focuses on e-learning process management and content delivery. In essence, an LMS is software for planning, delivering and managing learning events within an organization, including online, virtual classroom, and instructor-led courses. For example, an LMS can simplify global certification efforts, enable entities to align learning initiatives with strategic goals and provide a means for enterprise-level skills management. The focus of an LMS is to manage students, keeping track of their progress and performance across all types of training activities. It performs administrative tasks, such as reporting to instructors, HR and other ERP systems but it isn't used to create course content.

An LCMS is content–centric. Here, the focus is on the authoring and management of e-learning reusable content.

By contrast, LCMS solutions are ideally suited to create content-centric learning strategies, supporting multiple methods for gathering and organizing content, leveraging content for multiple purposes, and operation for mission critical purposes. LCMS technology can either be used in tandem with an LMS, or as a standalone application for learning initiatives that require rapid development and distribution of learning content.

Rather than developing entire courses and adapting them to multiple audiences, an LCMS is designed for managing learning content across an organization's various training development areas. It provides developers, authors, instructional designers, and subject matter experts the means to create and re-use e-learning content and reduce duplicated development efforts. An LCMS provides the ability for single course instances to be modified and republished for various audiences maintaining versions and history. The objects stored in the centralized repository can be made available to course developers and content experts throughout an organization for potential reuse and repurpose. This allows for the rapid assembly of customized content.

In addition, Brandon Hall believes that:

When LCMS technology is appropriately applied and matched to an orchestrated e-learning strategy, with a complete instructional design plan for designing and using learning objects, great efficiencies can and will be achieved, such as:

- The ability to make instantaneous, company-wide changes to critical learning content
- Rapid and productive content development efforts
- Seamless collaboration among subject matter experts and course designers
- The ability to create multiple, derivative versions of content applicable to different audiences from senior management to line-level workers
- Access to find and reuse learning content, 'just-in-time' and 'just enough'
- Ultimate reusability of content by making it available through a wide array of output types such as structured e-learning courses, CD-ROM courses, learning material available from a Palm device or PocketPC, print-based learning for use in classroom settings, and so on.

1.9.1 Computer-Aided Assessment

Computer-aided Assessment, ranging from automated multiple-choice tests to more sophisticated systems is becoming increasingly common. With some systems, feedback can be geared towards a student's specific mistakes or the computer can navigate the student through a series of questions adapting to what the student appears to have learned or not learned.

The best examples follow a Formative Assessment structure and are called "Online Formative Assessment". This involves making an initial formative assessment by sifting out the incorrect answers. The author/teacher will then explain what the pupil should have done with each question. It will then give the pupil at least one practice at each slight variation of sifted out questions. This is the formative learning stage. The next stage is to make a Summative Assessment by a new set of questions only covering the topics previously taught. Some will take this even further and repeat the cycle such as BOFA which is aimed at the Eleven plus exam set in the UK.

The term learning design has sometimes come to refer to the type of activity enabled by software such as the open-source system LAMS which supports sequences of activities that can be both adaptive and collaborative. The IMS Learning Design specification is intended as a standard format for learning designs, and IMS LD Level A is supported in LAMS V2.elearning has been replacing the traditional settings due to its cost effectiveness.

1.9.2 Electronic Performance Support Systems (EPSS)

Electronic performance support systems (EPSS) is a "computer-based system that improves worker productivity by providing on-the-job access to integrated information, advice, and learning experiences".

1.10 CONTENT ISSUES

Content is a core component of E-learning and includes issues such as pedagogy and learning object re-use.

1.10.1 Pedagogical Elements

Pedagogical elements are an attempt to define structures or units of educational material. For example, this could be a lesson, an assignment, a multiple choice question, a quiz, a discussion group or a case study. These units should be format independent, so although it may be in any of the following methods, pedagogical structures would not include a textbook, a web page, a video conference or Podcast.

When beginning to create E-Learning content, the pedagogical approaches need to be evaluated. Simple pedagogical approaches make it easy to create content, but lack flexibility, richness and downstream functionality. On the other hand, complex pedagogical approaches can be difficult to set up and slow to develop, though they have the potential to provide more engaging learning experiences for students. Somewhere between these extremes is an ideal pedagogy that allows a particular educator to effectively create educational materials while simultaneously providing the most engaging educational experiences for students.

1.10.2 Pedagogical Approaches or Perspectives

It is possible to use various pedagogical approaches for eLearning which include:

- Social-constructivist – This pedagogy is particularly well afforded by the use of discussion forums, blogs, wiki and on-line collaborative activities. It is a collaborative approach that opens educational content creation to a wider group including the students themselves. The One Laptop Per Child Foundation attempted to use a constructivist approach in its project
- Laurillard's Conversational Model is also particularly relevant to eLearning, and Gilly Salmon's Five-Stage Model is a pedagogical approach to the use of discussion boards.
- Cognitive perspective focuses on the cognitive processes involved in learning as well as how the brain works.
- Emotional perspective focuses on the emotional aspects of learning, like motivation, engagement, fun, etc.

- Behavioural perspective focuses on the skills and behavioural outcomes of the learning process. Role-playing and application to on-the-job settings.
- Contextual perspective focuses on the environmental and social aspects which can stimulate learning. Interaction with other people, collaborative discovery and the importance of peer support as well as pressure.
- Mode Neutral Convergence or promotion of 'transmodal' learning where online and classroom learners can coexist within one learning environment thus encouraging interconnectivity and the harnessing of collective intelligence.

1.11 REUSABILITY, STANDARDS AND LEARNING OBJECTS

Much effort has been put into the technical reuse of electronically based teaching materials and in particular creating or re-usingLearning Objects. These are self contained units that are properly tagged with keywords, or other metadata, and often stored in an XMLfile format. Creating a course requires putting together a sequence of learning objects. There are both proprietary and open, non-commercial and commercial, peer-reviewed repositories of learning objects such as the Merlot repository.

A common standard format for e-learning content is SCORM whilst other specifications allow for the transporting of "learning objects" or categorizing metadata (LOM).

These standards themselves are early in the maturity process with the oldest being 8 years old. They are also relatively vertical specific: SIF is primarily pK-12, LOM is primarily Corp, Military and Higher Ed, and SCORM is primarily Military and Corp with some Higher Ed. PESC- the Post-Secondary Education Standards Council- is also making headway in developing standards and learning objects for the Higher Ed space, while SIF is beginning to seriously turn towards Instructional and Curriculum learning objects.

In the US pK12 space there are a host of content standards that are critical as well- the NCES data standards are a prime example. Each state government's content standards and achievement benchmarks are critical metadata for linking e-learning objects in that space.

An excellent example of e-learning that relates to knowledge management and reusability is Navy E-Learning, which is available to Active Duty, Retired, or Disable Military members. This on-line tool provides certificate courses to enrich the user in various subjects related to military training and civilian skill sets. The e-learning system not only provides learning objectives, but also evaluates the progress of the student and credit can be earned toward higher learning institutions. This reuse is an excellent example of knowledge retention and the cyclical process of knowledge transfer and use of data and records.

1.12 ONLINE EDUCATION PROCESS

Online education is a type of distance learning---taking courses without attending a brick-and-mortar school or university. Instead, online students and teachers interact over the Internet. To meet the definition of online education, according to education expert, a course of study must offer two-way communication between teacher and learner and fall under the oversight of an educational institution.

Online education is defined as the creation and proliferation of the personal computer, the globalization of ideas and other human acts, and the use of technology in exchanging ideas and providing access to more people. Audio, video, computer, and networking technologies are often combined to create a multifaceted instructional delivery system. The fundamental method to unite the distance learning instructor with the distance learner is the network. Networks suitable for distance learning implementations include satellite, cable modem, digital subscriber lines (DSL), and wireless cable.

Greenberg (1998) defines contemporary distance learning as "a planned teaching/learning experience that uses a wide spectrum of technologies to reach learners at a distance and is designed to encourage learner interaction and certification of learning" . Teaster and Blieszner (1999) say "the term distance learning has been applied to many instructional methods: however, its primary distinction is that the teacher and the learner are separate in space and possibly time". Desmond Keegan (1995) provides another definition. He states that distance education and training result from the technological separation of teacher and learner which frees the student from the necessity of traveling to "a fixed place, at a fixed time, to meet a fixed person, in order to be trained". From these definitions we can see that the student and teacher are separated by space, but not necessarily by time.

There are many terms for on-line education. Some of them are virtual education, internet-based education, web-based education, education via computer-mediated communication. The web-edu project uses a definition of online education that is based on Desmond Keegan's (1988) definition. It is by:

1. The separation of teachers and learners which distinguishes it from face-to-face education;
2. The influence of an educational organization which distinguishes it from self-study and private tutoring;
3. The use of a computer network to present or distribute some educational content; and
4. The provision of tw0-way communication via a computer network so that students may benefit from communication with each other, teachers and staff.

1.12.1 History of Online Education

A few years ago, online education was unthinkable; now it is a reality and it has expanded beyond imagination. The Internet has allowed us to cross boundaries that took a long time to cross; technology has allowed us to learn and grow with people from around the world. It has given access to new opportunities in work, learning and in socializing. We are now witnessing a transformation in the way people learn. The future of education in general, and college education in particular, will be of more access, more educational choices, and new fields in educational research.

Distance learning was once only possible by corresponding through the mail. In the late 1970s and 1980s, higher education institutions in the U.S. and Europe began delivering instructional content to distance learners over cable and satellite TV. From the mid-1990s onwards, the Internet rapidly became the most common method of delivering distance education.

Online education has created possibilities that previous generations couldn't even fathom.

Literally, students can earn their entire degree at home, by working when it's convenient for them, while wearing their pajamas. This amazing innovation has allowed for greater access to universities and targeted specializations that may not be locally available. It has also been especially beneficial for working adults or stay at home parents who are eager to earn a degree.

The history of online education extends back further than you may think, with the very first virtual classroom environments being created in the 1960s. University of Illinois scientists created a classroom system based in linked computer terminals. There, students were able to access informational resources while listening to a professor whose lectures were brought in remotely, via some form of television or audio device.

Certainly not a form of "online learning" that stands up to the web learning of today, but it was the beginning of enhanced distance learning and the utilization of computer resources for educational purposes.

Universities quickly began to take advantage of these new resources by offering distance learning courses, using computer networking for information and resource sharing, and more. By the mid 1980s, college resources frequently included online access to course information and student networking tools.

Online only courses began emerging in the late 1980s, with some moderate success. The concept was further popularized as major corporations began using similar utilities to trim their training budgets. While businesses began with software training programs, the largest corporations started utilizing online tools to minimize software distribution costs.

Another phenomenon that contributed to online learning was the correspondence school. The original correspondence schools worked in a very straightforward way: You registered by mail, received materials by mail, then mailed the course work back for grading upon completion.

As the digital age swept across the nation, the correspondence school became more grounded in the virtual world, and the first online correspondence school, the University of Phoenix, made its way onto the scene in 1989. It was not a fully accredited institution at that time, however, and it wasn't until 1993 that the first accredited university, the Jones International University, really opened the floodgates.

It was at this same time that a new innovation in the online world made more universities of this kind possible: the Mosaic web interface. This was the first graphic interface that reached out to more common users, allowing for unprecedented access and support. Since that time, hundreds of standard universities have started offering a variety of online courses.

Many institutions, as well as a number of digital correspondence schools, offer full degrees online. As the web continued to open doors, these universities expanded their degree selection. These days, it's literally possible to graduate with the degree of your choice without ever having to set foot in a classroom.

1.12.2 Expansion of Online Education

In the last 20 years, with the advancement in technology, independent study has become more accessible for distance education students. The ease with which modern communications technologies can link educational institutions to homes, work-sites, and community centers has made college, adult education and lifelong learning matters of national policy

At the same time, the loads and responsibilities of adults have become of interest to experts and educators in distance learning. Feasley (1983) stated that individuals who must learn at a distance have ongoing obligations such as employment, family responsibilities, handicaps, or live in geographically isolated area. The 1970s and 1980s introduced the related concept "distance education" which posed new challenges to traditional independent study, forcing a reexamination and redefinition of the place of independent study in this new international movement.

In the late 1970s and early 1980s, cable and satellite television came into use as a delivery medium for distance education courses. During the 1980s, many quality telecourse offerings were available by using cable and satellite delivery. But as Munshi (1980) said, "Unfortunately, systematic efforts to evaluate telecourses have been the exception rather than the rule." In the fall of 1991, eighteen institutions, including the University of California, the University of Oklahoma, Penn State, and Washington State, used the Mind Extension University (MEU), Educational Network to deliver video course materials for independent study courses. Women's desire and participation in distance education helped the growth of distance education in the 1980s and 1990s. The report of the survey of telecourse enrollments in five states showed 67% of the participants in the distance education were women (Instructional Telecommunication Consortium, 1984). Participation of women in distance learning was directly related to political and social changes in women's position within the family and society, technological changes in the work place, and the economic necessity of participation, and the job market and new job opportunities, (Vision Quest Team: Lopez, Milon and Bebawi, The Future of Educational Institutions, Capella University, 2003).

With the recent development and expansion of new technology, it has become expected that computers will play an integral part of the process of education. The future of education lies within the capabilities of this new and growing technology.

1.13 TYPES

Online education is "synchronous" if the teacher and student have some direct, simultaneous contact. For instance, a teacher might meet with students in a chat forum for a discussion. Another example of synchronous distance learning is a teacher delivering a lecture at a scheduled time while students watch it simultaneously via a webcam.

Distance learning also allows for "asynchronous" learning, where instructor and learner do not meet in time or space. For instance, a student may go to a website to read or watch the week's lectures at any point during the week. Students may use email to submit assignments to the teacher or ask questions. Asynchronous learning opens up enormous possibilities by divorcing education from the constraints of time as well as place.

1.13.1 Audience

Online education makes more subjects of study available to more students. According to the U.S. Department of Education, in 2002, 78 percent of family households had a connection to the Internet. Online classes can reach individuals who traditionally found access to learning difficult, such as people with full-time jobs, women with family responsibilities, people in remote locations and students with medical or developmental challenges.

1.13.2 Scope

Online education originated at the college level, but today many professional certifications are available online. U.S. Department of Education surveys show that online classes are popular with adult learners of all races, with all levels of prior education. Online career and continuing education reaches learners from trade and service careers as from professional careers.

During the academic year 2006-2007, the U.S. Department of Education found that 65 percent of two-year and four-year post-secondary institutions offered college-level online learning for credit. Community colleges make the greatest use of online learning to cut costs and reach a wide audience of learners. A full 97 percent of two-year public institutions offer credit-granting online learning.

1.13.3 Potential

Today online education is making inroads into kindergarten through 12th grade. During the academic year 2002-2003, independent researchers at Eduventures found that 300,000

American high school students took classes online. Most of these students used online classes to fill gaps in the courses available at their public high schools. Public school systems increasingly use online learning. For instance, West Virginia schools provide students with online foreign language instruction when they cannot locate or afford new Spanish teachers, say Edutopia researchers.

1.14 THE BENEFITS OF ONLINE EDUCATION

It is far from a disruptive use of telecommunications computing technology to broadcast one's lectures over the Web and convert paper-and-pencil exams to self-graded, online learning management systems.

Our successful online programs at Siena Heights University recognize that students are individuals with a wide variety of learning styles. One style, like lectures and exams, cannot fit all students; there is much evidence to show that this model is one of the least effective ways to learn.

Online students benefit from increased time-on-task through daily online guided discussion, interaction with their peers in problem-based learning activities, writing across the curriculum aided by social media, and by the use of teaching-learning activities geared to a variety of learning styles.

Educational research has shown that there are distinct and emerging differences between effective online and on-ground learning, and that these need to be designed into the teaching process for the technology to be effective.

For centuries, a college education meant "going away to school." It meant ivy-encrusted campuses, dorms and fraternities, and all-nighters at the library cramming for a chemistry test. But recently, prospective students are facing a new kind of college experience — online education. The purpose of this article is to inform students about some of the potential benefits of this new kind of college education in which students take classes and work toward their degrees over the internet.

1. **Accessibility:** Traditionally, if a student wanted a college education they had to relocate or commute to campus, reduce hours at work, or even postpone careers entirely. But not anymore. Online education offers the same quality education, the same courses, and the same degrees as traditional education, but in a more convenient setting. With online education, you can get a college education on your schedule. All you need is a computer and an internet connection and you can go to college in the comfort of your own home.
2. **Flexibility:** In addition to being more accessible, online education is also more flexible than traditional education, especially for students who work. With online education, you can cater your courses, homework, and school correspondence around your work or family schedule. Study when you want and where you want. The flexibility of an online education allows you the ability to maintain your priorities and your income while still earning a college degree.

3. **Work-Ability:** Many people fear that starting or finishing their college education will interfere with their existing careers. Traditionally, going to college meant going to school full-time during the day, which made it difficult to work. Not so with online education. By going to school online, you can keep your current job and continue earning the money you need. Online programs allow you to take courses at your own pace, which in turn allows you the flexibility to work full-time or part-time while still maintaining a balance among work, school, and your social life.
4. **Applicability:** One of the oft-overlooked advantages of working while going to school is the potential applicability that studies may have on your job. In other words, it's one thing to go to class and learn about something in theory, and it's another to take that theory and put it into practice. Students who work can apply their newly acquired knowledge immediately to their jobs; they can also focus their studies on the kinds of real-world problems that professionals face daily in the workplace.
5. **Speed:** The accessibility and flexibility of online education makes it possible to shave months, even years off your graduation date. Motivated students can earn prestigious degrees online in half the time it would have taken in a traditional classroom setting.
6. **Variety:** One of the great myths regarding online education is that there aren't enough degrees to choose from. Not true — at least, not anymore. Colleges and universities are now offering scores of degrees in a variety of different areas including business, criminal justice, education, engineering, health care, hospitality, law, liberal arts, science, and web design, to name but a few. Furthermore, within these areas you can obtain associate degrees, bachelor's degrees, master's degrees, and other professional degrees in addition to a gamut of certificates and diplomas.
7. **Cost:** Finally, one of the most dramatic advantages of online education is the cost. Typically, the tuition of online programs is already less expensive than traditional programs. When you add in the potential savings associated with housing, transportation, books, and lost wages, the difference is enormous. Furthermore, if students continue to work while taking classes online, the need for student loans decreases, which greatly eases the financial strain of college after graduation. Whether you experience college in a brick-and-mortar classroom or a virtual one, your education will be one of the most important investments you will make in your life. So as you prepare for this important decision, make sure you consider all the options, including the unique possibilities offered by online education. Whatever you choose, you are certain to have a genuine "college experience," including more than a few all-nighters cramming for that chemistry test.

1.14.1 Reasons to Choose Online Education

Online education isn't the best choice for everyone. But, many students thrive in the online education environment. Here are 10 reasons why online education continues to grow in popularity.

1. **Choice:** Online education allows students to choose from a wide variety of schools and programs not available in their area.
2. **Flexibility:** Online education offers flexibility for students who have other commitments.
3. **Networking Opportunities:** Students enrolled in online education programs network with peers from all over the nation.
4. **Pacing:** Many online education programs allow pupils to work at their own pace.
5. **Open Scheduling:** Online education allows professionals to continue their careers while working towards a degree.
6. **Savings:** Online education programs often charge less than traditional schools.
7. **Lack of Commute:** Students who choose online education save on gas and commuting time.
8. **Connections:** Some online education programs connect students with top-notch professors and guest lecturers from around the world.
9. **Teaching & Testing Options:** The variety of online education programs available means that students are able to choose a learning and evaluation format that works for them.
10. **Effectiveness:** Online education is effective. A 2009 meta-study from the Department of Education found that students taking online courses outperformed their peers in traditional classrooms.

1.15 ONLINE MACHINE LEARNING

In machine learning, online learning is a model of induction that learns one instance at a time. The goal in online learning is to predict labels for instances. For example, the instances could describe the current conditions of the stock market, and an online algorithm predicts tomorrow's value of a particular stock. The key defining characteristic of online learning is that soon after the prediction is made, the true label of the instance is discovered. This information can then be used to refine the prediction hypothesis used by the algorithm. The goal of the algorithm is to make predictions that are close to the true labels.

More formally, an online algorithm proceeds in a sequence of trials. Each trial can be decomposed into three steps. First the algorithm receives an instance. Second the algorithm predicts the label of the instance. Third the algorithm receives the true label of the instance. The third stage is the most crucial as the algorithm can use this label feedback to update its hypothesis for future trials. The goal of the algorithm is to minimize some performance criteria. For example, with stock market prediction the algorithm may attempt to minimize sum of the square distances between the predicted and true value of a stock. Another popular performance criterion is to minimize the number of mistakes when dealing with classification problems.

Because online learning algorithms continually receive label feedback, the algorithms are able to adapt and learn in difficult situations. Many online algorithms can give strong guarantees on performance even when the instances are not generated by a distribution. As long as a reasonably good classifier exists, the online algorithm will learn to predict correct labels. This good classifier must come from a previously determined set that depends on the algorithm. For example, two popular on-line algorithms perceptron and winnow can perform well when a hyperplane exists that splits the data into two categories. These algorithms can even be modified to do provably well even if the hyperplane is allowed to infrequently change during the online learning trials.

Unfortunately, the main difficulty of online learning is also a result of the requirement for continual label feedback. For many problems it is not possible to guarantee that accurate label feedback will be available in the near future. For example, when designing a system that learns how to do optical character recognition, typically some expert must label previous instances to help train the algorithm. In actual use of the OCR application, the expert is no longer available and no inexpensive outside source of accurate labels is available. Fortunately, there is a large class of problems where label feedback is always available. For any problem that consists of predicting the future, an online learning algorithm just needs to wait for the label to become available. This is true in our previous example of stock market prediction and many other problems.

1.16 LEARNING MANAGEMENT SYSTEM

A Learning Management System (LMS) is a software application for the administration, documentation, tracking, and reporting of training programs, classroom and online events, e-learning programs, and training content. A robust LMS should be able to do the following:

- Centralize and automate administration
- Use self-service and self-guided services
- Assemble and deliver learning content rapidly
- Consolidate training initiatives on a scalable web-based platform
- Support portability and standards
- Personalize content and enable knowledge reuse.

LMSs range from systems for managing training and educational records, to software for distributing courses over the Internet with features for online collaboration. Corporate training use LMSs to automate record-keeping and employee registration. Student self-service, training workflow, the provision of on-line learning, on-line assessment, management of Continuous Professional Education (CPE), collaborative learning, and training resource management, are dimensions to Learning Management Systems.

Some LMSs are Web-based to facilitate access to learning content and administration. LMSs are used by regulated industries for compliance training. They are also used by educational institutions to enhance and support classroom teaching and offering courses to a larger population of learners across the globe.

Some LMS providers include "performance management systems", which encompass employee appraisals, competency management, skills-gap analysis, succession planning, and multi-rater assessments. Modern techniques now employcompetency-based learning to discover learning gaps and guide training material selection.

For the commercial market, some Learning and Performance Management Systems include recruitment and reward functionality.

1.16.1 Characteristics

LMSs cater to educational, administrative, and deployment requirements. While an LMS for corporate learning, for example, may share many characteristics with a VLE, or virtual learning environment, used by educational institutions, they each meet unique needs. The virtual learning environment used by universities and colleges allow instructors to manage their courses and exchange information with students for a course that in most cases will last several weeks and will meet several times during those weeks. In the corporate setting a course may be much shorter in length, completed in a single instructor-led event or online session.

The characteristics shared by both types of LMSs include:

- Manage users, roles, courses, instructors, facilities, and generate reports
- Course calendar
- Learning Path
- Student messaging and notifications
- Assessment and testing handling before and after testing
- Display scores and transcripts
- Grading of coursework and roster processing, including wait listing
- Web-based or blended course delivery

Characteristics more specific to corporate learning, which sometimes includes franchisees or other business partners, include:

- Auto enrollment (enrolling Students in courses when required according to predefined criteria, such as job title or work location)
- Manager enrollment and approval
- Boolean definitions for prerequisites or equivalencies
- Integration with performance tracking and management systems
- Planning tools to identify skill gaps at departmental and individual level
- Curriculum, required and elective training requirements at an individual and organizational level
- Grouping students according to demographic units (geographic region, product line, business size, etc.)
- Assign corporate and partner employees to more than one job title at more than one demographic unit

1.16.2 Technical Aspects

Most LMSs are web-based, built using a variety of development platforms, like Java/J2EE, Microsoft.NET or PHP. They usually employ the use of a database like MySQL, Microsoft SQL Server or Oracle as back-end. Although most of the systems are commercially developed and have commercial software licenses there are several systems that have an open-source license.

1.16.3 Learning Content Management System (LCMS)

A Learning Content Management System (LCMS) is a related technology to the learning management system in that it is focused on the development, management and publishing of the content that will typically be delivered via an LMS. An LCMS is a multi-user environment where developers may create, store, reuse, manage, and deliver digital learning content from a central object repository. The LMS cannot create and manipulate courses; it cannot reuse the content of one course to build another. The LCMS, however, can create, manage and deliver not only training modules but also manage and edit all the individual pieces that make up a catalog of training. LCMS applications allow users to create, import, manage, search for and reuse small units or "chunks" of digital learning content and assets, commonly referred to as learning objects. These assets may include media files developed in other authoring tools, assessment items, simulations, text, graphics or any other object that makes up the content within the course being created. An LCMS manages the process of creating, editing, storing and delivering e-learning content, ILT materials and other training support deliverables such as job aids.

LCMS have the ability to assemble and consolidate learning objects into lengthier "learning paths" or learning experiences that are personalized to a learner's profile, job description, assessment results, or requests.

By separating content, style, and flow, and integrating extensibility, an extended Learning Content Management System allows courseware authors to leverage their learning content and present it in countless different ways for a wide variety of target platforms and in a remarkably short timeframe.

1.16.4 Drawbacks to Learning Management Systems

Certain learning tasks are well suited for an LMS (centralized functions like learner administration and content management). Learning itself is different – it is not a process to be managed. Learning is by nature multi-faceted and chaotic. Organizations that now lock into enterprise-level systems will be able to do an excellent job of delivering courses. They won't, however, be positioning themselves well for informal learning, performance support, or knowledge management. The concept is simple: one tool can't do it all without losing functionality. The more feature-rich an individual tool becomes, the more it loses its usefulness to the average user. Connected specialization, modularization, and decentralization are learning foundations capable of adjusting to varied information climate changes.

1.16.5 Learning Management Industry

In the relatively new LMS market, commercial vendors for corporate and education applications range from new entrants to those that entered the market in the nineties. In addition to commercial packages, many open source solutions are available, including Moodle,Sakai, and Instructure.

LMSs represent an $860 million market, made up of more than 60 different providers. The six largest LMS product companies constitute approximately 50% of the market. In addition to the remaining smaller LMS product vendors, training outsourcing firms, enterprise resource planning vendors, and consulting firms all compete for part of the learning management market. Approximately 40 percent of US training organizations reported that they have an LMS installed, a figure that has not changed significantly over the past two years. The small business market offers the greatest opportunity for growth, as only 36 percent of these companies are using an LMS. Many of these businesses would like a low-cost, easy-to-use, easy-to-maintain system – but, as yet, they are not willing to make the commitment. An LMS is still a nontrivial investment in money and resources.

According to a 2009 report by American Society for Training and Development (ASTD) 91 percent of ASTD respondents are using LMSs in their organizations, with more than half purchasing rather than building their systems, and one-fifth of respondents opting to go with a hosted platform. And whether built or bought, the majority of respondents are satisfied with their current LMS, with 22.2 percent very satisfied, 31.1 percent satisfied, and 25.6 percent somewhat satisfied. Still, some 13.3 said they were unsatisfied, and 8.8 said they were very unsatisfied.

Most buyers of LMSs utilize an authoring tool to create their e-learning content, which is then hosted on an LMS. In many cases LMSs include a primitive authoring tool for basic content manipulation. For advanced content creation buyers must choose an authoring software that integrates with their LMS in order for their content to be hosted. There are authoring tools on the market, which meet AICC and SCORM standards and therefore content created in tools such as these can be hosted on an AICC or SCORM certified LMS. By May 2010, ADL had validated 301 SCORM-certified products while 329 products were compliant.

Evaluation of LMSs is a complex task and significant research supports different forms of evaluation, including iterative processess where students' experiences and approaches to learning are evaluated.

1.16.6 Trends

Another upcoming trend in this technology is 'Channel Learning' where organizations are sharing online contents and learning from their partner firms. According to a survey by trainingindustry.com, for many buyers channel learning is not their number one priority, but often there is a gap when the HR department oversees training and development initiatives, where the focus is consolidated inside traditional corporate boundaries. Software technology companies are at the front end of this curve, placing higher priority on channel trainings.

Today the biggest trend in the e-learning market is for these systems to be integrated with 'Talent Management Systems'. A talent management software serves towards the process of recruiting, managing, assessing, developing and maintaining an organization's most important resources. Bersin research shows that in 2009 more than 70 percent of large companies have an LMS already and almost one third of these companies are considering replacing or upgrading these systems with integrated talent management systems.

A growing trend in today's market is the ability for publishers to sell training/courses on their site with syndicated training. Syndicated training courses are hosted by a third party learning management system. This allows publishers to sell their courses via a turn key syndication process. The rise and popularity of social media has allowed many content/course creators to syndicate content on their own sites.

To facilitate knowledge sharing, KM must understand the requirements of the users, as well as the complexities and potential problems with managing knowledge and knowledge sources. Very broadly speaking, management must therefore implement the right processes, frameworks, and systems that enable knowledge sharing. They must also foster a knowledge sharing culture that ensures that these investments are fully utilized.

For explicit knowledge, seven issues have been identified that KM must consider, these are: articulation, awareness, access, guidance, completeness. IT has been identified as a key component of this type of knowledge sharing, facilitating and lowering the cost of the storage, access, retrieval, and variety of explicit knowledge.

Tacit knowledge sharing depends on socialization and practice. KM must offer the means for this to take place by providing the right forums (primarily physical, but also virtual), supporting networks and communities, and accepting unstructured work environments. Generalists, known as knowledge managers, should be used to gain an understanding of the location of knowledge sources and to bridge the gaps between communities and networks.

In order to support the transfer of tacit knowledge, KMS must support the socialization functions, while at the same time not enforcing strict managerial practices/routines/hierarchies/etc. One of its roles is as an expert finder, and it can also help in the direct transfer of tacit knowledge through the support of rich and varied methods of communication, which preferably include informal communication channels.

Embedded knowledge sharing is a process whereby embedded knowledge is passed on from one product, routine, or process to another. Several tools have been described that can help management understand the effects of embedded knowledge and help in its transfer. These were: scenario planning, after action reviews, and management training.

CHAPTER

KNOWLEDGE SHARING METHODS 2

2.1 INTRODUCTION

There are endless number of business challenges across the world, but the solutions mostly remain localized – not learning from the experiences. So, what is the major difference between the companies that progress and fall? The answer to this complex question is rather simple – knowledge sharing within organizations, i.e., captured knowledge needs to be disseminated, scaled up and replicated.

Incorporating a knowledge sharing culture is mandatory for organizations to succeed because there is always a risk of losing or forgetting the acquired knowledge. The conduit of knowledge sharing needs to be shared rather than just storing or documenting it because when your staff struggles to access information employees need and can't find it on time, the bottom line of your company suffers.

Now when you know the importance of knowledge sharing, now is the time to make it happen. Watch this video to learn 10 knowledge management best practices to bring you success.

Whether it is verbal or digital, sharing leads to a better knowledge base of employees and fosters a culture of knowledge management. Hence, it is crucial to boost such a culture that facilitates employees to use digital platforms for sharing best knowledge and practices.

The ultimate key is developing a knowledge sharing platform where employees feel comfortable in putting up their opinions, ideas, personal viewpoints, and seek assistance of peers/seniors/experts when needed.

Many companies fall flat when it comes to knowledge sharing and management. When your customer is faced with a struggle to find information, your company can suffer. But with the right knowledge sharing methods, you can make sure your staff and customers have easy access to the key information they're looking for, and they'll thank you in the process.

Knowledge sharing has the potential to revolutionize how your business operates, enhancing the potential of what you know, and magnifying the value you can extract and utilize to deliver your proposition.

2.2 KNOWLEDGE SHARING IN A NUTSHELL

Knowledge sharing can bring endless benefits to your company. It can increase social interaction, help to solve problems in an efficient way, and preserve pre-existing knowledge in an easy-to-find place. Your team will thank you for being able to find the information they need, when they need it, therefore speeding up 'response times'.

Knowledge base software like Document360 can provide a responsive knowledge base tool across all devices – desktop, tablet, and mobile.

Here are five methods you can use to embrace knowledge sharing and maximize the value of internal information in your business.

2.2.1 Peer Assists

During a peer assist, your team comes together to share experiences, insights, and knowledge to identify problems, challenges, and 'wins'. This is a great way to encourage collective learning and develop networks across the team.

You can translate this method to customers too. By creating a public editable knowledge base, you can encourage customers to interact, help resolve issues, and share their experiences in the system. This helps all involved and ensures the asset is always evolving and delivering greater value.

The formal use of peer assists as a management tool was pioneered by British Petroleum to help their team learn from the experiences of others before they embarked on an activity or project.

2.2.2 After Action Review

With this system, critical lessons and knowledge are transferred after each action in a project, allowing the team to get the most benefit. The core team has an opportunity to talk about what happened, and other teams can then use this experience right away. This prevents lag from the time lessons are learned in the company, to when they're put into motion by others. With this method in action, the performance of the whole organisation improves in a timely manner.

An AAR Is a Structured Meeting That Does the Following:

- Focuses on why things happened
- Compares intended results with what was actually accomplished
- Encourages participation
- Emphasizes trust and the value of feedback

2.2.3 Storytelling

Storytelling has become a useful marketing approach, and is a great knowledge sharing method.

Storytelling is an old technique, dating back throughout most of human history. The practice is embedded into our culture. Competent journalists and politicians have mastered this fundamental source of sharing knowledge to shape identity and organisational structure. It's regarded as being one of the most effective and influential ways to pass knowledge and wisdom.

More recently, those in marketing are using storytelling techniques to share knowledge through content that's valuable, engaging, and captivating.

Storytelling Can

- Help to share norms and values
- Develop trust and commitment
- Generate emotional connections

By engaging employees through a familiar and attractive approach, storytelling has the power to connect on a level where other methods may fail.

2.2.4 Mentoring

Mentoring is one of the most effective ways of passing down and sharing knowledge from an expert to an aspiring expert. This is a relationship oriented way of building knowledge.

Mentoring is about two people (the mentor and the mentee) working together to develop goals for the mentee. Mentoring looks to the future. Its aim is career development. It's a key process for knowledge management. Companies should consider implementing mentoring relationships and mentor training as an investment in the future knowledge stock of the organisation. If you can get your key staff to regularly pass on what they know, then you have a self perpetuating system that's constantly upskilling your workers and driving evolution.

2.2.5 Coaching

Not to be confused with mentoring. Where mentoring is relationship focus, coaching is task focused. Coaching focuses on concrete issues, such as managing more effectively, speaking more articulately, and learning how to think strategically. This requires a content expert (coach) who is capable of teaching the coachee(s) how to develop these skills.

Coaching is much more structured and focuses on specific objectives within a set period of time – it's mainly concerned with performance and the development of certain skills. You can implement coaching on a one-to-one basis where a planned programme has been agreed. Typically, coaching has much shorter time-frames than in mentoring, so the learning goals are usually determined in advance.

Mentoring and coaching can be 'stand alone' activities, but they can also be used to complement each other for optimal impact too.

2.2.6 Knowledge is Power

Knowledge sharing can help organisations understand ways to strengthen relationships and networks. Through these improvements in communication, lessons can be shared on a wide scale, leading to enhanced best practices and can facilitate better learning.

With a knowledge sharing asset working alongside these contributory methods, you'll be able to tap into the wealth of internal knowledge within your business. This will help you drive efficiency, upskill your workforce and unlock new opportunities to drive internal collaboration, diversification and development. Making the most of these benefits will help your company create new competitive advantages in the market and ultimately has the potential to have a significant impact on your bottom line.

Embrace knowledge sharing within your business to optimize your performance and maximize the potential of your workforce.

1. **Proprietary Online Training:** The Internet cannot provide information about your business to your employees. That's why many organizations have developed a proprietary training program for their staff. It helps individuals learn about their company's products and its roadmap for the future.

Suggested Tools to Use

- **Lessonly:** LMS provides training and practice sessions for the customer and sales representatives. It focuses on the best practices to serve your customers.
- **Eloomi:** Eloomi can provide a detailed performance review of your staff. It will also help you improve the employee engagement of your company.
- **Cloud Tutorial:** Cloud Tutorial knowledge management system can help the employees get answers to their questions quickly. It has a quick and smart search to browse the content they need.

2. **AI-Powered Decision Making:** Artificial intelligence (AI) can deliver better insights about the business and market to the employees.

Often new employees face difficulty in decision-making due to their lack of experience. In such situations, AI can guide them in deciding which project they should work for in the office.

Suggested Tools to Use

- **Faraday:** It's a platform for AI predictions and decisions. Faraday focuses on B2C growth.
- **Element AI Knowledge Scout:** AI decision-making platform for software and tech organizations.

3. **Link Management:** A Knowledge worker visits many websites seeking knowledge to complete their project. An organization may leave it up to the employee to manage these resources through bookmarks. At some point, such bookmarkswill become unscalable and ineffective.

Link management can solve this issue by providing access to essential resources faster and can expand across the organization.

Suggested Tools to Use

- **Go Links:** It's enterprise-grade software for secure short links. These links are easy to remember for team members. They will be able to find and share information quickly with such links.
- **Workona:** It's a link management dashboard. If your activities get scattered across the browser, Workona will organize them with one-click collaboration. It keeps a team project well organized.

4. **Project Management Software:** Project Management Software helps a team exchange knowledge and stay on the same page in a specific project. It has individual task cards where everyone finds relevant data and files for that particular project.

Suggested Tools to Use

- **Asana:** A task management tool for marketing team members.
- **Jira:** It is software that keeps every department and team of a company on the same tool.
- **Clickup:** A project management software with spreadsheets, chat, and docs.

5. **Meetings and Verbal Knowledge Sharing:** Meetings such as sales calls, project meetings, and team meetings get conducted regularly in the office. These tools can help you schedule and manage all of these with ease.

Suggested Tools to Use

- **Zoom:** Webinar and Web conferencing software for all types of teams.
- **Wingman**: The platform offers call feedback and conversation intelligence for a company. It is essential for the sales team members.
- **Panopto:** It's a platform that fulfills all kinds of video requirements such as video management, hosting, video search, and live streaming.

6. **Chat Platforms:** Chat is useful if it gets organized into channels with different sections. Here, essential files can be shared and discovered.

Suggested Software to Use

- **Slack:** Communication and Chat platform with video and voice calling. It also has useful integrations and file sharing.

- **Microsoft Teams:** It is a group chat software that offers collaboration features for everyone and team meetings. It can also integrate with other Microsoft programs.

7. **Digital Asset Management:** What if your essential files go missing in email threads, slack channels, or in old task management software? It can get prevented with a digital asset management system. This system provides searchable phrases and tags, which is essential for a big company. Employees will be able to search and find the required assets they need quickly.

Suggested Tools to Use

- **Box:** It's a digital asset management system for all types of files. Box comes with features such as searching, permissions, and tagging.
- **Canto:** It's a platform for storing and sharing brand assets.
- **Aprimo:** For managing work and digital assets, primarily meant for the digital marketing department.

8. **Standard Operating Procedures and Project Documentation:** Any process used by an organization needs to get documented. These tools can help you develop and share such SOPs with your employees.

Suggested Software to Use

- **Process Street:** It is a process and workflow management system. It can process templates, checklists, and track progress.
- **Trainual:** A robust platform for training and onboarding. It also contains process documentation, SOPs, wiki, and learning management systems.
- **Notion:** It's an all-in-one platform that lets you add project documentation and SOPs besides task management.
- **Cloud Tutorial:** Cloud Tutorial is a fully customized platform. It allows companies to create FAQ pages, help desk, and SOP for any processes.

9. **Screen Recordings:** Video meetings, email, or chat aren't always necessary. Screen recordings can also help for communication purposes. One can create short video content and share it with everyone in the team. It can also be added in SOPs and other documentation.

Suggested Software to Use

- **Loom**: It's an easy tool for sharing screen recordings with others. You can use it for training, feedback, and assigning tasks to everyone.
- **Vidyard:** It's an excellent screen recording tool for connecting remote employees. Also useful for marketing and sales objectives.

10. Shared Digital Whiteboards: Whiteboards can be used in creating a visual representation of processes and requirements. It's an excellent tool for brainstorming sessions and to keep visual work on track.

Suggested Software to Use

- **Miro:** It's an online whiteboard platform with canvases. You can use it to create anything, such as mind maps and wireframes.
- **Sketchboard:** It's a collaborative online whiteboard. One can use it to sketch UX flows and give presentations.

2.2.7 Knowledge Sharing Best Practices

Considering the huge benefits of sharing knowledge in the workplace, it is no secret that it is one of the best ways to improve the productivity and performance of an organization. Sharing best practices helps in filling the knowledge gaps and improving efficiency at the workplace.

The question here is, how to improve knowledge sharing in the organization? Here are some of the most effective practices to encourage knowledge sharing.

Establish Knowledge Sharing Habits

The key to effective knowledge sharing practices is not just to educate about sharing practices but help them understand the potential benefits from their fellow worker's experience. The knowledge sharing methods helps in automating and standardizing the knowledge management, but the most prominent challenge is to create a knowledge sharing culture. A knowledge lifecycle helps in building the processes and stimulate knowledge transfer within the organization. Let's understand the lifecycle of knowledge first.

The lifecycle of knowledge is mainly concerned with the organization of data and outlines the building, storing, pooling, and extending the knowledge. Here, the role of technology becomes very important to support this learning community. Employing technology helps you streamline internal communication, discussions, knowledge dissemination, and much more.

Go Cloud to Share Best Practices

Accessibility is the key to the best knowledge management. And by keeping the resources on the cloud can help you make the knowledge easily accessible across the organization. Some of the key features of your content management system includes:

- Online or cloud access that allows you to access the resources anytime, anywhere.
- Intuitive user experience that tunes with the employees and does not require intensive training
- Defined authoring process and direct link sharing

- Mobile-friendly
- Manage multiple roles and permissions for content access within the organization
- Integrate seamlessly with social and collaboration tools.

Incentivize the Knowledge Sharing Activities

Now, who does not love rewards? There are many different ways to reward your team members who embody the knowledge sharing practices. To start with, a social media post on the company page, an appreciation email, or an announcement can be done for the team member. Their valuable contribution needs to be valued as it benefits the fellow-workers as well as the organization.

Specify the content that has been shared by the team member with some tangible benefits that encourages everyone to make their part of the contribution. You can also consider giving a bonus to the employee who share the most important information in the quarter or year.

Enhance Onboarding and Training Practices

The onboarding and training seem to be unrelated here at first glance. However, knowledge sharing platform is one of the most useful resources for new hires. Often, they spend a lot of time to contribute their ideas and feel nervous to express in the group setting. As a result, they lose their interactive skills and knowledge over time.

The contribution and collaboration of new hires are as important as existing employees. And knowledge management can fulfill this purpose. For example, a mentor can be allocated for each hire so that they feel empowered to speak up in the group. Never assume that they don't want to contribute but always encourage them to provide their opinion.

Use State-of-the-Art Knowledge Sharing Tool

The selection of a knowledge sharing platform is one of the major business decisions as it directly impacts the productivity of employees and business performance. The utilization effective knowledge sharing tools allow you to streamline the business processes, search for content quickly, store documents and media content easily, locate experts, ask questions, and much more. The right selection of a knowledge sharing platform can maximize the impact of valuable contributions made by every employee in the organization.

2.3 TOP KNOWLEDGE SHARING TOOLS

2.3.1 Project Portfolio Solution to Manage Projects

Most businesses juggle endless tasks, people, projects, and goals. Having an integrated portfolio management solution ensures that everything is organized while planning and implementing the projects. It helps a team share best practices and project related knowledge and stay on the same page. BizPortals 365 portfolio management solution supports the ever-changing needs of the project management environment. The ready-to-use features and capabilities of Microsoft 365 help in streamlining key activities of project portfolios. It also offers seamless real-time integration with external systems like ERP, CRM, and line of business applications.

2.3.2 Re-usable Templates for Link Management

We will start this with an analogy here – Despite having feature rich DSLR camera, why most people take photographs using their mobile phones? The reason is accessibility and serving the purpose of capturing the moment.

Same goes with the knowledge sharing platforms. When you select a knowledge management tool, concentrate on the must-have features like quick link sharing, accessibility, responsiveness, social collaboration, authoring, role-based access permissions and, rest all is a bonus. Like, BizPortals 365 platform offers multiple content options like resources, modules, courses, knowledge sheets, etc. across different subject genres. These templates are re-usable, saves time and provide an overview of possibilities to the organization.

2.3.3 Meetings for Knowledge Sharing

Meetings like sales calls, team meetings get conducted on a regular basis. The right knowledge sharing tools can help you manage and schedule the tasks, discuss projects, share ideas in real-time. With BizPortals 365, you can leverage Microsoft Teams for 1:1 chat, group chat, calls, meetings, or screen share at any time, from any device. The knowledge sharing tool offers excellent collaboration features and team meetings. It can also integrate with other Microsoft programs.

2.3.4 Digital Asset Management

Never let your essential files go missing in email threads, old task management software, or communication channels. The integrated Microsoft 365 platform provides searchable phrases and tags and a centralized repository to manage documents efficiently. The employees can search, tag, categorize, and find the digital assets they need without any hassles.

2.4 WHY ADOPT A KNOWLEDGE SHARING PLATFORM?

2.4.1 Reuse the Best Problem-Solving Experiences

Reusing what others have already learned and created can save a lot of time and money, increase work productivity, and minimize risks. Sharing best practices helps in streamlining the work and increasing the productivity of employees. Some knowledge sharing examples include user manuals, training documents, used methodologies, best-proven practices, storytelling, lessons learned, e-learning.

2.4.2 Boosts Competence and Efficiency

Did you know that your employees could take a substantial amount of time to look for the right information or locate the relevant search result? It means that a lot of productive time is spent unproductively to seek information.

The knowledge management practices in an organization shrink most of the unproductive time spent in searching for the information. And at the same time, all the employees will have easy access to the right information, whenever and wherever they need it.

2.4.3 Stimulate Workplace Innovation

Sharing the best knowledge management practices encourage your employees to share their innovative ideas and help deliver better results. The stimulation of knowledge and increased idea sharing helps the employees to be more productive and on the cusp of new trends and markets.

2.4.4 Faster and Better Decision Making

Sharing best practices across teams is not only beneficial to your employees but also fruitful for business performance. When all the tasks are performed efficiently in the organization and every member works in a streamlined manner, it ensures faster, better decision making and eventually improves the productivity and performance of the organization.

2.4.5 Improve Sales and Customer Relationships

The importance of customer cannot be overstated as it is ranked before finance and product to achieve business success. Knowledge management plays a crucial role in managing customer relations. For example, when a customer service agent spends a lot of time to search for the relevant information to resolve a problem or answer a question, customers will end up being frustrated and ultimately dissatisfied. With a knowledge-sharing platform, the search effort and time can be reduced drastically. It provides access to consolidated information, making it easier to use.

2.4.6 Reduce Know-How Losses

Know-how is a very important asset for the organization and its management directly impacts the business performance. The knowledge sharing practices can capture best of the knowledge and make it accessible to employees.

It makes scarce resources readily available across the organization. Earlier, the presentations, trainings, white papers and case studies fulfilled these needs but now, central streamline internal communication are the necessity to make information accessible.

2.4.7 Build a Corporate Community

Sharing knowledge is one of the best intuitive ways to form a closely-knit community. A dedicated platform for information sharing and management helps businesses to capture and store knowledge in the most accessible ways. Building a community also ensures the consistency of knowledge sharing within the organization.

2.4.8 Reduce Cost and Time

Knowledge sharing best practices allows employees to share important information they have along with their achievements and experience. It eliminates the redundant effort of employees and saves them from committing the same mistakes. Moreover, they can get the ready solution at the right time. In addition to saving time, it also reduces the cost that your business may incur to solve the problems.

2.5 BENEFITS OF KNOWLEDGE SHARING IN ORGANIZATIONS

Simply put, knowledge sharing is the exchange of valuable information between the employees of an organization. It's a fundamental part of every company's knowledge management efforts.

Knowledge sharing can happen in the form of employee handbooks, manuals, mentoring sessions, and even informal discussions between workers.

Studies have found that knowledge sharing leads to greater creativity, more innovation, improved collaboration, and better performance, for individuals, teams, and organizations. There are many reasons why companies would want to encourage it.

2.5.1 Knowledge Sharing Prevents the "Brain Drain"

Your long-time employees have accumulated a lot of valuable know-how over the years. Unless they document or share that knowledge with other employees, they will take it with them when they leave. Making up for that knowledge loss is not cheap either. It has been estimated that it costs more than $30,000 to replace a member of staff, resulting from the loss of productivity in the 28 weeks it takes to bring a new recruit up to speed.

2.5.2 Employees are Better Equipped to do Their Jobs

In 2012, McKinsey reported that on average, "employees spend 9.3 hours per week searching and gathering information". And wasted time is just part of the problem. When knowledge is not shared, decisions take longer, the same mistakes are made over and over again, work gets duplicated, and overall quality of work suffers. When employees have access to the information they need, when they need it, they get things done faster.

2.5.3 New Hires Ramp up Productivity Faster

When a new employee joins a team, there is an overwhelming amount of things they need to learn: the tools, the workflows, the company culture. Knowledge sharing between new and experienced employees helps them get up to speed and learn the ropes sooner.

2.5.4 Knowledge Sharing Tools

Establishing a knowledge-sharing culture in your organization is not an easy task which can't be solved by technology alone. But choosing the right knowledge sharing tool is an important first step.

If the tool you choose turns out to be slow, complex, or buggy, it's going to be a lot more difficult to encourage your team to use it. On the other hand, if the tool is intuitive and fun to use, knowledge sharing can turn from a chore into a pleasant, rewarding activity. An ideal knowledge sharing tool (for example, a knowledge base or an intranet portal) needs to:

- Provide an instant and reliable search function.
- Have intuitive navigation and content hierarchy.
- Be easily editable even by non-technical users, ideally, in real time.
- Have a reliable version history.
- Have permissions and access rights management.
- Allow easy linking between pages.
- Integrate with other tools to keep all content in sync.
- Have enterprise-level security.

2.5.5 Sharing Knowledge Through an Intranet Portal (Nuclino)

One such knowledge sharing tool is Nuclino, a unified workspace for all your team's knowledge, docs, and projects. It focuses on essential features and offers a clean, intuitive interface that can be easily set up even by non-technical users.

Teams use Nuclino to share and collaborate on business memos, SOP documents, process documentation, employee onboarding checklists, meeting minutes, project plans and more. It works like a collective brain, allowing you to bring all your team's work together in one place and collaborate without the chaos of files and folders, context switching, or silos.

2.5.6 Best Practices for Knowledge Sharing

As mentioned above, technology alone is not enough to make knowledge sharing an integral part of your company culture. "If you build it, they will come" is rarely how it goes with corporate knowledge bases. It needs to be a continuous process that requires discipline and commitment from your entire team.

Fortunately, there are several effective measures you can take to motivate your colleagues:

Keep your Knowledge Base Up-to-Date

Your team will be a lot more likely to engage with your knowledge management system if it makes their day-to-day jobs easier. If you are introducing a new knowledge base, make sure that the information it contains is helpful, up-to-date, and easy to retrieve.

Make Knowledge Sharing a Part of the Onboarding Process

To make knowledge sharing a core part of your company culture, start with your new hires. Introduce them to your knowledge base and show them how to update it. Pair them with a mentor they can turn to with questions. Allow them to shadow someone in a similar position and let them learn through observation.

2.6 EMBRACE ASYNCHRONOUS COMMUNICATION

Knowledge silos exist because in most companies information is mainly exchanged in meetings, without getting documented. Communicating asynchronously through thoughtful long-worm write-ups automatically creates internal documentation and adds to your team knowledge base, increasing clarity and transparency and benefiting everyone, including your future employees.

2.6.1 Provide Incentives

Before knowledge sharing turns into a habit, motivating your team may require some effort. Make it a team KPI and come up with appropriate rewards for the most active contributors to your team knowledge base.

2.6.2 Pay Attention to Feedback

Cultural shifts don't happen overnight and it may be difficult to get it right the first time. Make sure to monitor your team and identify potential areas of improvement. Are there repetitive questions that could be documented in the knowledge base? Is the content kept up-to-date? Are new hires struggling to find the information they need? Use your team's input to continuously iterate on your knowledge sharing workflows, making your employees feel included, valued, and heard.

2.7 COMMUNITY OF PRACTICE

A community of practice (CoP) is a group of people who "share a concern or a passion for something they do and learn how to do it better as they interact regularly". The concept was first proposed by cognitive anthropologist Jean Lave and educational theorist Etienne Wenger in their 1991 book Situated Learning. Wenger then significantly expanded on the concept in his 1998 book Communities of Practice.

A CoP can evolve naturally because of the members' common interest in a particular domain or area, or it can be created deliberately with the goal of gaining knowledge related to a specific field. It is through the process of sharing information and experiences with the group that members learn from each other, and have an opportunity to develop personally and professionally.

CoPs can exist in physical settings, for example, a lunchroom at work, a field setting, a factory floor, or elsewhere in the environment, but members of CoPs do not have to be co-located. They form a "virtual community of practice" (VCoP) when they collaborate online, such as within discussion boards, newsgroups, or the various chats on social media, such as #musochat centered on contemporary classical music performance. A "mobile community of practice" (MCoP) is when members communicate with one another via mobile phones and participate in community work on the go.

Communities of practice are not new phenomena: this type of learning has existed for as long as people have been learning and sharing their experiences through storytelling. The idea is rooted in American pragmatism, especially C. S. Peirce's concept of the "community of inquiry" , but also John Dewey's principle of learning through occupation (Wallace 2007).

For Etienne Wenger, learning is central to human identity. A primary focus of Wenger's more recent work is on learning as social participation – the individual as an active participant in the practices of social communities, and in the construction of his/her identity through these communities. In this context, a community of practice is a group of individuals participating in communal activity, and experiencing/continuously creating their shared identity through engaging in and contributing to the practices of their communitics.

The structural characteristics of a community of practice are again redefined to a domain of knowledge, a notion of community and a practice:

- **Domain:** A domain of knowledge creates common ground, inspires members to participate, guides their learning and gives meaning to their actions.
- **Community:** The notion of a community creates the social fabric for that learning. A strong community fosters interactions and encourages a willingness to share ideas.
- **Practice:** While the domain provides the general area of interest for the community, the practice is the specific focus around which the community develops, shares and maintains its core of knowledge.

In many organizations, communities of practice have become an integral part of the organization structure. These communities take on knowledge stewarding tasks that were formerly covered by more formal organizational structures. In some organizations, there are both formal and informal communities of practice. There is a great deal of interest within organizations to encourage, support, and sponsor communities of practice in order to benefit from shared knowledge that may lead to higher productivity (Wenger 2004). Communities of practice are now viewed by many in the business setting as a means to capturing the tacit knowledge, or the know-how that is not so easily articulated.

An important aspect and function of communities of practice is increasing organization performance. Lesser & Storck (2001, p. 836) identify four areas of organizational performance that can be affected by communities of practice:

- Decreasing the learning curve of new employees
- Responding more rapidly to customer needs and inquiries
- Reducing rework and preventing "reinvention of the wheel"
- Spawning new ideas for products and services

2.7.1 Compared to Functional or Project Teams

Collaboration constellations differ in various ways. Some are under organizational control others, like CoPs, are self-organized or under the control of individuals. For examples of how these and other collaboration types vary in terms of their temporal or boundary focus and the basis of their members' relationships.

A project team differs from a community of practice in several significant ways.

- A project team is driven by deliverables with shared goals, milestones and results.
- A project team meets to share and exchange information and experiences just as the community of practice does, but team membership is defined by task.
- A project team typically has designated members who remain consistent in their roles during the project.
- A project team is dissolved once its mission is accomplished.
- A community of practice is often organically created, with as many objectives as members of that community.
- Community membership is defined by the knowledge of the members.
- CoP membership changes and members may take on new roles within the community as interests and needs arise.
- A community of practice can exist as long as the members believe they have something to contribute to it, or gain from it.

2.8 VERSUS COMMUNITIES OF INTEREST

In addition to the distinction between CoP and other types of organizational groupings found in the workplace, in some cases, it is useful to differentiate CoP from community of interest (CoI).

2.8.1 Community of Interest

- A group of people interested in sharing information and discussing a particular topic that interests them.
- Members are not necessarily experts or practitioners of the topic around which the CoI has formed.
- The purpose of the CoI is to provide a place where people who share a common interest can go and exchange information, ask questions, and express their opinions about the topic.
- Membership in a CoI is not dependent upon expertise – one only needs to be interested in the subject.

2.8.2 Community of Practice

- A CoP, in contrast, is a group of people who are active practitioners.
- CoP participation is not appropriate for non-practitioners.
- The purpose of a CoP, as discussed above, is to provide a way for practitioners to share tips and best practices, ask questions of their colleagues, and provide support for each other.
- Membership is dependent on expertise – one should have at least some recent experience performing in the role or subject area of the CoP.

2.9 BENEFITS

2.9.1 Social Capital

Social capital is said to be a multi-dimensional concept, with both public and private facets. That is, social capital may provide value to both the individual and the group as a whole. Through informal connections that participants build in their community of practice, and in the process of sharing their expertise, learning from others, and participating in the group, members are said to be acquiring social capital – especially those members who demonstrate expertise and experience.

2.9.2 Knowledge Management

Wasko & Faraj (2000) describe three kinds of knowledge: "knowledge as object", "knowledge embedded within individuals", and "knowledge embedded in a community". Communities of Practice have become associated with finding, sharing, transferring, and archiving knowledge, as well as making explicit "expertise", or tacit knowledge. Tacit knowledge is considered to be those valuable context-based experiences that cannot easily be captured, codified and stored.

Because knowledge management is seen "primarily as a problem of capturing, organizing, and retrieving information, evoking notions of databases, documents, query languages, and data mining", the community of practice, collectively and individually, is considered a rich potential source of helpful information in the form of actual experiences; in other words, best practices.

Thus, for knowledge management, a community of practice is one source of content and context that if codified, documented and archived can be accessed for later use.

2.10 FACTORS

2.10.1 Individuals

Members of communities of practice are thought to be more efficient and effective conduits of information and experiences. While organizations tend to provide manuals to meet the training needs of their employees, CoPs help foster the process of storytelling among colleagues which, in turn, helps them strengthen their skills on the job.

Studies have shown that workers spend a third of their time looking for information and are five times more likely to turn to a co-worker rather than an explicit source of information (book, manual, or database). Time is saved by conferring with members of a CoP. Members of the community have tacit knowledge, which can be difficult to store and retrieve outside. For example, one person can share the best way to handle a situation based on his experiences, which may enable the other person to avoid mistakes and shorten the learning curve. In a CoP, members can openly discuss and brainstorm about a project, which can lead to new capabilities. The type of information that is shared and learned in a CoP is boundless. Duguid (2005) clarifies the difference between tacit knowledge, or knowing how, and explicit knowledge, or knowing what. Performing optimally in a job requires being able to convert theory into practice. Communities of practice help the individual bridge the gap between knowing what and knowing how.

As members of communities of practice, individuals report increased communication with people (professionals, interested parties, hobbyists), less dependence on geographic proximity, and the generation of new knowledge.

2.10.2 Social Presence

Communicating with others in a community of practice involves creating social presence. Tu (2002) defines social presence as "the degree of salience of another person in an interaction and the consequent salience of an interpersonal relationship". It is believed that social presence affects how likely an individual is of participating in a CoP (especially in online environments and virtual communities of practice) (Tu 2002). Management of a community of practice often faces many barriers that inhibit individuals from engaging in knowledge exchange. Some of the reasons for these barriers are egos and personal attacks, large overwhelming CoPs, and time constraints.

2.10.3 Motivation

Motivation to share knowledge is critical to success in communities of practice. Studies show that members are motivated to become active participants in a CoP when they view knowledge as meant for the public good, a moral obligation and/or as a community interest. Members of a community of practice can also be motivated to participate by using methods such as tangible returns, intangible returns and community interest.

2.10.4 Collaboration

Collaboration is essential to ensuring that communities of practice thrive. Research has found that certain factors can indicate a higher level of collaboration in knowledge exchange in a business network. Sveiby and Simons found that more seasoned colleagues tend to foster a more collaborative culture. Additionally they noted that a higher educational level also predicts a tendency to favor collaboration.

2.10.5 Community of Interest

A community of interest, or interest-based community, is a community of people who share a common interest or passion. These people exchange ideas and thoughts about the given passion, but may know (or care) little about each other outside this area. Participation in a community of interest can be compelling, entertaining and create a community where people return frequently and remain for extended periods. Frequently, they cannot be easily defined by a particular geographical area.

In other words, "a community of interest is a gathering of people assembled around a topic of common interest. Its members take part in the community to exchange information, to obtain answers to personal questions or problems, to improve their understanding of a subject, to share common passions or to play." In contrast to a spatial community, "a 'community of interest' is defined not by space, but by some common bond or entity".

"Online communities" connect to communities of interest in that often, they develop out of interests in a particular topic. A benefit of online communities over place-based communities is that of non-physical access to group involvement.

2.11 COMPUTER NETWORK

A computer network is a set of computers sharing resources located on or provided by network nodes. The computers use common communication protocols over digital interconnections to communicate with each other. These interconnections are made up of telecommunication network technologies, based on physically wired, optical, and wireless radio-frequency methods that may be arranged in a variety of network topologies.

The nodes of a computer network may include personal computers, servers, networking hardware, or other specialised or general-purpose hosts. They are identified by network addresses, and may have hostnames. Hostnames serve as memorable labels for the nodes, rarely changed after initial assignment. Network addresses serve for locating and identifying the nodes by communication protocols such as the Internet Protocol.

Computer networks may be classified by many criteria, including the transmission medium used to carry signals, bandwidth, communications protocols to organize network traffic, the network size, the topology, traffic control mechanism, and organizational intent.

Computer networks support many applications and services, such as access to the World Wide Web, digital video, digital audio, shared use of application and storage servers, printers, and fax machines, and use of email and instant messaging applications.

Computer networking may be considered a branch of computer science, computer engineering, and telecommunications, since it relies on the theoretical and practical application of the related disciplines. Computer networking was influenced by a wide array of technology developments and historical milestones.

- In the late 1950s, a network of computers was built for the U.S. military Semi-Automatic Ground Environment (SAGE) radar system using the Bell 101 modem. It was the first commercial modem for computers, released by AT&T Corporation in 1958. The modem allowed digital data to be transmitted over regular unconditioned telephone lines at a speed of 110 bits per second.
- In 1959, Christopher Strachey filed a patent application for time-sharing and John McCarthy initiated the first project to implement time-sharing of user programs at MIT. Stratchey passed the concept on to J. C. R. Licklider at the inaugural UNESCO Information Processing Conference in Paris that year. McCarthy was instrumental in the creation of three of the earliest time-sharing systems (Compatible Time-Sharing System in 1961, BBN Time-Sharing System in 1962, and Dartmouth Time Sharing System in 1963).
- In 1959, Anatoly Kitov proposed to the Central Committee of the Communist Party of the Soviet Union a detailed plan for the re-organisation of the control of the Soviet armed forces and of the Soviet economy on the basis of a network of computing centres. Kitov's proposal was rejected, as later was the 1962 OGAS economy management network project.
- In 1960, the commercial airline reservation system semi-automatic business research environment (SABRE) went online with two connected mainframes.
- In 1963, J. C. R. Licklider sent a memorandum to office colleagues discussing the concept of the "Intergalactic Computer Network", a computer network intended to allow general communications among computer users.
- Throughout the 1960s, Paul Baran and Donald Davies independently developed the concept of packet switching to transfer information between computers over a

network. Davies pioneered the implementation of the concept. The NPL network, a local area network at the National Physical Laboratory (United Kingdom) used a line speed of 768 kbit/s and later high-speed T1 links (1.544 Mbit/s line rate).

- In 1965, Western Electric introduced the first widely used telephone switch that implemented computer control in the switching fabric.
- In 1969, the first four nodes of the ARPANET were connected using 50 kbit/s circuits between the University of California at Los Angeles, the Stanford Research Institute, the University of California at Santa Barbara, and the University of Utah. In the early 1970s, Leonard Kleinrock carried out mathematical work to model the performance of packet-switched networks, which underpinned the development of the ARPANET. His theoretical work on hierarchical routing in the late 1970s with student Farouk Kamoun remains critical to the operation of the Internet today.
- In 1972, commercial services were first deployed on public data networks in Europe, which began using X.25 in the late 1970s and spread across the globe. The underlying infrastructure was used for expanding TCP/IP networks in the 1980s.
- In 1973, the French CYCLADES network was the first to make the hosts responsible for the reliable delivery of data, rather than this being a centralized service of the network itself.
- In 1973, Robert Metcalfe wrote a formal memo at Xerox PARC describing Ethernet, a networking system that was based on the Aloha network, developed in the 1960s by Norman Abramson and colleagues at the University of Hawaii. In July 1976, Robert Metcalfe and David Boggs published their paper "Ethernet: Distributed Packet Switching for Local Computer Networks" and collaborated on several patents received in 1977 and 1978.
- In 1974, Vint Cerf, Yogen Dalal, and Carl Sunshine published the Transmission Control Protocol (TCP) specification, RFC 675, coining the term Internet as a shorthand for internetworking.
- In 1976, John Murphy of Datapoint Corporation created ARCNET, a token-passing network first used to share storage devices.
- In 1977, the first long-distance fiber network was deployed by GTE in Long Beach, California.
- In 1977, Xerox Network Systems (XNS) was developed by Robert Metcalfe and Yogen Dalal at Xerox.
- In 1979, Robert Metcalfe pursued making Ethernet an open standard.
- In 1980, Ethernet was upgraded from the original 2.94 Mbit/s protocol to the 10 Mbit/s protocol, which was developed by Ron Crane, Bob Garner, Roy Ogus, and Yogen Dalal.

- In 1995, the transmission speed capacity for Ethernet increased from 10 Mbit/s to 100 Mbit/s. By 1998, Ethernet supported transmission speeds of 1 Gbit/s. Subsequently, higher speeds of up to 400 Gbit/s were added. The scaling of Ethernet has been a contributing factor to its continued use.

2.11.1 Use

A computer network extends interpersonal communications by electronic means with various technologies, such as email, instant messaging, online chat, voice and video telephone calls, and video conferencing. A network allows sharing of network and computing resources. Users may access and use resources provided by devices on the network, such as printing a document on a shared network printer or use of a shared storage device. A network allows sharing of files, data, and other types of information giving authorized users the ability to access information stored on other computers on the network. Distributed computing uses computing resources across a network to accomplish tasks.

2.11.2 World Cafe

A world café is a structured conversational process for knowledge sharing in which groups of people discuss a topic at several small tables like those in a café. Some degree of formality may be retained to make sure that everyone gets a chance to speak. Although pre-defined questions have been agreed upon at the beginning, outcomes or solutions are not decided in advance. The assumption is that collective discussion can shift people's conceptions and encourage collective action. Events need to have at least twelve participants, but there is no upper limit. For example, in Israel in 2011 an event called 1000 Tables was hosted in several cities on a single day as part of a series of social justice protests held around that time, and around a thousand people participated.

2.11.3 Knowledge Cafe

A knowledge café, as developed by David Gurteen, has no tables, and no themes or questions for each of the small group discussions. Discussion is not led by a facilitator, and no summary is captured for subsequent feedback to the group—the aim is to maximise time spent in conversation, so time spent with one person presenting is minimised.

2.11.4 Modified World Cafe

Modified world café is a variant developed in 2019 and structured in two rounds which have the same length and an equal number of tables. Each group is provided with a goal to work on and each round is ended by plenary presentation. After the intermediate presentation, all members of each group except one (called the "host") are asked to move their seats to a new table and start a new round of discussion that is concluded by a final plenary presentation.

Application in Japanese clinical clerkship and postgraduate (residency) clinical teaching showed a relevant increase of the perceived usefulness and consent in respect of the product of the discussion groups.

2.11.5 Mentorship

Mentorship is the influence, guidance, or direction given by a mentor. A mentor is someone who teaches or gives help and advice to a less experienced and often younger person. In an organizational setting, a mentor influences the personal and professional growth of a mentee. Most traditional mentorships involve having senior employees mentor more junior employees, but mentors do not necessarily have to be more senior than the people they mentor. What matters is that mentors have experience that others can learn from.

Interaction with an expert may also be necessary to gain proficiency with cultural tools. Mentorship experience and relationship structure affect the "amount of psychosocial support, career guidance, role modeling and communication that occurs in the mentoring relationships in which the protégés and mentors engaged".

The person receiving mentorship may be referred to as a protégé (male), a protégée (female), an apprentice, a learner or, in the 2000s, a mentee. Mentoring is a process that always involves communication and is relationship-based, but its precise definition is elusive, with more than 50 definitions currently in use, such as:

Mentoring is a process for the informal transmission of knowledge, social capital, and the psychosocial support perceived by the recipient as relevant to work, career, or professional development; mentoring entails informal communication, usually face-to-face and during a sustained period of time, between a person who is perceived to have greater relevant knowledge, wisdom, or experience (the mentor) and a person who is perceived to have less (the protégé).

Mentoring in Europe has existed as early as Ancient Greek. The word's origin comes from Mentor, son of Alcimus in Homer's Odyssey. Since the 1970s it has spread in the United States mainly in training contexts, associated with important historical links to the movement advancing workplace equity for women and minorities and has been described as "an innovation in American management".

2.12 PROFESSIONAL BODIES AND QUALIFICATIONS

The European Mentoring and Coaching Council (EMCC) is the leading global body in terms of creating and maintaining a range of industry-standard frameworks, rules and processes for mentorship and related supervision and coaching fields.

2.12.1 Techniques

As the focus of mentorship is to develop the whole person, the techniques used are broad and require wisdom to be appropriately used. A 1995 study of mentoring techniques most commonly used in business found that the five most commonly used techniques among mentors were:

1. **Accompanying:** the mentor participates in the learning process alongside the learner and supports them.
2. **Sowing:** the mentor gives initially unclear or unacceptable advice to the learner that has value in a given situation.
3. **Catalyzing:** the mentor chooses to plunge the learner right into change to provoke a different way of thinking, a change in identity or a re-ordering of values.
4. **Showing:** the mentor teaches the learner by demonstrating a skill or activity.
5. **Harvesting:** the mentor assesses and defines the utility and value of the learner's skills.

Different techniques may be used by mentors according to the situation and the mindset of the mentee. The techniques used in modern organizations can be found in ancient education systems, from the Socratic technique of harvesting to the accompaniment used in the apprenticeship of itinerant cathedral builders during the Middle Ages. Leadership authors Jim Kouzes and Barry Z. Posner advise mentors to look for "teachable moments" in order to "expand or realize the potentialities of the people in the organizations they lead" and underline that personal credibility is as essential to quality mentoring as skill.

There are different types of mentors, such as:

- **Multiple mentors:** A new trend is for a learner to have multiple mentors. Having more than one mentor can expand the learner's knowledge, as different mentors may have different strengths.
- **Profession or trade mentor:** This is someone who is currently in the trade or profession the learner is entering. They know the trends, important changes, and new practices that newcomers should know to stay at the top of their career. A mentor like this would be someone a learner can discuss ideas with and also provides the learner the opportunity to network with other individuals in the trade or profession.
- **Industry mentor:** This is someone who does not only focus on the profession and can give insight on the industry as a whole, such as research, development, or key changes.
- **Organization mentor**: Politics in the organizations are constantly changing. It is important to be knowledgeable about the values, strategies, and products that are within the organisation, and when they change. An organization mentor can give clarity when needed, for example, on missions and strategies.
- **Work process mentor:** This mentor can cut through unnecessary work, explain the "ins and outs" of projects and day to day tasks, and eliminate unnecessary things in the learner's work day. This mentor can help finish tasks quickly and efficiently.

- **Technology mentor:** Technology has been rapidly improving and becoming more a part of day-to-day transactions within companies. A technology mentor can help with technical breakdowns, advise on systems that may work better than what the learner is currently using, and coach them in using new technology.

2.13 TYPES

2.13.1 Formal Mentoring

Formal mentoring relationships are set up by an administrative unit or office in a company or organization, which solicits and recruits qualified individuals who are willing to mentor, provides training to the mentors, and helps to match the mentors with a person in need of mentoring. While formal mentoring systems contain numerous structural and guidance elements, they usually allow the mentor and mentee to have an active role in choosing who they want to work with. Formal mentoring programs that simply assign mentors to mentees without allowing input from these individuals have not performed well. Even though a mentor and a mentee may seem perfectly matched "on paper", in practice, they may have different working or learning styles. As such, giving the mentor and the mentee the opportunity to help select who they want to work with is a widely used approach. For example, youth mentoring programs assign at-risk children or youth who lack role models and sponsors to mentors who act as role models and sponsors.

In business, formal mentoring is one of many talent management strategies that are used to groom key employees, newly hired graduates, high-potential employees, and future leaders. Matching mentors and mentees is often done by a mentoring coordinator with the help of a computerized database registry, which usually suggests matches based on the type of experience and qualifications being sought.

There are formal mentoring programs that are values-oriented, while social mentoring and other types focus specifically on career development. Some mentorship programs provide both social and vocational support. In well-designed formal mentoring programs, there are program goals, schedules, training (for both mentors and protégés), and evaluation.

2.13.2 Informal Mentoring

Informal mentoring occurs without the use of structured recruitment, mentor training and matching services. It can develop naturally between partners, such as business networking situations where a more experienced individual meets a new employee and the two build a rapport. Apart from these types, mentoring takes a dyadic structure in science, technology, engineering, mathematics, and medicine (STEMM).

2.14 MODELS

There are many kinds of mentoring relationships from school or community-based relationships to e-mentoring relationships. These mentoring relationships vary and can be influenced by the type of mentoring relationship. There are several models that have been used to describe and examine the sub-relationships that can emerge: for example, Cindy Buell describes how mentoring relationships can develop:

- **Cloning model:** The mentor teaches the learner as if they were a clone of the mentor.
- **Nurturing model:** The mentor assumes a parental role to create an open, supportive environment where the learner can learn and try things themselves.
- **Friendship model:** The mentor acts more as a peer "rather than being involved in a hierarchical relationship".
- **Apprenticeship model:** The mentor and learner predominantly have a professional relationship.

2.14.1 Other Types

- **Peer mentoring:** Relationships that involve individuals in similar positions. One person may be more knowledgeable in a certain aspect or another, and they can help each other progress in their work. In most cases, peer relationships provide a lot of support, empathy, and advice because the situations are quite similar.
- **Situational mentoring:** Short-term relationships in which a person mentors for a specific purpose. This could be a company bringing an expert in regarding social media, or internet safety. This expert can mentor employees to make them more knowledgeable about a specific topic or skill.
- **Supervisory mentoring:** This relationship involves a mentor with a higher position than the learner. The mentor can answer many questions and advise the best course of action.
- **Mentoring circles:** Participants from all levels of the organization propose and own[clarification needed] a topic before meeting in groups to discuss the topic, which motivates them to grow and become more knowledgeable. Flash mentoring is ideal for situations like job shadowing and reverse mentoring.
- **Flash mentoring:** A short-term form of mentoring that focuses on single meetings rather than a traditional, long-term mentoring relationship.

2.14.2 Benefits of Mentoring

A meta-analysis of 112 individual research studies found mentoring has significant behavioral, attitudinal, health-related, relational, motivational, and career benefits. For a learner, these benefits depend on the different functions being performed by the mentor. Originally, the concept of mentoring functions developed from qualitative research in a organizational context with functions that belong under two major factors: psychosocial support and career-related support. An early quantitative approach found role modeling to be a distinct third factor. In mentoring for college success, a fourth function concerning knowledge transfer was additionally identified, which was also discovered in the context of mentoring creativity.

There are also many benefits for an employer to develop a mentorship program for new and current employees:

- **Career development:** Setting up a career development mentoring program for employees enables an organization to help junior employees to learn the skills and behaviours from senior employees that the junior employees need to advance to higher-responsibility positions. This type of mentoring program can help to align organizational goals with employees' personal career goals of progressing within the organization. It gives employees the ability to advance professionally and learn more about their work. This collaboration also gives employees a feeling of engagement with the organization, which can lead to better retention rates and increased employee satisfaction.
- **High potential mentoring:** The most talented employees in organizations tend to be difficult to retain as they usually seek greater challenges and responsibilities and are likely to leave for a different organization if they do not feel that they are being given the opportunity to develop. Creating a mentoring program for high-potential employees that gives them one-on-one guidance from senior leaders can help engage employees, give them the opportunity to develop, and increase the likelihood of staying in the organization.
- **Diversity mentoring:** One of the top ways to innovate is by bringing in new ideas from senior employees and leaders from underrepresented groups (e.g., women, ethnic minorities, etc.). In many Western countries, women and ethnic minorities are significantly underrepresented in executive positions and boards of directors. However, in some traditionally gender segregated occupations, such as education and nursing, women may be the dominant gender in the workforce. Mentors from underrepresented groups can empower employees from similar groups to increase their confidence to accept higher-responsibility tasks and prepare for leadership roles. Developing employees from diverse groups can give the organization access to new ideas, problem-solving approaches, and perspectives. These relationships tend to lead to success within the organization and increased job satisfaction. Majority mentors are given the opportunity to learn about and empathize with the culture and experiences of the minority learning, but the mentoring relationship can be impeded if they are unwilling to adapt their cultural views. Members of the majority culture are perceived as more competent while members of the minority culture receive less credit for the same amount of work; therefore, a majority mentor, by virtue of their status, can assist a minority learner in receiving the recognition and job advancement they deserve. Minority mentors often feel pressure to work harder than other mentors to prove their worth within an organization. However, when paired with majority

learners, their perceived worth automatically increases due solely to the majority status of their peers. Minority mentors tend to impart emotional benefits onto their learners. In a 1958 study, Margaret Cussler showed that for each female executive she interviewed who did not own her own company, "something—or someone—gave her a push up the ladder while others halted on a lower rung." Cussler concluded that the relationship between the "sponsor and protégé" (the vocabulary of "mentorship" was not yet in common use) was the "magic formula" for success. By the late 1970s, numerous publications had established the centrality of mentorship to business success for everyone and particularly for women trying to enter the male-dominated business world. These publications noted the many benefits provided by mentorship, which included insider information, education, guidance, moral support, inspiration, sponsorship, protection, promotion, the ability to "bypass the hierarchy", the projection of the superior's "reflected power," access to otherwise invisible opportunities, and tutelage in corporate politics. The literature also showed the value of these benefits: for example, a Harvard Business Review survey of 1,250 top executives published in 1979 showed that most employees that had been mentored or sponsored and that those who received such assistance reported higher incomes, better education, quicker paths to achievement, and more job satisfaction than those who did not. The literature particularly emphasized the necessity of mentoring for businesswomen's success: although women comprised less than one percent of the executives in the Harvard Business Review survey, all of these women reported being mentored. In subsequent decades, as mentoring became a widely valued phenomenon in the United States, women and minorities in particular continued to develop mentoring relationships consciously as they sought professional advancement.

- **Reverse mentoring:** While mentoring typically involves a more experienced, typically older employee or leader providing guidance to a younger employee, the opposite approach can also be used. With the rise of digital innovations, Internet applications, and social media in the 2000s, new, younger employees may be more familiar with these technologies than senior employees in the organizations. The younger generations can help the older generations expand and grow with current trends.
- **Knowledge transfer mentoring:** Employees must have a certain set of skills in order to accomplish the tasks at hand. Mentoring can teach employees to be organized. It can also give them access to an expert that can provide feedback and answer questions.

2.15 ONLINE CHAT

Online chat may refer to any kind of communication over the Internet that offers a real-time transmission of text messages from sender to receiver. Chat messages are generally short in order to enable other participants to respond quickly. Thereby, a feeling similar to a spoken conversation is created, which distinguishes chatting from other text-based online communication forms such as Internet forums and email. Online chat may address point-to-point communications as well as multicast communications from one sender to many receivers and voice and video chat, or may be a feature of a web conferencing service.

Online chat in a less stringent definition may be primarily any direct text-based or video-based (webcams), one-on-one chat or one-to-many group chat (formally also known as synchronous conferencing), using tools such as instant messengers, Internet Relay Chat (IRC), talkers and possibly MUDs or other online games. The expression online chat comes from the word chat which means "informal conversation". Online chat includes web-based applications that allow communication – often directly addressed, but anonymous between users in a multi-user environment. Web conferencing is a more specific online service, that is often sold as a service, hosted on a web server controlled by the vendor.

The first online chat system was called Talkomatic, created by Doug Brown and David R. Woolley in 1973 on the PLATO System at the University of Illinois. It offered several channels, each of which could accommodate up to five people, with messages appearing on all users' screens character-by-character as they were typed. Talkomatic was very popular among PLATO users into the mid-1980s. In 2014, Brown and Woolley released a web-based version of Talkomatic.

The first online system to use the actual command "chat" was created for The Source in 1979 by Tom Walker and Fritz Thane of Dialcom, Inc.

Other chat platforms flourished during the 1980s. Among the earliest with a GUI was BroadCast, a Macintosh extension that became especially popular on university campuses in America and Germany.

The first transatlantic Internet chat took place between Oulu, Finland and Corvallis, Oregon in February 1989.

The first dedicated online chat service that was widely available to the public was the CompuServe CB Simulator in 1980, created by CompuServe executive Alexander "Sandy" Trevor in Columbus, Ohio. Ancestors include network chat software such as UNIX "talk" used in the 1970s.

Chat is implemented in many video-conferencing tools. A study of chat use during work-related Video conferencing found that chat during meetings allows participants to communicate without interrupting the meeting, plan action around common resources, and enables greater inclusion. The study also found that chat can cause distractions and information asymmetries between participants.

2.15.1 Chatiquette

The term chatiquette (chat etiquette) is a variation of netiquette (Internet etiquette) and describes basic rules of online communication. These conventions or guidelines have been created to avoid misunderstandings and to simplify the communication between users. Chatiquette varies from community to community and generally describes basic courtesy. As an example, it is considered rude to write only in upper case, because it appears as if the user is shouting. The word "chatiquette" has been used in connection with various chat systems (e.g. Internet Relay Chat) since 1995.

Chatrooms can produce a strong sense of online identity leading to impression of subculture.

Chats are valuable sources of various types of information, the automatic processing of which is the object of chat/text mining technologies.

2.15.2 Social Criticism

Criticism of online chatting and text messaging include concern that they replace proper English with shorthand or with an almost completely new hybrid language.

Writing is changing as it takes on some of the functions and features of speech. Internet chat rooms and rapid real-time teleconferencing allow users to interact with whoever happens to coexist in cyberspace. These virtual interactions involve us in 'talking' more freely and more widely than ever before. With chatrooms replacing many face-to-face conversations, it is necessary to be able to have quick conversation as if the person were present, so many people learn to type as quickly as they would normally speak. Some critics are wary that this casual form of speech is being used so much that it will slowly take over common grammar; however, such a change has yet to be seen.

With the increasing population of online chatrooms there has been a massive growth of new words created or slang words, many of them documented on the website Urban Dictionary. Sven Birkerts wrote:

"as new electronic modes of communication provoke similar anxieties amongst critics who express concern that young people are at risk, endangered by a rising tide of information over which the traditional controls of print media and the guardians of knowledge have no control on it".

In Guy Merchant's journal article Teenagers in Cyberspace: An Investigation of Language Use and Language Change in Internet Chatrooms; Merchant says

"that teenagers and young people are in the leading the movement of change as they take advantage of the possibilities of digital technology, drastically changing the face of literacy in a variety of media through their uses of mobile phone text messages, e-mails, web-pages and on-line chatrooms. This new literacy develops skills that may well be important to the labor market but are currently viewed with suspicion in the media and by educationalists."

Merchant also says "Younger people tend to be more adaptable than other sectors of society and, in general, quicker to adapt to new technology. To some extent they are the innovators, the forces of change in the new communication landscape." In this article he is saying that young people are merely adapting to what they were given.

2.16 WIKI

A wiki is a hypertext publication collaboratively edited and managed by its own audience directly. A typical wiki contains multiple pages for the subjects or scope of the project and could be either open to the public or limited to use within an organization for maintaining its internal knowledge base.

Wikis are enabled by wiki software, otherwise known as wiki engines. A wiki engine, being a form of a content management system, differs from other web-based systems such as blog software, in that the content is created without any defined owner or leader, and wikis have little inherent structure, allowing structure to emerge according to the needs of the users. Wiki engines usually allow content to be written using a simplified markup language and sometimes edited with the help of a rich-text editor. There are dozens of different wiki engines in use, both standalone and part of other software, such as bug tracking systems. Some wiki engines are open source, whereas others are proprietary. Some permit control over different functions; for example, editing rights may permit changing, adding, or removing material. Others may permit access without enforcing access control. Other rules may be imposed to organize content.

The online encyclopedia project, Wikipedia, is the most popular wiki-based website, and is one of the most widely viewed sites in the world, having been ranked in the top twenty since 2007. Wikipedia is not a single wiki but rather a collection of hundreds of wikis, with each one pertaining to a specific language. In addition to Wikipedia, there are hundreds of thousands of other wikis in use, both public and private, including wikis functioning as knowledge management resources, notetaking tools, community websites, and intranets. The English-language Wikipedia has the largest collection of articles: as of February 2020, it has over 6 million articles. Ward Cunningham, the developer of the first wiki software, WikiWikiWeb, originally described wiki as "the simplest online database that could possibly work." "Wiki" is a Hawaiian word meaning "quick."

2.16.1 Characteristics

In their book The Wiki Way: Quick Collaboration on the Web, Ward Cunningham and co-author Bo Leuf described the essence of the Wiki concept:

- "A wiki invites all users—not just experts—to edit any page or to create new pages within the wiki Web site, using only a standard "plain-vanilla" Web browser without any extra add-ons."
- "Wiki promotes meaningful topic associations between different pages by making page link creation intuitively easy and showing whether an intended target page exists or not."

- "A wiki is not a carefully crafted site created by experts and professional writers and designed for casual visitors. Instead, it seeks to involve the typical visitor/user in an ongoing process of creation and collaboration that constantly changes the website landscape."

A wiki enables communities of editors and contributors to write documents collaboratively. All that people require to contribute is a computer, Internet access, a web browser, and a basic understanding of a simple markup language. A single page in a wiki website is referred to as a "wiki page", while the entire collection of pages, which are usually well-interconnected by hyperlinks, is "the wiki". A wiki is essentially a database for creating, browsing, and searching through information. A wiki allows non-linear, evolving, complex, and networked text, while also allowing for editor argument, debate, and interaction regarding the content and formatting. A defining characteristic of wiki technology is the ease with which pages can be created and updated. Generally, there is no review by a moderator or gatekeeper before modifications are accepted and thus lead to changes on the website. Many wikis are open to alteration by the general public without requiring registration of user accounts. Many edits can be made in real-time and appear almost instantly online, but this feature facilitates abuse of the system. Private wiki servers require user authentication to edit pages, and sometimes even to read them. Maged N. Kamel Boulos, Cito Maramba, and Steve Wheeler write that the open wikis produce a process of Social Darwinism. "... because of the openness and rapidity that wiki pages can be edited, the pages undergo an evolutionary selection process, not unlike that which nature subjects to living organisms. 'Unfit' sentences and sections are ruthlessly culled, edited and replaced if they are not considered 'fit', which hopefully results in the evolution of a higher quality and more relevant page."

2.16.2 Source Editing

Some wikis have an Edit button or link directly on the page being viewed if the user has permission to edit the page. This can lead to a text-based editing page where participants can structure and format wiki pages with a simplified markup language, sometimes known as wikitext, wiki markup or wikicode. For example, starting lines of text with asterisks could create a bulleted list. The style and syntax of wikitexts can vary greatly among wiki implementations, some of which also allow HTML tags.

2.16.3 Layout Consistency

Wikis have favored plain-text editing, with fewer and simpler conventions than HTML for indicating style and structure. Although limiting access to HTML and Cascading Style Sheets (CSS) of wikis limits user ability to alter the structure and formatting of wiki content, there are some benefits. Limited access to CSS promotes consistency in the look and feel, and having JavaScript disabled prevents a user from implementing code that may limit other users' access.

2.16.4 Visual Editing

Wikis can also make WYSIWYG editing available to users, usually through a JavaScript control that translates graphically entered formatting instructions into the corresponding HTML tags or wikitext. In those implementations, the markup of a newly edited, marked-up version of the page is generated and submitted to the server transparently, shielding the user from this technical detail. WYSIWYG controls do not, however, always provide all the features available in wikitext, and some users prefer not to use a WYSIWYG editor. Hence, many of these sites offer some means to edit the wikitext directly.

2.16.5 Version History

Some wikis keep a record of changes made to wiki pages; often, every version of the page is stored. This means that authors can revert to an older version of the page should it be necessary because a mistake has been made, such as the content accidentally being deleted or the page has been vandalized to include offensive or malicious text or other inappropriate content.

2.16.6 Edit Summary

Many wiki implementations, such as MediaWiki, the software that powers Wikipedia, allow users to supply an edit summary when they edit a page. This is a short piece of text summarizing the changes they have made. It is not inserted into the article's main text but is stored along with that revision of the page, allowing users to explain what has been done and why. This is similar to a log message when making changes in a revision-control system. This enables other users to see which changes have been made by whom and why, often in a list of summaries, dates and other short, relevant content, a list which is called a "log" or "history."

2.16.7 Navigation

Within the text of most pages, there are usually many hypertext links to other pages within the wiki. This form of non-linear navigation is more "native" to a wiki than structured/formalized navigation schemes. Users can also create any number of index or table-of-contents pages, with hierarchical categorization or whatever form of organization they like. These may be challenging to maintain "by hand", as multiple authors and users may create and delete pages in an ad hoc, unorganized manner. Wikis can provide one or more ways to categorize or tag pages to support the maintenance of such index pages. Some wikis, including the original, have a backlink feature, which displays all pages that link to a given page. It is also typically possible in a wiki to create links to pages that do not yet exist, as a way to invite others to share what they know about a subject new to the wiki. Wiki users can typically "tag" pages with categories or keywords, to make it easier for other users to find the article. For example, a user creating a new article on cold-weather biking might "tag" this page under the categories of commuting, winter sports and bicycling. This would make it easier for other users to find the article.

2.16.8 Linking and Creating Pages

Links are created using a specific syntax, the so-called "link pattern". Originally, most wikis used CamelCase to name pages and create links. These are produced by capitalizing words in a phrase and removing the spaces between them. While CamelCase makes linking easy, it also leads to links in a form that deviates from the standard spelling. To link to a page with a single-word title, one must abnormally capitalize one of the letters in the word (e.g. "WiKi" instead of "Wiki"). CamelCase-based wikis are instantly recognizable because they have many links with names such as "Table of Contents" and "Beginner Questions." a wiki can render the visible anchor of such links "pretty" by reinserting spaces, and possibly also reverting to lower case. This reprocessing of the link to improve the readability of the anchor is, however, limited by the loss of capitalization information caused by CamelCase reversal. For example, "RichardWagner" should be rendered as "Richard Wagner", whereas "PopularMusic" should be rendered as "popular music". There is no easy way to determine which capital letters should remain capitalized. As a result, many wikis now have "free linking" using brackets, and some disable CamelCase by default.

2.16.9 Searching

Most wikis offer at least a title search, and sometimes a full-text search. The scalability of the search depends on whether the wiki engine uses a database. Some wikis, such as PmWiki, use flat files. MediaWiki's first versions used flat files, but it was rewritten by Lee Daniel Crocker in the early 2000s (decade) to be a database application. Indexed database access is necessary for high speed searches on large wikis. Alternatively, external search engines such as Google Search can sometimes be used on wikis with limited searching functions to obtain more precise results.

2.17 STORYTELLING

Storytelling is the social and cultural activity of sharing stories, sometimes with improvisation, theatrics or embellishment. Every culture has its own stories or narratives, which are shared as a means of entertainment, education, cultural preservation or instilling moral values. Crucial elements of stories and storytelling include plot, characters and narrative point of view. The term "storytelling" can refer specifically to oral storytelling but also broadly to techniques used in other media to unfold or disclose the narrative of a story.

Storytelling, intertwined with the development of mythologies, predates writing. The earliest forms of storytelling were usually oral, combined with gestures and expressions. Some archaeologists believe that rock art, in addition to a role in religious rituals, may have served as a form of storytelling for many ancient cultures. The Australian aboriginal people painted symbols which also appear in stories on cave walls as a means of helping the storyteller remember the story. The story was then told using a combination of oral narrative, music, rock art and dance, which bring understanding and meaning to human existence through the remembrance and enactment of stories. People have used the carved trunks of living trees and ephemeral media to record folktales in pictures or with writing. Complex forms of tattooing may also represent stories, with information about genealogy, affiliation and social status.

Folktales often share common motifs and themes, suggesting possible basic psychological similarities across various human cultures. Other stories, notably fairy tales, appear to have spread from place to place, implying memetic appeal and popularity.

Groups of originally oral tales can coalesce over time into story cycles (like the Arabian Nights), cluster around mythic heroes (like King Arthur), and develop into the narratives of the deeds of the gods and saints of various religions. The results can be episodic (like the stories about Anansi), epic (as with Homeric tales), inspirational (note the tradition of vitae) and/or instructive (as in many Buddhist or Christian scriptures).

With the advent of writing and the use of stable, portable media, storytellers recorded, transcribed and continued to share stories over wide regions of the world. Stories have been carved, scratched, painted, printed or inked onto wood or bamboo, ivory and other bones, pottery, clay tablets, stone, palm-leaf books, skins, bark cloth, paper, silk, canvas and other textiles, recorded on film and stored electronically in digital form. Oral stories continue to be created, improvisationally by impromptu and professional storytellers, as well as committed to memory and passed from generation to generation, despite the increasing popularity of written and televised media in much of the world.

2.17.1 Contemporary Storytelling

Modern storytelling has a broad preview. In addition to its traditional forms (fairytales, folktales, mythology, legends, fables etc.), it has extended itself to representing history, personal narrative, political commentary and evolving cultural norms. Contemporary storytelling is also widely used to address educational objectives. New forms of media are creating new ways for people to record, express and consume stories. Tools for asynchronous group communication can provide an environment for individuals to reframe or recast individual stories into group stories. Games and other digital platforms, such as those used in interactive fiction or interactive storytelling, may be used to position the user as a character within a bigger world. Documentaries, including interactive web documentaries, employ storytelling narrative techniques to communicate information about their topic. Self-revelatory stories, created for their cathartic and therapeutic effect, are growing in their use and application, as in Psychodrama, Drama Therapy and Playback Theatre. Storytelling is also used as a means by which to precipitate psychological and social change in the practice of transformative arts.

Some people also make a case for different narrative forms being classified as storytelling in the contemporary world. For example, digital storytelling, online and dice-and-paper-based role-playing games. In traditional role-playing games, storytelling is done by the person who controls the environment and the non-playing fictional characters, and moves the story elements along for the players as they interact with the storyteller. The game is advanced by mainly verbal interactions, with dice roll determining random events in the fictional universe, where the players interact with each other and the storyteller. This type of game has many genres, such as sci-fi and fantasy, as well as alternate-reality worlds based on the current reality, but with different setting and beings such as werewolves, aliens, daemons, or hidden societies. These oral-based role-playing games were very popular in the 1990s among circles of youth in many countries before computer and console-based online MMORPG's took their place. Despite the prevalence of computer-based MMORPGs, the dice-and-paper RPG still has a dedicated following.

2.17.2 Oral Traditions

Oral traditions of storytelling are found in several civilizations; they predate the printed and online press. Storytelling was used to explain natural phenomena, bards told stories of creation and developed a pantheon of gods and myths. Oral stories passed from one generation to the next and storytellers were regarded as healers, leaders, spiritual guides, teachers, cultural secrets keepers and entertainers. Oral storytelling came in various forms including songs, poetry, chants and dance.

Albert Bates Lord examined oral narratives from field transcripts of Yugoslav oral bards collected by Milman Parry in the 1930s, and the texts of epics such as the Odyssey. Lord found that a large part of the stories consisted of text which was improvised during the telling process.

Lord identified two types of story vocabulary. The first he called "formulas": "Rosy-fingered Dawn", "the wine-dark sea" and other specific set phrases had long been known of in Homer and other oral epics. Lord, however, discovered that across many story traditions, fully 90% of an oral epic is assembled from lines which are repeated verbatim or which use one-for-one word substitutions. In other words, oral stories are built out of set phrases which have been stockpiled from a lifetime of hearing and telling stories.

The other type of story vocabulary is theme, a set sequence of story actions that structure a tale. Just as the teller of tales proceeds line-by-line using formulas, so he proceeds from event-to-event using themes. One near-universal theme is repetition, as evidenced in Western folklore with the "rule of three": Three brothers set out, three attempts are made, three riddles are asked. A theme can be as simple as a specific set sequence describing the arming of a hero, starting with shirt and trousers and ending with headdress and weapons. A theme can be large enough to be a plot component.

The story was described by Reynolds Price, when he wrote:

A need to tell and hear stories is essential to the species Homo sapiens – second in necessity apparently after nourishment and before love and shelter. Millions survive without love or home, almost none in silence; the opposite of silence leads quickly to narrative, and the sound of story is the dominant sound of our lives, from the small accounts of our day's events to the vast incommunicable constructs of psychopaths.

In contemporary life, people will seek to fill "story vacuums" with oral and written stories. "In the absence of a narrative, especially in an ambiguous and/or urgent situation, people will seek out and consume plausible stories like water in the desert. It is our innate nature to connect the dots. Once an explanatory narrative is adopted, it's extremely hard to undo," whether or not it is true.

2.17.3 Märchen and Sagen

Folklorists sometimes divide oral tales into two main groups: Märchen and Sagen. These are German terms for which there are no exact English equivalents, however we have approximations:

Märchen, loosely translated as "fairy tale(s)" or little stories, take place in a kind of separate "once-upon-a-time" world of nowhere-in-particular, at an indeterminate time in the past. They are clearly not intended to be understood as true. The stories are full of clearly defined incidents, and peopled by rather flat characters with little or no interior life. When the supernatural occurs, it is presented matter-of-factly, without surprise. Indeed, there is very little effect, generally; bloodcurdling events may take place, but with little call for emotional response from the listener.

Sagen, translated as "legends", are supposed to have actually happened, very often at a particular time and place, and they draw much of their power from this fact. When the supernatural intrudes (as it often does), it does so in an emotionally fraught manner. Ghost and Lovers' Leap stories belong in this category, as do many UFO stories and stories of supernatural beings and events.

Another important examination of orality in human life is Walter J. Ong's Orality and Literacy: The Technologizing of the Word (1982). Ong studies the distinguishing characteristics of oral traditions, how oral and written cultures interact and condition one another, and how they ultimately influence human epistemology.

2.17.4 Storytelling and Learning

Storytelling is a means for sharing and interpreting experiences. Peter L. Berger says human life is narratively rooted, humans construct their lives and shape their world into homes in terms of these groundings and memories. Stories are universal in that they can bridge cultural, linguistic and age-related divides. Storytelling can be adaptive for all ages, leaving out the notion of age segregation. Storytelling can be used as a method to teach ethics, values and cultural norms and differences. Learning is most effective when it takes place in social environments that provide authentic social cues about how knowledge is to be applied. Stories function as a tool to pass on knowledge in a social context. So, every story has 3 parts. First, The setup (The Hero's world before the adventure starts). Second, The Confrontation (The hero's world turned upside down). Third, The Resolution (Hero conquers villain, but it's not enough for Hero to survive. The Hero or World must be transformed). Any story can be framed in such format.

Human knowledge is based on stories and the human brain consists of cognitive machinery necessary to understand, remember and tell stories. Humans are storytelling organisms that both individually and socially, lead storied lives. Stories mirror human thought as humans think in narrative structures and most often remember facts in story form. Facts can be understood as smaller versions of a larger story, thus storytelling can supplement analytical thinking. Because storytelling requires auditory and visual senses from listeners, one can learn to organize their mental representation of a story, recognize structure of language and express his or her thoughts.

Stories tend to be based on experiential learning, but learning from an experience is not automatic. Often a person needs to attempt to tell the story of that experience before realizing its value. In this case, it is not only the listener who learns, but the teller who also becomes aware of his or her own unique experiences and background. This process of storytelling is empowering as the teller effectively conveys ideas and, with practice, is able to demonstrate the potential of human accomplishment. Storytelling taps into existing knowledge and creates bridges both culturally and motivationally toward a solution.

Stories are effective educational tools because listeners become engaged and therefore remember. Storytelling can be seen as a foundation for learning and teaching. While the storylistener is engaged, they are able to imagine new perspectives, inviting a transformative and empathetic experience. This involves allowing the individual to actively engage in the story as well as observe, listen and participate with minimal guidance. Listening to a storyteller can create lasting personal connections, promote innovative problem solving and foster a shared understanding regarding future ambitions. The listener can then activate knowledge and imagine new possibilities. Together a storyteller and listener can seek best practices and invent new solutions. Because stories often have multiple layers of meanings, listeners have to listen closely to identify the underlying knowledge in the story. Storytelling is used as a tool to teach children the importance of respect through the practice of listening. As well as connecting children with their environment, through the theme of the stories, and give them more autonomy by using repetitive statements, which improve their learning to learn competence. It is also used to teach children to have respect for all life, value inter-connectedness and always work to overcome adversity. To teach this a Kinesthetic learning style would be used, involving the listeners through music, dream interpretation, or dance.

2.18 KNOWLEDGE SHARING: CHALLENGES

Knowledge management facilitates streamlining of solved problems, ideas, product deployment, and new projects. Many employees believe that transferring company-specific data and knowledge is a big challenge. Such knowledge is unique and cannot be found on search engines. Below listed are some of the knowledge sharing challenges:

Problems associated with knowledge sharing aren't easy to solve. All the issues fall into two main categories.

- **Lack of knowledge-sharing systems in the office:** There is no proper procedure for an employee to log and store knowledge. It could also be that they are using ineffective knowledge management software.
- **Lack of adoption for knowledge sharing systems:** Teams are clueless about the internal knowledge-sharing methods they need to use. Even if they do know about these methods, it could be that they don't like such methods and prefer not using them.
- **Updating Shared Data:** Another challenge that you might face is the moderation of your content. Useful data produced by your users may require updating and verification regularly. You can keep your data updated by scheduling validation notifications for your moderators.

CHAPTER

KNOWLEDGE MANAGEMENT 3

3.1 INTRODUCTION

Knowledge Management (KM) is the process of organizing, creating, using, and sharing collective knowledge within an organization. Successful knowledge management includes maintaining information in a place where it is easy to access.

Only a few initiatives are able to truly transform how an organization operates, and knowledge management is one of them.

Knowledge Management (KM) is the collection of methods relating to creating, sharing, using and managing the knowledge and information of an organization. It refers to a multidisciplinary approach to achieve organisational objectives by making the best use of knowledge.

An established discipline since 1991, KM includes courses taught in the fields of business administration, information systems, management, library, and information science. Other fields may contribute to KM research, including information and media, computer science, public health and public policy. Several universities offer dedicated master's degrees in knowledge management.

Many large companies, public institutions and non-profit organisations have resources dedicated to internal KM efforts, often as a part of their business strategy, IT, or human resource management departments. Several consulting companies provide advice regarding KM to these organizations.

Knowledge management efforts typically focus on organisational objectives such as improved performance, competitive advantage, innovation, the sharing of lessons learned, integration and continuous improvement of the organisation. These efforts overlap with organisational learning and may be distinguished from that by a greater focus on the management of knowledge as a strategic asset and on encouraging the sharing of knowledge. KM is an enabler of organizational learning.

The most complex scenario for knowledge management may be found in the context of supply chain as it involves multiple companies without an ownership relationship or hierarchy between them, being called by some authors as transorganizational or interorganizational knowledge. That complexity is additionally increased by industry 4.0 (or 4th industrial revolution) and digital transformation, as new challenges emerge from both the volume and speed of information flows and knowledge generation.

Knowledge management is the conscious process of defining, structuring, retaining, and sharing the knowledge and experience of employees within an organization.

As organizations evolve, expand into new areas, and define their approach to business, they develop significant institutional knowledge. This information is invaluable to the company. Imparting it to new or less experienced staff is vital for maintaining successful operations.

The primary goal of knowledge management is facilitating the connection of staff looking for information, or institutional knowledge, with the people who have it.

With practical knowledge management in place, organizations can spread information and raise the level of expertise held by specific individuals or teams to improve the efficiency of their practices.

It often refers to training and learning in an organization or of its customers. It consists of a cycle of creating, sharing, structuring, and auditing knowledge to maximize the effectiveness of an organization's collective expertise.

3.2 HISTORY OF KNOWLEDGE MANAGEMENT

Knowledge management efforts have a long history, including on-the-job discussions, formal apprenticeship, discussion forums, corporate libraries, professional training, and mentoring programs. With increased use of computers in the second half of the 20th century, specific adaptations of technologies such as knowledge bases, expert systems, information repositories, group decision support systems, intranets, and computer-supported cooperative work have been introduced to further enhance such efforts.

In 1999, the term personal knowledge management was introduced; it refers to the management of knowledge at the individual level.

In the enterprise, early collections of case studies recognised the importance of knowledge management dimensions of strategy, process and measurement. Key lessons learned include people and the cultural norms which influence their behaviors are the most critical resources for successful knowledge creation, dissemination and application; cognitive, social and organisational learning processes are essential to the success of a knowledge management strategy; and measurement, benchmarking and incentives are essential to accelerate the learning process and to drive cultural change. In short, knowledge management programs can yield impressive benefits to individuals and organisations if they are purposeful, concrete and action-orientated.

The concept and the terminology of KM sprouted within the management consulting community. When the Internet arose, those organizations quickly realized that an intranet, an in-house subset of the Internet, was a wonderful tool with which to make information accessible and to share it among the geographically dispersed units of their organizations. Not surprisingly, they quickly realized that in building tools and techniques such as dashboards, expertise locators, and best practice databases, they had acquired an expertise which was in effect a new product that they could market to other organizations, particularly to organizations which were large, complex, and dispersed. However, a new product needs a name, and the name that emerged was Knowledge Management. The term apparently was first used in its current context at McKinsey in 1987 for an internal study on their information handling and utilization. KM went public, as it were, at a conference in Boston in 1993 organized by Ernst and Young (Prusak 1999). Note that Davenport was at E&Y when he wrote the definition above.

Those consulting organizations quickly disseminated the principles and the techniques of KM to other organizations, to professional associations, and to disciplines. The timing was propitious, as the enthusiasm for intellectual capital in the 1980s, had primed the pump for the recognition of information and knowledge as essential assets for any organization.

3.3 TYPES OF KNOWLEDGE MANAGEMENT

When discussing knowledge management, it is helpful to consider the different types of knowledge and how it is possible to share them within an organization.

The information knowledge management covers can generally be broken down into three main types:

1. Explicit knowledge is knowledge and information that can be easily codified and taught, such as how to change the toner in a printer and mathematical equations.
2. Implicit knowledge is knowledge that explains how best to implement explicit knowledge. For example, consider discussing a task with an experienced co-worker. They may provide explicit steps detailing how to complete the job. But they may also use their understanding of the situation to consider different options and decide the best approach for your given circumstances. The experienced employee utilizes and shares their implicit knowledge to improve how the team operates.
3. Tacit knowledge is knowledge gained through experience. Therefore, it is more intuitive and less easy to share with others. Examples of tacit knowledge are "know-hows", innovative thinking, and understanding body language.

While knowledge management for implicit and tacit knowledge can be harder to implement, with correct procedures in place, you can ensure all relevant information is shared around the company and retained as staff retire or move on.

Utilizing all the expertise in your company benefits the business as a whole, creating best practices for everyday tasks, improving situational awareness, developing employee intuition for course corrections, and enhancing organizational capacity.

3.4 EXAMPLES OF KNOWLEDGE MANAGEMENT

3.4.1 Staff Retiring

An employee's knowledge and skillset grow as they spend time with an organization. As a result, staff typically retire with a wealth of expertise that the company needs to mine using efficient knowledge management processes in order to reduce disruption and prevent workforce knowledge gaps.

This means identifying and capturing the meaningful information that needs to be retained by the organization and determining the best approach for storing and distribution.

3.4.2 Employee Transfer or Promotion

When staff change positions within a company, they must develop additional skillsets and expertise to match their new role.

Efficient knowledge management procedures simplify delivering this information to create a seamless transition from one position to another.

3.5 IMPORTANCE OF KNOWLEDGE MANAGEMENT

Knowledge management is important because it boosts the efficiency of an organization's decision-making ability.

By making sure that all employees have access to the overall expertise held within the organization, a smarter workforce is built that is more able to make quick, informed decisions, benefiting the entire company.

Knowledge management allows innovation to grow within the organization, customers benefit from increased access to best practices, and employee turnover is reduced.

The importance of knowledge management is growing every year. As the marketplace becomes ever more competitive, one of the best ways to stay ahead of the curve is to build your organization in an intelligent, flexible manner. You must have the ability to spot issues from a distance and be able to respond quickly to new information and innovations.

Companies begin the knowledge management process for many different reasons.

1. A merger or acquisition could spur the need for codifying knowledge and encouraging teams to share their expertise.

2. The imminent retirement of key employees could demonstrate the need to capture their knowledge.
3. An upcoming recruitment drive shows the wisdom in using knowledge management to assist in training new employees.

52% of respondents in Deloitte's 2021 Global Human Capital Trends Survey stated workforce movement as the driving force behind proactively developing knowledge management strategies.

Whatever the reason is, implementing knowledge management processes offers tangible benefits that drive value. This is backed up by research, showing knowledge management positively influences dynamic capabilities and organizational performance.

3.6 KNOWLEDGE MANAGEMENT PROCESS

While some academics summarize the knowledge management process as involving knowledge acquisition, creation, refinement, storage, transfer, sharing and utilization. This process can be synthesized this a little further. Effective knowledge management system typically goes through three main steps:

1. **Knowledge Creation:** During this step, organizations identify and document any existing or new knowledge that they want to circulate across the company.
2. **Knowledge Storage:** During this stage, an information technology system is typically used to host organizational knowledge for distribution. Information may need to be formatted in a particular way to meet the requirements of that repository.
3. **Knowledge Sharing:** In this final stage, processes to share knowledge are communicated broadly across the organization. The rate in which information spreads will vary depending on organizational culture. Companies that encourage and reward this behavior will certainly have a competitive advantage over other ones in their industry.

3.7 KNOWLEDGE MANAGEMENT TOOLS

There are a number tools that organizations utilize to reap the benefits of knowledge management. Examples of knowledge management systems can include:

- Document Management Systems act as a centralized storage system for digital documents, such as PDFs, images, and word processing files. These systems enhance employee workflows by enabling easy retrieval of documents, such as lessons learned.
- Content Management Systems (CMS) are applications which manage web content where end users can edit and publish content. These are commonly confused

with document management systems, but CMSs can support other media types, such as audio and video.

- Intranets are private networks that exist solely within an organization, which enable the sharing of enablement, tools, and processes within internal stakeholders. While they can be time-consuming and costly to maintain, they provide a number of groupware services, such as internal directories and search, which facilitate collaboration.
- Wikis can be a popular knowledge management tool given its ease of use. They make it easy to upload and edit information, but this ease can lead to concerns about misinformation as workers may update them with incorrect or outdated information.
- Data warehouses aggregate data from different sources into a single, central, consistent data store to support data analysis, data mining, artificial intelligence (AI), and machine learning. Data is extracted from these repositories so that companies can derive insights, empowering employees to make data-driven decisions.

3.7.1 Strategies to Accelerate Knowledge Management

While knowledge management solutions can be helpful in facilitating knowledge transfer across teams and individuals, they also depend on user adoption to generate positive outcomes. As a result, organizations should not minimize the value of human elements that enable success around knowledge management.

- **Organizational Culture:** Management practices will affect the type of organization that executives lead. Managers can build learning organizations by rewarding and encouraging knowledge sharing behaviors across their teams. This type of leadership sets the groundwork for teams to trust each other and communicate more openly to achieve business outcomes.
- **Communities of practice:** Centers of excellence in specific disciplines provide employees with a forum to ask questions, facilitating learning and knowledge transfer. In this way, organizations increase the number of subject matter experts in a given area of the company, reducing dependencies on specific individuals to execute certain tasks.

3.7.2 Knowledge Management Use Cases

Armed with the right tools and strategies, knowledge management practices have seen success in specific applications, such as:

- **Onboarding employees:** Knowledge management systems help to address the huge learning curve for new hires. Instead of overwhelming new hires with a 'data dump' in their first weeks, continually support them with knowledge tools that will give them useful information at any time. Learn more.

- **Day-to-day employee tasks**: Enable every employee to have access to accurate answers and critical information. Access to highly relevant answers at the right time, for the right person, allows workforces to spend less time looking for information and more time on activities that drive business. Learn more.
- **Self-serve customer service:** Customers repeatedly say they'd prefer to find an answer themselves, rather than pick up the phone to call support. When done well, a knowledge management system helps businesses decrease customer support costs and increase customer satisfaction. Learn more.

3.8 BENEFITS OF KNOWLEDGE MANAGEMENT

Companies experience a number of benefits when they embrace knowledge management strategies. Some key advantages include:

- **Identification of skill gaps:** When teams create relevant documentation around implicit or tacit knowledge or consolidate explicit knowledge, it can highlight gaps in core competencies across teams. This provides valuable information to management to form new organizational structures or hire additional resources.
- **Make better informed decisions:** Knowledge management systems arm individuals and departments with knowledge. By improving accessibility to current and historical enterprise knowledge, your teams can upskill and make more information-driven decisions that support business goals.
- **Maintains enterprise knowledge:** If your most knowledgeable employees left tomorrow, what would your business do? Practicing internal knowledge management enables businesses to create an organizational memory. Knowledge held by your long-term employees and other experts, then make it accessible to your wider team.
- **Operational efficiencies:** Knowledge management systems create a go-to place that enable knowledge workers to find relevant information more quickly. This, in turn, reduces the amount of time on research, leading to faster decision-making and cost-savings through operational efficiencies. Increase productivity not only saves time, but also reduces costs.
- **Increased collaboration and communication:** Knowledge management systems and organizational cultures work together to build trust among team members. These information systems provide more transparency among workers, creating more understanding and alignment around common goals. Engaged leadership and open communication create an environment for teams to embrace innovation and feedback.
- **Data Security:** Knowledge management systems enable organizations to customize permission control, viewership control and the level of document-security to ensure that information is shared only in the correct channels or with

selected individuals. Give your employees the autonomy access knowledge safely and with confidence.

The more effectively and efficiently a company shares its information with its employees, the better the business will perform. The benefits of knowledge management include:

- Faster decision-making
- Efficient access to knowledge and information
- Increased collaboration and idea generation
- Enhanced communication throughout your organization
- Improved quality of information and data
- More security for intellectual property
- Optimized training

3.9 HOW KNOWLEDGE MANAGEMENT HELPS ORGANIZATIONS?

When an organization is able to easily access, share, and update business knowledge, it can become more productive and cost-efficient. The ability to access the right knowledge at the right time, via a robust knowledge management system, informs accurate decision-making and stimulates collaboration and innovation.

3.9.1 Will Knowledge Management Improve Work Performance?

A McKinsey Global Institute Report indicates that a robust knowledge management system can reduce information search time by as much as 35 percent and raise organization wide productivity by 20 to 25 percent. Findings culled from the International Data Corp also corroborate the value of a knowledge management system, highlighting that Fortune 500 companies lose roughly $31.5 billion a year by failing to share knowledge.

As your enterprise grows, so too will the need to access a reliable knowledge database in order to effectively run your business, serve your clients, and increase revenue. Without a knowledge management system in place, your employees will be forced to learn and relearn processes and information. That's an inefficient and costly practice. Plus, you may also run the risk of losing those processes or information if a knowledge leader or legacy employee leaves your company.

3.9.2 Research

KM emerged as a scientific discipline in the early 1990s. It was initially supported by individual practitioners, when Skandia hired Leif Edvinsson of Sweden as the world's first Chief Knowledge Officer (CKO). Hubert Saint-Onge (formerly of CIBC, Canada), started investigating KM long before that. The objective of CKOs is to manage and maximise the intangible assets of their organizations. Gradually, CKOs became interested in practical and theoretical aspects of KM, and the new research field was formed. The KM idea has been taken up by academics, such as Ikujiro Nonaka (Hitotsubashi University), Hirotaka Takeuchi (Hitotsubashi University), Thomas H. Davenport (Babson College) and Baruch Lev (New York University).

In 2001, Thomas A. Stewart, former editor at Fortune magazine and subsequently the editor of Harvard Business Review, published a cover story highlighting the importance of intellectual capital in organizations. The KM discipline has been gradually moving towards academic maturity. First, is a trend toward higher cooperation among academics; single-author publications are less common. Second, the role of practitioners has changed. Their contribution to academic research declined from 30% of overall contributions up to 2002, to only 10% by 2009. Third, the number of academic knowledge management journals has been steadily growing, currently reaching 27 outlets.

Multiple KM disciplines exist; approaches vary by author and school. As the discipline matured, academic debates increased regarding theory and practice, including:

- Techno-centric with a focus on technology, ideally those that enhance knowledge sharing and creation.
- Organisational with a focus on how an organisation can be designed to facilitate knowledge processes best.
- Ecological with a focus on the interaction of people, identity, knowledge, and environmental factors as a complex adaptive system akin to a natural ecosystem.

Regardless of the school of thought, core components of KM roughly include people/culture, processes/structure and technology. The details depend on the perspective. KM perspectives include:

- Community of practice
- Social network analysis
- Intellectual capital
- Information theory
- Complexity science
- Constructivism

The practical relevance of academic research in KM has been questioned with action research suggested as having more relevance and the need to translate the findings presented in academic journals to a practice.

3.9.3 Dimensions

Different frameworks for distinguishing between different 'types of' knowledge exist. One proposed framework for categorising the dimensions of knowledge distinguishes tacit knowledge and explicit knowledge. Tacit knowledge represents internalised knowledge that an individual may not be consciously aware of, such as to accomplish particular tasks. At the opposite end of the spectrum, explicit knowledge represents knowledge that the individual holds consciously in mental focus, in a form that can easily be communicated to others.

Ikujiro Nonaka proposed a model (SECI, for Socialisation, Externalisation, Combination, Internalisation) which considers a spiraling interaction between explicit knowledge and tacit knowledge. In this model, knowledge follows a cycle in which implicit knowledge is 'extracted' to become explicit knowledge, and explicit knowledge is 're-internalised' into implicit knowledge.

Hayes and Walsham (2003) describe knowledge and knowledge management as two different perspectives. The content perspective suggests that knowledge is easily stored; because it may be codified, while the relational perspective recognises the contextual and relational aspects of knowledge which can make knowledge difficult to share outside the specific context in which it is developed.

Early research suggested that KM needs to convert internalised tacit knowledge into explicit knowledge to share it, and the same effort must permit individuals to internalise and make personally meaningful any codified knowledge retrieved from the KM effort.

Subsequent research suggested that a distinction between tacit knowledge and explicit knowledge represented an oversimplification and that the notion of explicit knowledge is self-contradictory. Specifically, for knowledge to be made explicit, it must be translated into information. More recently, together with Georg von Krogh and Sven Voelpel, Nonaka returned to his earlier work in an attempt to move the debate about knowledge conversion forward.

A second proposed framework for categorising knowledge dimensions distinguishes embedded knowledge of a system outside a human individual from embodied knowledge representing a learned capability of a human body's nervous and endocrine systems.

A third proposed framework distinguishes between the exploratory creation of "new knowledge" (i.e., innovation) vs. the transfer or exploitation of "established knowledge" within a group, organisation, or community. Collaborative environments such as communities of practice or the use of social computing tools can be used for both knowledge creation and transfer.

3.9.4 Strategies

Knowledge may be accessed at three stages: before, during, or after KM-related activities. Organisations have tried knowledge capture incentives, including making content submission mandatory and incorporating rewards into performance measurement plans. Considerable controversy exists over whether such incentives work and no consensus has emerged.

One strategy to KM involves actively managing knowledge. In such an instance, individuals strive to explicitly encode their knowledge into a shared knowledge repository, such as a database, as well as retrieving knowledge they need that other individuals have provided. Another strategy involves individuals making knowledge requests of experts associated with a particular subject on an adhoc basis. In such an instance, expert individual(s) provide insights to requestor (personalisation). When talking about strategic knowledge management, the form of the knowledge and activities to share it defines the concept between codification and personalization. The form of the knowledge means that it's either tacit or explicit. Data and information can be considered as explicit and know-how can be considered as tacit.

Hansen et al. defined the two strategies (codification and personalisation). Codification means a system-oriented method in KM strategy for managing explicit knowledge with organizational objectives. Codification strategy is document-centered strategy, where knowledge is mainly codified as "people-to-document" method. Codification relies on information infrastructure, where explicit knowledge is carefully codified and stored. Codification focuses on collecting and storing codified knowledge in electronic databases to make it accessible. Codification can therefore refer to both tacit and explicit knowledge. In contrast, personalisation encourages individuals to share their knowledge directly. Personification means human-oriented KM strategy where the target is to improve knowledge flows through networking and integrations related to tacit knowledge with knowledge sharing and creation. Information technology plays a less important role, as it only facilitates communication and knowledge sharing.

Other knowledge management strategies and instruments for companies include:

- Knowledge sharing (fostering a culture that encourages the sharing of information, based on the concept that knowledge is not irrevocable and should be shared and updated to remain relevant)
    - Make knowledge-sharing a key role in employees' job description
    - Inter-project knowledge transfer
    - Intra-organisational knowledge sharing
    - Inter-organisational knowledge sharing
    - Knowledge retention also known as Knowledge Continuation: activities addressing the challenge of knowledge loss as a result of people leaving
    - Mapping knowledge competencies, roles and identifying current or future predicted gaps.
    - Defining for each chosen role the main knowledge that should be retained, and building rituals in which the knowledge is documented or transferred on, from the day they start their job.

- o Transfer of knowledge and information prior to employee departure by means of sharing documents, shadowing, mentoring, and more,

- Proximity & architecture (the physical situation of employees can be either conducive or obstructive to knowledge sharing)
- Storytelling (as a means of transferring tacit knowledge)
- Cross-project learning
- After-action reviews
- Knowledge mapping (a map of knowledge repositories within a company accessible by all)
- Communities of practice
- Expert directories (to enable knowledge seeker to reach to the experts)
- Expert systems (knowledge seeker responds to one or more specific questions to reach knowledge in a repository)
- Best practice transfer
- Knowledge fairs
- Competency-based management (systematic evaluation and planning of knowledge related competences of individual organisation members)
- Master–apprentice relationship, Mentor-mentee relationship, job shadowing
- Collaborative software technologies (wikis, shared bookmarking, blogs, social software, etc.)
- Knowledge repositories (databases, bookmarking engines, etc.)
- Measuring and reporting intellectual capital (a way of making explicit knowledge for companies)
- Knowledge brokers (some organisational members take on responsibility for a specific "field" and act as first reference on a specific subject)
- Knowledge farming (using note-taking software to cultivate a knowledge graph, part of knowledge agriculture)

3.9.5 Motivations

Multiple motivations lead organisations to undertake KM. Typical considerations include:

- Making available increased knowledge content in the development and provision of products and services
- Achieving shorter development cycles
- Facilitating and managing innovation and organisational learning

- Leveraging expertises across the organisation
- Increasing network connectivity between internal and external individuals
- Managing business environments and allowing employees to obtain relevant insights and ideas appropriate to their work
- Solving intractable or wicked problems
- Managing intellectual capital and assets in the workforce (such as the expertise and know-how possessed by key individuals or stored in repositories)

3.9.6 KM Technologies

Knowledge Management (KM) technology can be categorised:

- **Groupware**—Software that facilitates collaboration and sharing of organisational information. Such applications provide tools for threaded discussions, document sharing, organisation-wide uniform email, and other collaboration-related features.
- **Workflow systems**—Systems that allow the representation of processes associated with the creation, use and maintenance of organisational knowledge, such as the process to create and utilise forms and documents.
- **Content management and document management systems**—Software systems that automate the process of creating web content and/or documents. Roles such as editors, graphic designers, writers and producers can be explicitly modeled along with the tasks in the process and validation criteria. Commercial vendors started either to support documents or to support web content but as the Internet grew these functions merged and vendors now perform both functions.
- **Enterprise portals**—Software that aggregates information across the entire organisation or for groups such as project teams.
- **eLearning**—Software that enables organisations to create customised training and education. This can include lesson plans, monitoring progress and online classes.
- **Planning and scheduling software**—Software that automates schedule creation and maintenance. The planning aspect can integrate with project management software.
- **Telepresence**—Software that enables individuals to have virtual "face-to-face" meetings without assembling at one location. Video conferencing is the most obvious example.
- **Semantic technology such as ontologies**—Systems that encode meaning alongside data to give machines the ability to extract and infer information.

These categories overlap. Workflow, for example, is a significant aspect of a content or document management systems, most of which have tools for developing enterprise portals.

Proprietary KM technology products such as Lotus Notes defined proprietary formats for email, documents, forms, etc. The Internet drove most vendors to adopt Internet formats. Open-source and freeware tools for the creation of blogs and wikis now enable capabilities that used to require expensive commercial tools.

KM is driving the adoption of tools that enable organisations to work at the semantic level, as part of the Semantic Web. Some commentators have argued that after many years the Semantic Web has failed to see widespread adoption, while other commentators have argued that it has been a success.

Knowledge Barriers

Just like knowledge transfer and knowledge sharing, the term "knowledge barriers" is not a uniformly defined term and differs in its meaning depending on the author. Knowledge barriers can be associated with high costs for both companies and individuals.

Knowledge Retention

Knowledge retention is part of knowledge management. Knowledge retention is needed when expert knowledge workers leave the organization after a long career. Retaining knowledge prevents losing intellectual capital.

Knowledge retention projects are usually introduced in three stages: decision making, planning and implementation. There are differences among researchers on the terms of the stages. For example, Dalkir talks about knowledge capture, sharing and acquisition and Doan et al. introduces initiation, implementation and evaluation. Furthermore, Levy introduces three steps (scope, transfer, integration) but also recognizes a "zero stage" for initiation of the project.

3.10 WHAT IS KM TRYING TO ACCOMPLISH?

3.10.1 Rich, Deep, and Open Communication

First, KM can very fruitfully be seen as the undertaking to replicate, indeed to create, the information environment known to be conducive to successful R&D—rich, deep, and open communication and information access—and to deploy it broadly across the firm. It is almost trite now to observe that we are in the post-industrial information age and that we are all information workers. Furthermore, the researcher is, after all, the quintessential information worker. Peter Drucker once commented that the product of the pharmaceutical industry wasn't pills, it was information. The research domain, and in particular the pharmaceutical industry, has been studied in depth with a focus on identifying the organizational and cultural environmental aspects that lead to successful research. The salient aspect that emerges with overwhelming importance is that of rich, deep, and open communications, not only within the firm, but also with the outside world. The logical conclusion, then, is to attempt to apply those same successful environmental aspects to knowledge workers at large, and that is precisely what KM attempts to do.

3.10.2 Situational Awareness

Second, Situational Awareness is a term only recently, beginning in 2015, used in the context of KM. The term, however, long precedes KM. It first gained some prominence in the cold war era when studies were commissioned by all of the major potential belligerents to try to identify what characteristics made a good fighter pilot. The costs of training a fighter pilot were huge, and if the appropriate characteristics leading to success could be identified, that training could be directed to the most appropriate candidates, and of those trained the most appropriate could be selected for front-line assignment. However, the only solid conclusion of those studies was that the salient characteristic of a good fighter pilot was excellent "situational awareness." The problem was that no good predictive test for situational awareness could be developed.

The phrase then retreated into relative obscurity until it was resuscitated by Jeff Cooper, a firearms guru, and others in the context of self-defense. How do you defend and protect yourself? The first step is to be alert and to establish good situational awareness. From there the phrase entered the KM vocabulary. The role of KM is to create the capability for the organization to establish excellent situational awareness and consequently to make the right decisions.

3.10.3 A New Definition of KM

A few years after the Davenport definition, the Gartner Group created another definition of KM, which has become the most frequently cited one, and it is given below:

"Knowledge management is a discipline that promotes an integrated approach to identifying, capturing, evaluating, retrieving, and sharing all of an enterprise's information assets. These assets may include databases, documents, policies, procedures, and previously un-captured expertise and experience in individual workers."

The one real lacuna of this definition is that it, too, is specifically limited to an organization's own information and knowledge assets. KM as conceived now, and this expansion arrived early on, includes relevant information assets from wherever relevant. Note, however, the breadth implied for KM by calling it a "discipline."

Both definitions share a very organizational and corporate orientation. KM, historically at least, was primarily about managing the knowledge of and in organizations. Rather quickly, however, the concept of KM became much broader than that.

3.11 WHAT DOES KM ACTUALLY CONSIST OF?

In short, what are the operational components of a KM system? This is, in a way, the most straightforward way of explaining what KM is—to delineate what the operational components are that constitute what people have in mind when they talk about a KM system.

3.11.1 Content Management

So what is involved in KM? The most obvious is the making of the organization's data and information available to the members of the organization through dashboards, portals, and with the use of content management systems. Content Management, sometimes known as Enterprise Content Management, is the most immediate and obvious part of KM. For a wonderful graphic snapshot of the content management domain go to realstorygroup.com and look at their Content Technology Vendor Map. This aspect of KM might be described as Librarianship 101, putting your organization's information and data up online, plus selected external information, and providing the capability to seamlessly shift to searching, more or less, the entire web. The term most often used for this is Enterprise Search. This is now not just a stream within the annual KMWorld Conference, but has become an overlapping conference in its own right. See the comments below under the "Third Stage of KM" section.

3.11.2 Expertise Location

Since knowledge resides in people, often the best way to acquire the expertise that you need is to talk with an expert. Locating the right expert with the knowledge that you need, though, can be a problem, particularly if, for example, the expert is in another country. The basic function of an expertise locator system is straightforward: it is to identify and locate those persons within an organization who have expertise in a particular area. These systems are now commonly known as expertise location systems. In the early days of KM the term 'Yellow Pages" was commonly used, but now that term is fast disappearing from our common vocabulary, and expertise location is, in any case, rather more precise.

There are typically three sources from which to supply data for an expertise locator system: (1) employee resumes, (2) employee self-identification of areas of expertise (typically by being requested to fill out a form online), and (3) algorithmic analysis of electronic communications from and to the employee. The latter approach is typically based on email traffic but can include other social networking communications such as Twitter, Facebook, and Linkedin. Several commercial software packages to match queries with expertise are available. Most of them have load-balancing schemes so as not to overload any particular expert. Typically such systems rank the degree of presumed expertise and will shift a query down the expertise ranking when the higher choices appear to be overloaded. Such systems also often have a feature by which the requester can flag the request as a priority, and the system can then match high priority to high expertise rank.

3.11.3 Lessons Learned

Lessons Learned databases are databases that attempt to capture and make accessible knowledge, typically "how to do it" knowledge, that has been operationally obtained and normally would not have been explicitly captured. In the KM context, the emphasis is upon capturing knowledge embedded in personal expertise and making it explicit. The lessons learned concept or practice is one that might be described as having been birthed by KM, as there is very little in the way of a direct antecedent. Early in the KM movement, the phrase most often used was "best practices," but that phrase was soon replaced with "lessons learned." The reasons were that "lessons learned" was a broader and more inclusive term and because "best practice" seemed too restrictive and could be interpreted as meaning there was only one best practice in a situation. What might be a best practice in North American culture, for example, might well not be a best practice in another culture. The major international consulting firms were very aware of this and led the movement to substitute the new more appropriate term. "Lessons Learned" became the most common hallmark phrase of early KM development.

The idea of capturing expertise, particularly hard-won expertise, is not a new idea. One antecedent to KM that we have all seen portrayed was the World War II debriefing of pilots after a mission. Gathering military intelligence was the primary purpose, but a clear and recognized secondary purpose was to identify lessons learned, though they were not so named, to pass on to other pilots and instructors. Similarly, the U. S. Navy Submarine Service, after a very embarrassing and lengthy experience of torpedoes that failed to detonate on target, and an even more embarrassing failure to follow up on consistent reports by submarine captains of torpedo detonation failure, instituted a mandatory system of widely disseminated "Captain's Patrol Reports." The intent, of course, was to avoid any such fiasco in the future. The Captain's Patrol Reports, however, were very clearly designed to encourage analytical reporting, with reasoned analyses of the reasons for operational failure and success. It was emphasized that a key purpose of the report was both to make recommendations about strategy for senior officers to mull over, and recommendations about tactics for other skippers and submariners to take advantage of.

The military has become an avid proponent of the lessons learned concept. The phrase the military uses is "After Action Reports." The concept is very simple: make sure that what has been learned from experience is passed on, and don't rely on the participant to make a report. There will almost always be too many things immediately demanding that person's attention after an action. There must be a system whereby someone, typically someone in KM, is assigned the responsibility to do the debriefing, to separate the wheat from the chaff, to create the report, and then to ensure that the lessons learned are captured and disseminated. The experiences in Iraq, Afghanistan, and Syria have made this process almost automatic in the military.

The concept is by no means limited to the military. Larry Prusak (2004) maintains that in the corporate world the most common cause of KM implementation failure is that so often the project team is disbanded and the team members almost immediately reassigned elsewhere before there is any debriefing or after-action report assembled. Any organization where work is often centered on projects or teams needs to pay very close attention to this issue and set up an after-action mechanism with clearly delineated responsibility for its implementation.

A particularly instructive example of a "lesson learned" is one recounted by Mark Mazzie (2003), a well known KM consultant. The story comes from his experience in the KM department at Wyeth Pharmaceuticals. Wyeth had recently introduced a new pharmaceutical agent intended primarily for pediatric use. Wyeth expected it to be a notable success because, unlike its morning, noon, and night competitors, it needed to be administered only once a day, and that would make it much easier for the caregiver to ensure that the child followed the drug regimen, and it would be less onerous for the child. Sales of the drug commenced well but soon flagged. One sales rep, however, by chatting with her customers, discovered the reason for the disappointing sales and also recognized the solution. The problem was that kids objected strenuously to the taste of the drug, and caregivers were reporting to prescribing physicians that they couldn't get their kid to continue taking the drug, so the old stand-by would be substituted. The simple solution was orange juice, a swig of which quite effectively masked the offensive taste. If the sales rep were to explain to the physician that the therapy should be conveyed to the caregiver as the pill and a glass of orange juice taken simultaneously at breakfast, then there was no dissatisfaction and sales were fine.

The obvious question that arises is what is there to encourage the sales rep to share this knowledge? The sales rep is compensated based on salary (small), and bonus (large). If she shares the knowledge, she jeopardizes the size of her bonus, which is based on her comparative performance.

This raises the issue, discussed below, that KM is much more than content management. It extends to how does one structures the organizational culture to facilitate and encourage knowledge sharing, and that extends to how one structures the organization's compensation scheme.

The implementation of a lessons learned system is complex both politically and operationally. Many of the questions surrounding such a system are difficult to answer. Are employees free to submit to the system un-vetted? Who, if anyone, is to decide what constitutes a worthwhile lesson learned? Most successful lessons learned implementations have concluded that such a system needs to be monitored and that there needs to be a vetting and approval mechanism for items that are posted as lessons learned.

How long do items stay in the system? Who decides when an item is no longer salient and timely? Most successful lessons learned systems have an active weeding or stratification process. Without a clearly designed process for weeding, the proportion of new and crisp items inevitably declines, the system begins to look stale, and usage and utility falls. Deletion, of course, is not necessarily loss and destruction. Using carefully designed stratification principles, items removed from the foreground can be archived and moved to the background but still made available. However, this procedure needs to be in place before things start to look stale, and a good taxonomically based retrieval system needs to be created.

These questions need to be carefully thought out and resolved, and the mechanisms designed and put in place, before a lessons-learned system is launched. Inattention can easily lead to failure and the creation of a bad reputation that will tar subsequent efforts.

3.11.4 Communities of Practice (CoPs)

CoPs are groups of individuals with shared interests that come together in person or virtually to tell stories, to share and discuss problems and opportunities, discuss best practices, and talk over lessons learned. Communities of practice emphasize, build upon, and take advantage of the social nature of learning within or across organizations. In small organizations, conversations around the water cooler are often taken for granted, but in larger, geographically distributed organizations, the water cooler needs to become virtual. Similarly, organizations find that when workers relinquish a dedicated company office to work online from home or on the road, the natural knowledge sharing that occurs in social spaces needs to be replicated virtually. In the context of KM, CoPs are generally understood to mean electronically linked communities. Electronic linkage is not essential, of course, but since KM arose in the consulting community from the awareness of the potential of intranets to link geographically dispersed organizations, this orientation is understandable.

A classic example of the deployment of CoPs comes from the World Bank. When James Wolfensohn became president in 1995, he focused on the World Bank's role in disseminating knowledge about development; he was known to say that the principal product of the World Bank was not loans, but rather the creation of knowledge about how to accomplish development. Consequently, he encouraged the development of CoPs and made that a focus of his attention. One World Bank CoP, for example, was about road construction and maintenance in arid countries and conditions. That CoP was encouraged to include and seek out not only participants and employees from the World Bank and its sponsored projects and from the country where the relevant project was being implemented, but also experts from elsewhere who had expertise in building roads in arid conditions, such as, for example, staff from the Australian Road Research Board and the Arizona Department of Highways. This is also a good example of the point that despite the fact that KM developed first in a very for-profit corporate context, it is applicable far more broadly, such as in the context of government and civil society.

The organization and maintenance of CoPs is not a simple or an easy task to undertake. As Durham (2004) points out, there are several key roles to be filled. She describes the key roles as manager, moderator, and thought leader. They need not necessarily be three separate people, but in some cases they will need to be. Some questions that need to be thought about and resolved are:

- Who fills the various roles of: manager, moderator, and thought leader?
- How is the CoP managed, and who will fill the management role?
- Who will have overall responsibility for coordinating and overseeing the various CoPs?
- Who looks for new members or suggests that the CoP may have outlived its usefulness?
- Who reviews the CoP for activity?
- Are postings open or does someone vet or edit the postings?
- How is the CoP kept fresh and vital?
- When and how (under what rules) are items removed?
- How are those items archived?
- How are the CoP files made retrievable? How do CoP leaders coordinate with the enterprise search/taxonomy function?

3.12 ANOTHER WAY TO VIEW KM IS TO LOOK AT THE STAGES OF KM'S DEVELOPMENT

3.12.1 First Stage of KM: Information Technology

KM was initially driven primarily by IT, information technology, and the desire to put that new technology, the Internet, to work and see what it was capable of. That first stage has been described using a horse breeding metaphor as "by the internet out of intellectual capital," the sire and the dam. The concept of intellectual capital, the notion that not just physical resources, capital, and manpower, but also intellectual capital (knowledge) fueled growth and development, provided the justification, the framework, and the seed. The availability of the internet provided the tool. As described above, the management consulting community jumped at the new capabilities provided by the Internet, using it first for themselves, realizing that if they shared knowledge across their organization more effectively they could avoid reinventing the wheel, underbid their competitors, and make more profit. The central point is that the first stage of KM was about how to deploy that new technology to accomplish more effective use of information and knowledge.

The first stage might be described as the "If only Texas Instruments knew what Texas Instruments knew" stage, to revisit a much quoted KM mantra. The hallmark phrase of Stage 1 was first "best practices," later replaced by the more politic "lessons learned."

3.12.2 Second Stage of KM: HR and Corporate Culture

Within a few years the second stage of KM emerged when it became apparent that simply deploying new technology was not sufficient to effectively enable information and knowledge sharing. It became obvious that human and cultural dimensions needed to be incorporated. The second stage can be described as the "'If you build it they will come' is a fallacy" stage. In other words, there was the recognition that "If you build it they will come" is a recipe that can easily lead to quick and embarrassing failure if human factors are not sufficiently taken into account.

It became clear that KM implementation would involve changes in the corporate culture, in many cases rather significant changes. Consider the case above of the new pediatric medicine and the discovery of the efficacy of adding orange juice to the recipe. Pharmaceutical sales reps are compensated primarily not by salary, but by bonuses based on sales results. What is in it for that sales rep to share her new discovery when the most likely result is that next year her bonus would be substantially reduced? The changes needed in corporate culture to facilitate and encourage information and knowledge sharing can be major and profound.

KM therefore extends far beyond just structuring information and knowledge and making it more accessible. In particular, the organizational culture needs to be examined in terms of how it rewards information and knowledge sharing. In many cases the examination will reveal that the culture needs to be modified and enriched. Often this will involve examining and modifying how the compensation scheme rewards information and knowledge sharing.

This implies a role for KM that very few information professionals have had to be involved with in the past. The implication is clear that KM leaders should be involved in the decision making process for designing the organization's compensation policy, a process that is very sensitive politically and fraught with difficulty.

A major component of this second stage was the design of easy-to-use and user-friendly systems. The metaphor that was used was that the interface, the Desktop Interface, should appear almost intuitively obvious, like the dashboard of an automobile. Human factors design became an important component of KM.

As this recognition of the importance of human factors unfolded, two major themes from the business literature were brought into the KM domain. The first of these was Senge's work on the learning organization (The Fifth Discipline: The Art and Practice of the Learning Organization.) The second was Nonaka's work on "tacit" knowledge and how to discover and cultivate it the Knowledge-Creating Company: How Japanese Companies Create the Dynamics of Innovation. Both were not only about the human factors of KM implementation and use; they were also about knowledge creation as well as knowledge sharing and communication. The hallmark phrase of Stage 2 was "communities of practice," CoPs. A good indicator of the shift from the first to the second stage of KM is that for the 1998 Conference Board conference on KM, there was, for the first time, a noticeable contingent of attendees from HR, human resource departments. By the next year, 1999, HR was the largest single group, displacing IT attendees from first place.

3.12.3 Third Stage of KM: Taxonomy and Content Management

The third stage developed from the awareness of the importance of content, and in particular the awareness of the importance of the retrievability of that content, and therefore the importance of the arrangement, description, and the syndetic structure of that content. Since a good alternative description for the second stage of KM is the "it's no good if they don't use it" stage, then in that vein, perhaps the best description for the third stage is the "it's no good if they try to use it but can't find it" stage. Another bellwether is that TFPL's report of their October 2001 CKO (Chief Knowledge Officer) Summit reported that for the first time taxonomies emerged as a topic, and it emerged full blown as a major topic (TFPL, 2001 Knowledge Strategies – Corporate Strategies.) The hallmark phrases emerging for the third stage are content management and taxonomies. At the KMWorld 2000 Conference, a track on Content Management appeared for the first time, and by the 2001 KMWorld Conference, Content Management had become the dominant track. In 2006, KMWorld added a two-day workshop entitled Taxonomy Boot Camp, which not only still continues today, and is a day longer, but has also expanded to international locations. The hallmark terms for the third stage of KM are taxonomy and content.

The third stage continues today and is expanding. A major theme now is "data analytics" and "machine learning" for "enterprise search." The crux is to be able to effectively manage and retrieve your data without maintaining a stable full of taxonomists. A good recent example derives from Rolls Royce's sale of a subsidiary company. The buyer was entitled to voluminous files of company records, but how was Rolls Royce to separate those from other records with valuable proprietary data that was not part of the sale, and that Rolls Royce wanted to maintain as proprietary knowledge, amidst a sea of structured and unstructured data? The answer was a major project to taxonomize, organize, index, and retrieve massive amounts of data and records. Data analytics and machine learning were powerful tools to help accomplish this, but notice the word "help." Those tools will not replace the need for good and intelligent human guidance, training, and oversight.

The author is reminded of an occurrence some years ago at Mitre Corporation, a very information driven organization, before the term KM was even bruited about, when the organization wanted to create an expertise location "file/database." A senior Vice President's first thought was that just putting the employee's resumes online would suffice. A short demonstration convinced him otherwise. One sample search was for employees with expertise in "Defense Logistics," a topic relevant to an RFP that Mitre was bidding on. The clincher was a resume containing neither word, but with the phase "battlefield re-supply."

A good idea is to browse the KMWorld website (kmworld.com) for current reports, "white papers," webinars, etc. on topics such as "text analytics" or "big data" or "cognitive computing."

3.13 OTHER KM ISSUES

3.13.1 Tacit Knowledge

The KM community uses the term "tacit knowledge" to mean what is not "explicit knowledge," and in that usage what is usually meant by "tacit" is implicit knowledge, that which is not explicit or formally captured in some fashion, most obviously the knowledge in people's heads. A more useful and nuanced categorization is explicit, implicit, and tacit. There is indeed tacit knowledge which only resides in someone's head. Nonaka uses the story of the tacit knowledge that was necessary to develop a home bread maker. To understand what was needed to design a machine to knead dough properly, it was necessary for the engineers to work with bread makers to get the feel for how the dough needed to be manipulated.

But frankly the extent of knowledge that is truly tacit, like how to get up on water skis, that overlaps with the interests of KM systems is rather small. What is often very extensive is the amount of implicit information that could have been made explicit, but has not been. That it has not been is usually not a failure, but usually simply a cost-effective decision, usually taken unconsciously, that it is not worth the effort. The danger lies in assuming that explicit information is addressed by "collecting" and tacit information by "connecting," and not examining whether there is potentially important implicit information that could and should be made explicit. The after action comments above under Lessons Learned illustrate this important point.

3.13.2 Knowledge Retention and Retirees

One long standing KM issue is the need to retain the knowledge of retirees. The fact that the baby boomer bulge is now reaching retirement age is making this issue increasingly important. KM techniques are very relevant to this issue. The most obvious technique is the application of the lessons learned idea—just treat the retiree's career as a long project that is coming to its end and create an after action report, a massive data dump. This idea seems straightforward enough, and debriefing the retiree and those with whom he works closely about what issues they perceive as likely to surface or that could possibly arise is obvious common sense. But only in special cases is the full data dump approach likely to be very useful. When a current employee has a knowledge need, is he or she likely to look for the information, and if so how likely is it that the employee's search request will map onto the information in the retiree's data dump?

Much more likely to be useful is to keep the retiree involved, maintaining him or her in the CoPs, involved in the discussions concerning current issues, and findable through expertise locator systems. The real utility is likely to be found not directly in the information that the retiree leaves behind, but in new knowledge created by the interaction of the retiree with current employees. The retiree, in response to a current issue says "it occurs to me that..." and elicits a response something like "yes, the situation is somewhat similar, but here...," a discussion unfolds, the retiree contributes some of the needed expertise, and a solution is generated. The solution arises partially from the retiree's knowledge, but more from the interaction.

3.13.3 The Scope of KM

Another major development is the expansion of KM beyond the 20th century vision of KM as the organization's knowledge as described in the Gartner Group definition of KM. Increasingly KM is seen as ideally encompassing the whole bandwidth of information and knowledge likely to be useful to an organization, including knowledge external to the organization—knowledge emanating from vendors, suppliers, customers, etc., and knowledge originating in the scientific and scholarly community, the traditional domain of the library world. Looked at in this light, KM extends into environmental scanning and competitive intelligence.

The additional definition of KM above, "Yet One More Definition of KM," the forest of the trees, also makes the case that the definition of KM is now very broad.

CHAPTER

COLLECTIVE INTELLIGENCE AND TRANSFER OF LEARNING 4

4.1 INTRODUCTION

Collective intelligence evolves ideas and progress that would be tenuous when done alone. Assembling research in any given field of study is presented with three setbacks. The first is an inability to contrast work with someone assessing the same topic, a lack of controls during the information-gathering phase, and no associates to scrutinize the conclusions reached. Networking is possible but having a group centered on a single objective amasses knowledge from multiple people.

Collective intelligence is the body of knowledge that grows out of a group. When groups of people work together, they create intelligence that cannot exist on an individual level. Making decisions as a group, forming a consensus, getting ideas from different sources, and motivating people through competition are all components of collective intelligence.

Thomas Malone, the Patrick J. McGovern Professor of Management at MIT and the founding director at the MIT Center for Collective Intelligence, coined the term. In his book, "The Future of Work," Malone has theorized that businesses of the future will look very different from today's organizations because of collective information gathering. Artificial intelligence involving computers and other types of automation have produced collective intelligence as different types of groups connect to produce a body of knowledge.

The concept of Collective Intelligence (CI) is nothing new – it's crucial in defining the success of any group endeavor and is used daily in most organizations. When combining Artificial Intelligence (AI) with collective intelligence, companies can become even stronger, more profitable, and more efficient.

In the Artificial Intelligence: Implications for Business Strategy online short course from the MIT Sloan School of Management and the MIT Computer Science and Artificial Intelligence Laboratory (CSAIL), you'll learn how AI can support your organization and be integrated to increase efficiency and scalability. In just six weeks, this course provides the background needed to transform your organization into a business of the future. You'll learn how to harness AI and leadership for strategic decision making, and explore a road map for implementing AI in your business context.

Malone explains that groups of people working together create a 'supermind' with CI. Essentially, in the same way IQ describes individual intelligence, CI defines a body of knowledge on a broader scale. It's a dynamic concept, with changes spurred on by the increasing sophistication of AI technologies.

Under this paradigm, human-machine partnerships (AI with human input) enable and enhance CI. Organizations able to capitalize on these possibilities are likely to find a strategic advantage in doing so.

Collective Intelligence (CI) is shared or group intelligence that emerges from the collaboration, collective efforts, and competition of many individuals and appears in consensus decision making. The term appears in sociobiology, political science and in context of mass peer review and crowdsourcing applications. It may involve consensus, social capital and formalisms such as voting systems, social media and other means of quantifying mass activity. Collective IQ is a measure of collective intelligence, although it is often used interchangeably with the term collective intelligence. Collective intelligence has also been attributed to bacteria and animals.

It can be understood as an emergent property from the synergies among: 1) data-information-knowledge; 2) software-hardware; and 3) individuals (those with new insights as well as recognized authorities) that continually learns from feedback to produce just-in-time knowledge for better decisions than these three elements acting alone, or more narrowly as an emergent property between people and ways of processing information. This notion of collective intelligence is referred to as "symbiotic intelligence" by Norman Lee Johnson. The concept is used in sociology, business, computer science and mass communications: it also appears in science fiction. Pierre Lévy defines collective intelligence as, "It is a form of universally distributed intelligence, constantly enhanced, coordinated in real time, and resulting in the effective mobilization of skills. I'll add the following indispensable characteristic to this definition: The basis and goal of collective intelligence is mutual recognition and enrichment of individuals rather than the cult of fetishized or hypostatized communities." According to researchers Pierre Lévy and Derrick de Kerckhove, it refers to capacity of networked ICTs (Information Communication Technologies) to enhance the collective pool of social knowledge by simultaneously expanding the extent of human interactions. A broader definition was provided by Geoff Mulgan in a series of lectures and reports from 2006 onwards and in the book Big Mind which proposed a framework for analysing any thinking system, including both human and machine intelligence, in terms of functional elements (observation, prediction, creativity, judgement etc.), learning loops and forms of organisation. The aim was to provide a way to diagnose, and improve, the collective intelligence of a city, business, NGO or parliament.

Collective intelligence strongly contributes to the shift of knowledge and power from the individual to the collective. According to Eric S. Raymond (1998) and JC Herz (2005), open source intelligence will eventually generate superior outcomes to knowledge generated by proprietary software developed within corporations (Flew 2008). Media theorist Henry Jenkins sees collective intelligence as an 'alternative source of media power', related to convergence culture. He draws attention to education and the way people are learning to participate in knowledge cultures outside formal learning settings. Henry Jenkins criticizes schools which promote 'autonomous problem solvers and self-contained learners' while remaining hostile to learning through the means of collective intelligence. Both Pierre Lévy (2007) and Henry Jenkins (2008) support the claim that collective intelligence is important for democratization, as it is interlinked with knowledge-based culture and sustained by collective idea sharing, and thus contributes to a better understanding of diverse society.

Similar to the g factor (g) for general individual intelligence, a new scientific understanding of collective intelligence aims to extract a general collective intelligence factor c factor for groups indicating a group's ability to perform a wide range of tasks. Definition, operationalization and statistical methods are derived from g. Similarly as g is highly interrelated with the concept of IQ, this measurement of collective intelligence can be interpreted as intelligence quotient for groups (Group-IQ) even though the score is not a quotient per se. Causes for c and predictive validity are investigated as well.

Writers who have influenced the idea of collective intelligence include Francis Galton, Douglas Hofstadter (1979), Peter Russell (1983), Tom Atlee (1993), Pierre Lévy (1994), Howard Bloom (1995), Francis Heylighen (1995), Douglas Engelbart, Louis Rosenberg, Cliff Joslyn, Ron Dembo, Gottfried Mayer-Kress (2003), and Geoff Mulgan.

4.2 COLLECTIVE INTELLIGENCE AS A TOOL

Much as a hammer is a highly specialized tool for hitting a nail, the simplest expression of the human-machine partnership – the tool – refers to AI's ability to undertake specific, basic tasks with human input. For example, AI alone can be taught concepts, but you might not want AI to do complex and nuanced work with variables. In most instances, these tasks must be monitored throughout the process with humans, enhancing the partnership and effectiveness of using AI.

Examples of applications include word processors in, for example, your cellphone apps that offer autocomplete functions based on machine learning algorithms. Tools such as these allow humans to manipulate and communicate information more efficiently, and leverage collaboration between humans and machines on a larger scale.

Malone calls this large-scale collaboration 'hyperconnectivity'. As he explains in the course: "This may well be the most important way information technology helps create more intelligent organizations."

4.3 HISTORY OF COLLECTIVE INTELLIGENVE

The concept (although not so named) originated in 1785 with the Marquis de Condorcet, whose "jury theorem" states that if each member of a voting group is more likely than not to make a correct decision, the probability that the highest vote of the group is the correct decision increases with the number of members of the group. Many theorists have interpreted Aristotle's statement in the Politics that "a feast to which many contribute is better than a dinner provided out of a single purse" to mean that just as many may bring different dishes to the table, so in a deliberation many may contribute different pieces of information to generate a better decision. Recent scholarship, however, suggests that this was probably not what Aristotle meant but is a modern interpretation based on what we now know about team intelligence.

A precursor of the concept is found in entomologist William Morton Wheeler's observation that seemingly independent individuals can cooperate so closely as to become indistinguishable from a single organism (1910). Wheeler saw this collaborative process at work in ants that acted like the cells of a single beast he called a superorganism.

In 1912 Émile Durkheim identified society as the sole source of human logical thought. He argued in "The Elementary Forms of Religious Life" that society constitutes a higher intelligence because it transcends the individual over space and time. Other antecedents are Vladimir Vernadsky and Pierre Teilhard de Chardin's concept of "noosphere" and H.G. Wells's concept of "world brain". Peter Russell, Elisabet Sahtouris, and Barbara Marx Hubbard (originator of the term "conscious evolution") are inspired by the visions of a noosphere – a transcendent, rapidly evolving collective intelligence – an informational cortex of the planet. The notion has more recently been examined by the philosopher Pierre Lévy. In a 1962 research report, Douglas Engelbart linked collective intelligence to organizational effectiveness, and predicted that pro-actively 'augmenting human intellect' would yield a multiplier effect in group problem solving: "Three people working together in this augmented mode [would] seem to be more than three times as effective in solving a complex problem as is one augmented person working alone". In 1994, he coined the term 'collective IQ' as a measure of collective intelligence, to focus attention on the opportunity to significantly raise collective IQ in business and society.

The idea of collective intelligence also forms the framework for contemporary democratic theories often referred to as epistemic democracy. Epistemic democratic theories refer to the capacity of the populace, either through deliberation or aggregation of knowledge, to track the truth and relies on mechanisms to synthesize and apply collective intelligence.

Collective intelligence was introduced into the machine learning community in the late 20th century, and matured into a broader consideration of how to design "collectives" of self-interested adaptive agents to meet a system-wide goal. This was related to single-agent work on "reward shaping" and has been taken forward by numerous researchers in the game theory and engineering communities.

4.3.1 Collective Intelligence Today

The first step in understanding how AI influences CI in business is understanding the different types of intelligence.

By definition, CI refers to a group or a team's combined capacity and capability to perform various tasks and solve diverse problems. According to Anita Woolley and Ishani Aggarwal, "teams exhibit Collective Intelligence (CI), defined as a team's basic capacity to perform a wide variety of tasks, which is consistently predictive of future performance."

Broadly speaking, intelligence can be specialized (where you're able to perform tasks related to a single narrow area of focus) or general (where you're able to complete tasks across a broad focus area).

When a group of individuals gather for work, there's a flow to what they're doing. The group as a whole has CI. When individuals work in isolation, they are limited by their individual intelligence. By adding AI to the mix, the collective minds of the group can be made even more effective.

"We know that the future of work is all about collaboration and problem-solving," says Peter Baeck, who leads the Centre for Collective Intelligence Design at Nesta, a UK charity that funds and promotes research into groundbreaking ideas. "One of the most obvious opportunities is using AI to better create connections within often quite chaotic messy networks of people who are working on a common challenge."

AI technologies fall into the category of specialized intelligence; the algorithm behind the technology is excellent at completing a single task or type of task, but unable to perform very well beyond that. For example, a machine learning algorithm can be designed to recognize pictures of dogs, but you wouldn't want the same AI doing your taxes. By contrast, humans possess general intelligence – we can carry out a wide range of tasks successfully, although we may not be as good as AI at specialized tasks.

By pairing AI with humans in human-machine partnerships, it's possible to overcome the drawbacks of each: a human partner adds versatility, while AI contributes efficiency. Human-computer alliances can take many forms and demonstrate collective intelligence at its best. In his work, Malone provides a useful framework for understanding these interactions, arguing that AI can act as your tool, assistant, peer, or manager in business.

4.4 ARTIFICIAL INTELLIGENCE TAKES ON A PEER ROLE WITH COLLECTIVE INTELLIGENCE

The third rung of human-computer interaction places AI in the role of a peer. Essentially, this means that humans and AI perform the same or similar tasks. Machines are often able to perform these tasks much quicker than humans, but humans can solve problems that fall outside the scope of AI programming. Therefore, peer interactions often have a human partner overseeing and checking the operation of an AI application, doing only what is necessary.

Robotics provides an excellent example of human-computer interaction at the peer level. In many modern warehouses, autonomous robots bring goods to workers, cutting down on time spent walking the floor and searching for products. The human end of this interaction is still needed to make sure the correct product is retrieved.

In another application, the predictions of AI and humans are combined to forecast the next play in a game of football. The combined predictions prove to be more accurate and robust, showing AI's potential in contexts such as forecasting cybercrime or market conditions.

4.5 AI MANAGERS INCREASE TASK EFFICIENCY UTILIZING COLLECTIVE INTELLIGENCE

Although frightening to some, the concept of AI managers is a reality we already experience on a day-to-day basis – just look at traffic lights, which are controlled by algorithmic systems.

The role of AI as managers can include a simple division of labor – breaking tasks into smaller subtasks and assigning them to human workers best suited to them. The machine, in this case, essentially acts as a coordinator, using data to ensure a task is performed as efficiently and effectively as possible. Although these systems rely on sophisticated machine learning algorithms, when used correctly, they can lead to vastly improved operational performance – all thanks to augmented CI, or human-machine partnerships. For example, the use of AI in healthcare, as explained in the MIT Sloan Artificial Intelligence in Health Care online short course, can help with diagnosis and patient monitoring.

4.5.1 The Future of Collective Intelligence Combines Humans with AI

CI is on display in virtually every business, every day, although few may be aware of it. AI represents the opportunity for companies to augment CI in very real ways, improving their operations and strategic performance. But the human element remains vital – while many fear that AI will replace humans, the more likely future will see humans and computers interact in complex ways to improve the performance of both.

As augmented intelligence advances, business will evolve and scale with it – and for those who stand at the leading edge of this process, the rewards will be great. The American Medical Association defines augmented intelligence as "a conceptualization of artificial intelligence that focuses on AI's assistive role, emphasizing that its design enhances human intelligence, rather than replaces it." This concept is thoroughly covered in the MIT Sloan Building and Scaling Intelligent Enterprises With Artificial Intelligence online short course.

As Malone says, "All uses of computers occur within the context of people." The two work together to help solve problems and accelerate business. In the future, Malone anticipates that AI will be implemented by more businesses and have an increasingly significant impact: "We believe that businesses should focus on applying AI in ways that don't just replace people, but that create new jobs by providing novel kinds of products and services," he says. "We recommend that all schools include computer literacy and computational thinking in their curricula, and we believe that community colleges should offer more reskilling and online micro-degree programs, often including apprenticeships at local employers."

4.5.2 Dimensions

Howard Bloom has discussed mass behavior – collective behavior from the level of quarks to the level of bacterial, plant, animal, and human societies. He stresses the biological adaptations that have turned most of this earth's living beings into components of what he calls "a learning machine". In 1986 Bloom combined the concepts of apoptosis, parallel distributed processing, group selection, and the superorganism to produce a theory of how collective intelligence works. Later he showed how the collective intelligences of competing bacterial colonies and human societies can be explained in terms of computer-generated "complex adaptive systems" and the "genetic algorithms", concepts pioneered by John Holland.

Bloom traced the evolution of collective intelligence to our bacterial ancestors 1 billion years ago and demonstrated how a multi-species intelligence has worked since the beginning of life. Ant societies exhibit more intelligence, in terms of technology, than any other animal except for humans and co-operate in keeping livestock, for example aphids for "milking". Leaf cutters care for fungi and carry leaves to feed the fungi.

David Skrbina cites the concept of a 'group mind' as being derived from Plato's concept of panpsychism (that mind or consciousness is omnipresent and exists in all matter). He develops the concept of a 'group mind' as articulated by Thomas Hobbes in "Leviathan" and Fechner's arguments for a collective consciousness of mankind. He cites Durkheim as the most notable advocate of a "collective consciousness" and Teilhard de Chardin as a thinker who has developed the philosophical implications of the group mind.

Tom Atlee focuses primarily on humans and on work to upgrade what Howard Bloom calls "the group IQ". Atlee feels that collective intelligence can be encouraged "to overcome 'groupthink' and individual cognitive bias in order to allow a collective to cooperate on one process – while achieving enhanced intellectual performance." George Pór defined the collective intelligence phenomenon as "the capacity of human communities to evolve towards higher order complexity and harmony, through such innovation mechanisms as differentiation and integration, competition and collaboration." Atlee and Pór state that "collective intelligence also involves achieving a single focus of attention and standard of metrics which provide an appropriate threshold of action". Their approach is rooted in scientific community metaphor.

The term group intelligence is sometimes used interchangeably with the term collective intelligence. Anita Woolley presents Collective intelligence as a measure of group intelligence and group creativity. The idea is that a measure of collective intelligence covers a broad range of features of the group, mainly group composition and group interaction. The features of composition that lead to increased levels of collective intelligence in groups include criteria such as higher numbers of women in the group as well as increased diversity of the group.

Atlee and Pór suggest that the field of collective intelligence should primarily be seen as a human enterprise in which mind-sets, a willingness to share and an openness to the value of distributed intelligence for the common good are paramount, though group theory and artificial intelligence have something to offer. Individuals who respect collective intelligence are confident of their own abilities and recognize that the whole is indeed greater than the sum of any individual parts. Maximizing collective intelligence relies on the ability of an organization to accept and develop "The Golden Suggestion", which is any potentially useful input from any member. Groupthink often hampers collective intelligence by limiting input to a select few individuals or filtering potential Golden Suggestions without fully developing them to implementation.

Robert David Steele Vivas in The New Craft of Intelligence portrayed all citizens as "intelligence minutemen," drawing only on legal and ethical sources of information, able to create a "public intelligence" that keeps public officials and corporate managers honest, turning the concept of "national intelligence" on its head.

According to Don Tapscott and Anthony D. Williams, collective intelligence is mass collaboration. In order for this concept to happen, four principles need to exist:

(i) Openness - Sharing ideas and intellectual property: though these resources provide the edge over competitors more benefits accrue from allowing others to share ideas and gain significant improvement and scrutiny through collaboration.

(ii) Peering - Horizontal organization as with the 'opening up' of the Linux program where users are free to modify and develop it provided that they make it available for others. Peering succeeds because it encourages self-organization – a style of production that works more effectively than hierarchical management for certain tasks.

(iii) Sharing - Companies have started to share some ideas while maintaining some degree of control over others, like potential and critical patent rights. Limiting all intellectual property shuts out opportunities, while sharing some expands markets and brings out products faster.

(iv) Acting Globally - The advancement in communication technology has prompted the rise of global companies at low overhead costs. The internet is widespread, therefore a globally integrated company has no geographical boundaries and may access new markets, ideas and technology.

4.6 SOURCES OF COLLECTIVE INTELLIGENCE

Many different theories exist regarding where collective intelligence comes from and where it resides. The Co-Intelligence Institute notes that intelligence in a group dynamic involves many different approaches and perspectives and can include several factors. These can include:

- Experiencing the intelligence of groups of people as a larger body of intelligence that operates through individuals.
- The minds that comprise the intelligence collective influence the whole and those who access its common body of knowledge.
- An emergent property of a social system that includes information gathering, communication systems, learning systems, and similar cultural patterns.
- Is a group phenomenon in which the intelligence of each individual merges into a larger form of intelligence.

4.6.1 Intelligence as a Capacity and as Strategic Information

The ability to adapt and solve problems, such as problem-solving, reasoning, learning, prediction, etc. are all ascribed to intelligence as a collective capacity. Other components of intelligence as a capacity include perception, reasoning and logic, analysis, intuition, experience, consciousness and awareness, reflection, creation, and invention, among others.

Strategically using facts that have been gathered is another crucial component of intelligence. Think of the intelligence that countries gather as an example. The information gathered acts as a basis for crucial decision-making and affects society as a whole. While intelligence professionals only make up a small percentage of society at large, such individuals exist in societies on different levels and contribute to the larger sense of what intelligence is all about.

4.6.2 Ways Group Intelligence Emerges in Society

Answering, "What is collective intelligence?" requires some understanding of social groups.

There are several ways that group intelligence can emerge in society. Collaboration is a leading way. This involves a group of people working together on one project with a common goal in mind. Several scientists in one research lab could fall under the method of collaboration. With collaboration, there is typically a leader for the group, such as a principal investigator leading the lab. Collective efforts are another way intelligence can emerge. This usually involves people working separately from each other, but not competing. It is less efficient, and there is no central organization to the effort. Competition is another way a collection of intelligence can be assembled. With this method, different groups of people with the same goal stake out their own paths to figuring out the problem. Each group has a leader, and there is competition for scarce resources, such as funding.

4.7 A SHIFT OF KNOWLEDGE

Collective learning can only take place when an individual is willing to share what they learned. In this sense, group intelligence is a shift of information from individuals to a group. The members of the group change over time and membership is always in a state of flux.

A group might be people in a neighborhood, people who work for a particular company, or members of a professional organization. When people leave the group, they take the intelligence with them to the next group they join. People from outside groups can bring in new intelligence to the organization. Member attrition keeps ways of thinking fresh.

4.7.1 How Politics and Equity Affect Intelligence Sharing Across Society

The collective sharing of information in a society is often at odds with political power. In an authoritarian regime, group activities of the citizens are often discouraged. They are seen as a possible threat to authority. Coordination or unionization as a form of power is also against the ideals of communism.

In democratic political systems, there is often a reluctance to share information that could give a competitor an edge or an advantage. For group intelligence to work, it has to be equally accessible by everyone in society. Economic disparities, such as an inability to pay for internet service, have a considerable impact on access to group intelligence.

4.7.2 How Technology Fits into Collective Intelligence

Technology plays an increasingly important part in group intelligence. Technology facilitates the development and maintenance of platforms where people can come together as a collective and exchange information. The advanced technology available in smartphones allows a person to connect in traditional ways, such as through conversation. It also allows individuals to connect in large networks, such as through video conferencing apps, social media forums, websites with chat or forums, and more.

Today's smartphone is a single device that replaces multiple devices that used to be needed to gather a collection of information and share it with a group. A person no longer needs to have a landline phone, television, radio, daily newspaper, magazine subscriptions, or printed books to obtain and share knowledge with others. A caveat is that the technology for social intelligence is not free, and some people do not have the means to obtain the technology to participate in the sharing of information.

4.7.3 Role of the Internet in Collective Intelligence

Group intelligence has created some of the most widely-used platforms on the internet. Wikipedia is an online encyclopedia that anyone can add to or edit. A team of moderators and approved senior editors verifies information on a 24/7 basis. Online question and answer forums allow people to share and exchange information. Even scientists share their research online, allowing other researchers to access bits of genetic code or information on how to perform a particular test. Google is perhaps the most well-known collective intelligence platform on the internet.

4.8 ONLINE SOURCES OF GROUP INTELLIGENCE

4.8.1 Applications of Collective Learning

There are many applications of collective learning. These include:

- **Opinion aggregation:** An example is online product reviewing.
- **Idea collection:** This focuses on crowd-sourcing of solutions, designs or ideas.
- **Point estimates:** This aggregates individual estimates from a group.
- **Market judgment:** This relates to predicting demand, prices, and values of goods and services.
- **Political predictions:** This determines a collective opinion on an issue or candidate.

4.8.2 Level of Trust from Group Intelligence

Not everyone will trust the information they get from a group. The trustworthiness of the group depends on its history, its members, and its sources of data. Within any group, its members form networks of trust. Any individual is more likely to trust the information they get if it is from a person they know in real life. People are also more likely to trust information that is in line with what they already believe. It reiterates or reinforces their existing opinion, and they may develop a confirmation bias or avoid conflicting sources of information.

Any information that is not in agreement with their pre-determined beliefs may be ignored, argued, belittled, or berated. Within a group, subject matter experts may not always be given top priority as a trusted source of data. This is most often the case for a geographic-based group, such as people in a civic association or people who all live in the same town. These disagreements cause a breakdown in the sharing of knowledge.

4.8.3 Intelligence is Subjective

What seems intelligent to one group might seem downright stupid to another group. Group intelligence is a subjective assessment of information. According to The Edge, artificial intelligence is playing a growing role in the evaluation of group intelligence. Because the artificial intelligence algorithms do not have an emotional stake or any subjectivity, they may have a better method of evaluating what is collective intelligence.

For example, Google's algorithms scour the internet in search of answers to questions. The algorithms assemble the collected answers and return links to searchers who type a question into the search bar. This makes Google seem intelligent, even though it is relying on the filtered answers of individuals. In true group intelligence, all of the information is available, even the information that could be wrong, outdated, or disingenuous.

The idea of intelligence helps people understand the meaning of what it is to be human. Realizing intelligence is primarily a collective phenomenon helps people understand the meaning of collective intelligence and what it means to live in society as a whole.

4.9 COLLECTIVE INTELLIGENCE FACTOR

A new scientific understanding of collective intelligence defines it as a group's general ability to perform a wide range of tasks. Definition, operationalization and statistical methods are similar to the psychometric approach of general individual intelligence. Hereby, an individual's performance on a given set of cognitive tasks is used to measure general cognitive ability indicated by the general intelligence factor g extracted via factor analysis. In the same vein as g serves to display between-individual performance differences on cognitive tasks, collective intelligence research aims to find a parallel intelligence factor for groups 'c factor' (also called 'Collective Intelligence Factor' (CI)) displaying between-group differences on task performance. The collective intelligence score then is used to predict how this same group will perform on any other similar task in the future. Yet tasks, hereby, refer to mental or intellectual tasks performed by small groups even though the concept is hoped to be transferable to other performances and any groups or crowds reaching from families to companies and even whole cities. Since individuals' g factor scores are highly correlated with full-scale IQ scores, which are in turn regarded as good estimates of g, this measurement of collective intelligence can also be seen as an intelligence indicator or quotient respectively for a group (Group-IQ) parallel to an individual's Intelligence Quotient (IQ) even though the score is not a quotient per se.

Mathematically, c and g are both variables summarizing positive correlations among different tasks supposing that performance on one task is comparable with performance on other similar tasks. c thus is a source of variance among groups and can only be considered as a group's standing on the c factor compared to other groups in a given relevant population. The concept is in contrast to competing hypotheses including other correlational structures to explain group intelligence, such as a composition out of several equally important but independent factors as found in individual personality research.

Besides, this scientific idea also aims to explore the causes affecting collective intelligence, such as group size, collaboration tools or group members' interpersonal skills. The MIT Center for Collective Intelligence, for instance, announced the detection of The Genome of Collective Intelligence as one of its main goals aiming to develop a taxonomy of organizational building blocks, or genes, that can be combined and recombined to harness the intelligence of crowds.

4.9.1 Causes

Individual intelligence is shown to be genetically and environmentally influenced. Analogously, collective intelligence research aims to explore reasons why certain groups perform more intelligently than other groups given that c is just moderately correlated with the intelligence of individual group members. According to Woolley et al.'s results, neither team cohesion nor motivation or satisfaction is correlated with c. However, they claim that three factors were found as significant correlates: the variance in the number of speaking turns, group members' average social sensitivity and the proportion of females. All three had similar predictive power for c, but only social sensitivity was statistically significant.

The number speaking turns indicates that "groups where a few people dominated the conversation were less collectively intelligent than those with a more equal distribution of conversational turn-taking". Hence, providing multiple team members the chance to speak up made a group more intelligent.

Group members' social sensitivity was measured via the Reading the Mind in the Eyes Test (RME) and correlated.26 with c. Hereby, participants are asked to detect thinking or feeling expressed in other peoples' eyes presented on pictures and assessed in a multiple choice format. The test aims to measure peoples' Theory of Mind (ToM), also called 'mentalizing' or 'mind reading', which refers to the ability to attribute mental states, such as beliefs, desires or intents, to other people and in how far people understand that others have beliefs, desires, intentions or perspectives different from their own ones. RME is a ToM test for adults that shows sufficient test-retest reliability and constantly differentiates control groups from individuals with functional autism or Asperger Syndrome. It is one of the most widely accepted and well-validated tests for ToM within adults. ToM can be regarded as an associated subset of skills and abilities within the broader concept of emotional intelligence.

The proportion of females as a predictor of c was largely mediated by social sensitivity which is in vein with previous research showing that women score higher on social sensitivity tests. While a mediation, statistically speaking, clarifies the mechanism underlying the relationship between a dependent and an independent variable, Wolley agreed in an interview with the Harvard Business Review that these findings are saying that groups of women are smarter than groups of men. However, she relativizes this stating that the actual important thing is the high social sensitivity of group members.

It is theorized that the collective intelligence factor c is an emergent property resulting from bottom-up as well as top-down processes. Hereby, bottom-up processes cover aggregated group-member characteristics. Top-down processes cover group structures and norms that influence a group's way of collaborating and coordinating.

4.10 PROCESSES

4.10.1 Top-Down Processes

Top-down processes cover group interaction, such as structures, processes, and norms. An example of such top-down processes is conversational turn-taking. Research further suggest that collectively intelligent groups communicate more in general as well as more equally; same applies for participation and is shown for face-to-face as well as online groups communicating only via writing.

4.10.2 Bottom-Up Processes

Bottom-up processes include group composition, namely the characteristics of group members which are aggregated to the team level. An example of such bottom-up processes is the average social sensitivity or the average and maximum intelligence scores of group members. Furthermore, collective intelligence was found to be related to a group's cognitive diversity including thinking styles and perspectives. Groups that are moderately diverse in cognitive style have higher collective intelligence than those who are very similar in cognitive style or very different. Consequently, groups where members are too similar to each other lack the variety of perspectives and skills needed to perform well. On the other hand, groups whose members are too different seem to have difficulties to communicate and coordinate effectively.

4.10.3 Serial vs. Parallel Processes

For most of human history, collective intelligence was confined to small tribal groups in which opinions were aggregated through real-time parallel interactions among members. In modern times, mass communication, mass media, and networking technologies have enabled collective intelligence to span massive groups, distributed across continents and time-zones. To accommodate this shift in scale, collective intelligence in large-scale groups been dominated by serialized polling processes such as aggregating up-votes, likes, and ratings over time. In engineering, aggregating many engineering decisions allows for identifying typical good designs. While modern systems benefit from larger group size, the serialized process has been found to introduce substantial noise that distorts the collective output of the group. In one significant study of serialized collective intelligence, it was found that the first vote contributed to a serialized voting system can distort the final result by 34%.

To address the problems of serialized aggregation of input among large-scale groups, recent advancements collective intelligence have worked to replace serialized votes, polls, and markets, with parallel systems such as "human swarms" modeled after synchronous swarms in nature. Based on natural process of Swarm Intelligence, these artificial swarms of networked humans enable participants to work together in parallel to answer questions and make predictions as an emergent collective intelligence. In one high-profile example, a human swarm challenge by CBS Interactive to predict the Kentucky Derby.

The value of parallel collective intelligence was demonstrated in medical applications by researchers at Stanford University School of Medicine and Unanimous AI in a set of published studies wherein groups of human doctors were connected by real-time swarming algorithms and tasked with diagnosing chest x-rays for the presence of pneumonia. When working together as "human swarms," the groups of experienced radiologists demonstrated a 33% reduction in diagnostic errors as compared to traditional methods.

4.11 EVIDENCE

Woolley, Chabris, Pentland, Hashmi, & Malone (2010), the originators of this scientific understanding of collective intelligence, found a single statistical factor for collective intelligence in their research across 192 groups with people randomly recruited from the public. In Woolley et al.'s two initial studies, groups worked together on different tasks from the McGrath Task Circumplex, a well-established taxonomy of group tasks. Tasks were chosen from all four quadrants of the circumplex and included visual puzzles, brainstorming, making collective moral judgments, and negotiating over limited resources. The results in these tasks were taken to conduct a factor analysis. Both studies showed support for a general collective intelligence factor c underlying differences in group performance with an initial eigenvalue accounting for 43% of the variance, whereas the next factor accounted for only 18%. That fits the range normally found in research regarding a general individual intelligence factor g typically accounting for 40% to 50% percent of between-individual performance differences on cognitive tests.

Afterwards, a more complex task was solved by each group to determine whether c factor scores predict performance on tasks beyond the original test. Criterion tasks were playing checkers against a standardized computer in the first and a complex architectural design task in the second study. In a regression analysis using both individual intelligence of group members and c to predict performance on the criterion tasks, c had a significant effect, but average and maximum individual intelligence had not. While average and maximum intelligence of individual group members were moderately correlated with c, c was still a much better predictor of the criterion tasks. According to Woolley et al., this supports the existence of a collective intelligence factor c, because it demonstrates an effect over and beyond group members' individual intelligence and thus that c is more than just the aggregation of the individual IQs or the influence of the group member with the highest IQ.

Engel et al. (2014) replicated Woolley et al.'s findings applying an accelerated battery of tasks with a first factor in the factor analysis explaining 49% of the between-group variance in performance with the following factors explaining less than half of this amount. Moreover, they found a similar result for groups working together online communicating only via text and confirmed the role of female proportion and social sensitivity in causing collective intelligence in both cases. Similarly to Wolley et al., they also measured social sensitivity with the RME which is actually meant to measure people's ability to detect mental states in other peoples' eyes. The online collaborating participants, however, did neither know nor see each other at all. The authors conclude that scores on the RME must be related to a broader set of abilities of social reasoning than only drawing inferences from other people's eye expressions.

A collective intelligence factor c in the sense of Woolley et al. was further found in groups of MBA students working together over the course of a semester, in online gaming groups as well as in groups from different cultures and groups in different contexts in terms of short-term versus long-term groups. None of these investigations considered team members' individual intelligence scores as control variables.

Note as well that the field of collective intelligence research is quite young and published empirical evidence is relatively rare yet. However, various proposals and working papers are in progress or already completed but (supposedly) still in a scholarly peer reviewing publication process.

4.11.1 Predictive Validity

Next to predicting a group's performance on more complex criterion tasks as shown in the original experiments, the collective intelligence factor c was also found to predict group performance in diverse tasks in MBA classes lasting over several months. Thereby, highly collectively intelligent groups earned significantly higher scores on their group assignments although their members did not do any better on other individually performed assignments. Moreover, highly collective intelligent teams improved performance over time suggesting that more collectively intelligent teams learn better. This is another potential parallel to individual intelligence where more intelligent people are found to acquire new material quicker.

Individual intelligence can be used to predict plenty of life outcomes from school attainment and career success to health outcomes and even mortality. Whether collective intelligence is able to predict other outcomes besides group performance on mental tasks has still to be investigated.

4.11.2 Potential Connections to Individual Intelligence

Gladwell (2008) showed that the relationship between individual IQ and success works only to a certain point and that additional IQ points over an estimate of IQ 120 do not translate into real life advantages. If a similar border exists for Group-IQ or if advantages are linear and infinite, has still to be explored. Similarly, demand for further research on possible connections of individual and collective intelligence exists within plenty of other potentially transferable logics of individual intelligence, such as, for instance, the development over time or the question of improving intelligence. Whereas it is controversial whether human intelligence can be enhanced via training, a group's collective intelligence potentially offers simpler opportunities for improvement by exchanging team members or implementing structures and technologies. Moreover, social sensitivity was found to be, at least temporarily, improvable by reading literary fiction as well as watching drama movies. In how far such training ultimately improves collective intelligence through social sensitivity remains an open question.

There are further more advanced concepts and factor models attempting to explain individual cognitive ability including the categorization of intelligence in fluid and crystallized intelligence or the hierarchical model of intelligence differences. Further supplementing explanations and conceptualizations for the factor structure of the Genomes of collective intelligence besides a general 'c factor', though, are missing yet.

4.12 CONTROVERSIES

Other scholars explain team performance by aggregating team members' general intelligence to the team level instead of building an own overall collective intelligence measure. Devine and Philips (2001) showed in a meta-analysis that mean cognitive ability predicts team performance in laboratory settings as well as field settings – note that this is only a small effect. Suggesting a strong dependence on the relevant tasks, other scholars showed that tasks requiring a high degree of communication and cooperation are found to be most influenced by the team member with the lowest cognitive ability. Tasks in which selecting the best team member is the most successful strategy, are shown to be most influenced by the member with the highest cognitive ability.

Since Woolley et al.'s results do not show any influence of group satisfaction, group cohesiveness, or motivation, they, at least implicitly, challenge these concepts regarding the importance for group performance in general and thus contrast meta-analytically proven evidence concerning the positive effects of group cohesion, motivation and satisfaction on group performance.

Noteworthy is also that the involved researchers among the confirming findings widely overlap with each other and with the authors participating in the original first study around Anita Woolley.

4.12.1 Machines are Transforming Superminds

Today, several organizations use superminds that employ human-machine collaboration to power their core business offerings. Malone shares Google Search as a case in point. Everything that happens from the moment a user types in a search query until they get their results is performed entirely by computers. No human appears in the loop for this operational process.

They tell the machines what to do. Google programmers are like employee training specialists—but here, the "employees" are machines. People instruct the machines through direct programming logic and by training machine-learning algorithms.

With ML, machines use historical queries from users to surface the most relevant search results. Of course, the web pages that a Google search returns were mostly created by people, highlighting another critical role that humans play in this supermind.

Once you consider everyday products and services, there are many similar examples of superminds that blend human-machine abilities seamlessly. Digital-native companies such as Netflix, Pandora, and Uber have deep human-machine collaborations that power not just their customer-facing offerings but also their internal operations.

While there are many instances of organizations using superminds to drive their operational workflows today, the area of strategic decision-making is less explored.

4.12.2 How Enterprises can Use Superminds for Strategic Decisions?

Strategic Decisions

A Harvard Business School report outlines that 85% of executive leadership teams spend under one hour per month discussing strategy, and 50% spend no time at all. Strategy planning is primarily restricted to an annual exercise with participation from a few senior leaders.

It's no wonder that 95% of a company's employees don't understand its strategy. Ultimately, 90% of businesses fail to meet their strategic targets.

Superminds can transform this dated process of corporate strategic planning, says Malone. Today, machines' involvement in this process is restricted to automating a few computations or tracking metrics. He envisions a new approach that leverages greater human-machine collaboration.

Malone outlines four significant steps to rethink strategic planning:

1. Increase human involvement : Thanks to hyperconnectivity, almost everyone within a company can have a say in the strategic planning process. Each employee can be empowered to share inputs on corporate plans, recommend strategic offerings, or suggest features in the product roadmap.

While this sounds great in principle, how do you get people to participate? Gamification can turn the planning process into a live contest. In fact, several enterprises have used gamification to improve employee engagement radically across their business.

For example, Spotify gamified the dreaded annual appraisal process through live scorecards and badges shared on an internal social network. Consequently, over 90% of employees participated voluntarily in reporting live performance scores throughout the year.

2. Inject objectivity: When a stream of ideas flows in, how do you evaluate them continuously and objectively? Borrow some best practices from prediction markets.

Early in their journey, Google built an internal system that works like a stock market. They let employees bet on probable outcomes using virtual money. Employees answered questions such as, "Will a project be finished on time?" or "How many users will Gmail have?" This trading system helped the Google hierarchy discover employees' uncensored opinions and gain insights that could have been overlooked.

The concept of prediction markets taps into the wisdom of crowds to discover the most effective outcomes. Through a similar setup, you can set up internal prediction markets with a defined audience to evaluate your strategic planning ideas.

3. Augment with artificial intelligence: At this point, you can bring in machines to augment the decisions. Machine learning models can observe this process of manual decision-making and learn from the outcomes. In case you're wondering whether machines can find patterns in such decisions, it has been done before.

Bridgewater Associates, the famed investment management firm founded by Ray Dalio, showed that algorithmic decision-making could be applied to run a large business. The firm's management coach system collects copious amounts of data to study employee behavior. The system bases judgments on continuous decisions made by employees across the firm. Dalio said that this collective decision-making approach helped turn the firm into one of the world's most successful hedge funds.

By studying examples of how humans evaluate strategic planning ideas, machines can start recognizing patterns in human judgments. Given enough decision volume and variety, ML models can be trained to make recommendations to humans. When machines reach an acceptable threshold of decision quality, you can delegate certain types of decisions entirely to them.

4. Scale across the organization: A gamified, machine-enabled strategic planning process can be replicated across all organizational levels, from individual product teams to the corporate level. Instead of creating strategic plans annually or quarterly, organizations can now make thousands of plans every single day.

"Most people think of strategy as an event, but that's not the way the world works," said Clayton Christensen, the Harvard Business School Professor. "More often than not, the strategy that leads to success emerges through a process that's at work 24/7 in almost every industry."

Whether it's because of a competitor launching a new offensive or the entire industry going into a decline during the pandemic, the strategy needs continual reassessment. This blueprint for a cyber-human strategy machine could enable organizations to respond continuously and rapidly to ongoing changes in their environment.

However, the approach does pose some inherent challenges. Culturally, it calls for organizations to switch from a hierarchical, closed planning process to one that's more flat and inclusive. From a technical perspective, machine learning stumbles when predicting scenarios with few historical examples or those involving nuanced decision-making, as they involve fewer digital trails.

However, with the proper executive support and technology investment, these roadblocks can be overcome. The potential upside of acquiring such an enhanced strategic capability will motivate organizations to make the switch. "A company that manages to build something even close to this has the potential to run circles around its competitors," says Malone.

Executives who aspire to apply superminds to rethink and rewire their organizational processes can tap into the supermind design methodology. This systematic process was developed at the MIT Center for Collective Intelligence. It helps organizations redesign their operations by leveraging novel approaches in human-machine collaboration.

4.13 ALTERNATIVE MATHEMATICAL TECHNIQUES

4.13.1 Computational Collective Intelligence

In 2001, Tadeusz (Tad) Szuba from the AGH University in Poland proposed a formal model for the phenomenon of collective intelligence. It is assumed to be an unconscious, random, parallel, and distributed computational process, run in mathematical logic by the social structure.

In this model, beings and information are modeled as abstract information molecules carrying expressions of mathematical logic. They are quasi-randomly displacing due to their interaction with their environments with their intended displacements. Their interaction in abstract computational space creates multi-thread inference process which we perceive as collective intelligence. Thus, a non-Turing model of computation is used. This theory allows simple formal definition of collective intelligence as the property of social structure and seems to be working well for a wide spectrum of beings, from bacterial colonies up to human social structures. Collective intelligence considered as a specific computational process is providing a straightforward explanation of several social phenomena. For this model of collective intelligence, the formal definition of IQS (IQ Social) was proposed and was defined as "the probability function over the time and domain of N-element inferences which are reflecting inference activity of the social structure". While IQS seems to be computationally hard, modeling of social structure in terms of a computational process as described above gives a chance for approximation. Prospective applications are optimization of companies through the maximization of their IQS, and the analysis of drug resistance against collective intelligence of bacterial colonies.

4.13.2 Collective Intelligence Quotient

One measure sometimes applied, especially by more artificial intelligence focused theorists, is a "collective intelligence quotient" (or "cooperation quotient") – which can be normalized from the "individual" intelligence quotient (IQ) – thus making it possible to determine the marginal intelligence added by each new individual participating in the collective action, thus using metrics to avoid the hazards of group think and stupidity.

4.13.3 Applications

There have been many recent applications of collective intelligence, including in fields such as crowd-sourcing, citizen science and prediction markets. The Nesta Centre for Collective Intelligence Design was launched in 2018 and has produced many surveys of applications as well as funding experiments. In 2020 the UNDP Accelerator Labs began using collective intelligence methods in their work to accelerate innovation for the Sustainable Development Goals.

4.13.4 Elicitation of Point Estimates

Here, the goal is to get an estimate (in a single value) of something. For example, estimating the weight of an object, or the release date of a product or probability of success of a project etc. as seen in prediction markets like Intrade, HSX or InklingMarkets and also in several implementations of crowdsourced estimation of a numeric outcome such as the Delphi method. Essentially, we try to get the average value of the estimates provided by the members in the crowd.

4.13.5 Opinion Aggregation

In this situation, opinions are gathered from the crowd regarding an idea, issue or product. For example, trying to get a rating (on some scale) of a product sold online (such as Amazon's star rating system). Here, the emphasis is to collect and simply aggregate the ratings provided by customers/users.

4.13.6 Idea Collection

In these problems, someone solicits ideas for projects, designs or solutions from the crowd. For example, ideas on solving a data science problem or getting a good design for a T-shirt or in getting answers to simple problems that only humans can do well. The objective is to gather the ideas and devise some selection criteria to choose the best ideas.

James Surowiecki divides the advantages of disorganized decision-making into three main categories, which are cognition, cooperation and coordination.

4.14 COGNITION

4.14.1 Market Judgment

Because of the Internet's ability to rapidly convey large amounts of information throughout the world, the use of collective intelligence to predict stock prices and stock price direction has become increasingly viable. Websites aggregate stock market information that is as current as possible so professional or amateur stock analysts can publish their viewpoints, enabling amateur investors to submit their financial opinions and create an aggregate opinion. The opinion of all investor can be weighed equally so that a pivotal premise of the effective application of collective intelligence can be applied: the masses, including a broad spectrum of stock market expertise, can be utilized to more accurately predict the behavior of financial markets.

Collective intelligence underpins the efficient-market hypothesis of Eugene Fama – although the term collective intelligence is not used explicitly in his paper. Fama cites research conducted by Michael Jensen in which 89 out of 115 selected funds underperformed relative to the index during the period from 1955 to 1964. But after removing the loading charge only 72 underperformed while after removing brokerage costs only 58 underperformed. On the basis of such evidence index funds became popular investment vehicles using the collective intelligence of the market, rather than the judgement of professional fund managers, as an investment strategy.

4.14.2 Predictions in Politics and Technology

Political parties mobilize large numbers of people to form policy, select candidates and finance and run election campaigns. Knowledge focusing through various voting methods allows perspectives to converge through the assumption that uninformed voting is to some degree random and can be filtered from the decision process leaving only a residue of informed consensus. Critics point out that often bad ideas, misunderstandings, and misconceptions are widely held, and that structuring of the decision process must favor experts who are presumably less prone to random or misinformed voting in a given context.

Companies such as Affinnova (acquired by Nielsen), Google, Innocentive, Marketocracy, and Threadless have successfully employed the concept of collective intelligence in bringing about the next generation of technological changes through their Research and Development (R&D), customer service, and knowledge management. An example of such application is Google's Project Aristotle in 2012, where the effect of collective intelligence on team makeup was examined in hundreds of the company's R&D teams.

4.15 COOPERATION

4.15.1 Networks of Trust

In 2012, the Global Futures Collective Intelligence System (GFIS) was created by The Millennium Project, which epitomizes collective intelligence as the synergistic intersection among data/information/knowledge, software/hardware, and expertise/insights that has a recursive learning process for better decision-making than the individual players alone.

New media are often associated with the promotion and enhancement of collective intelligence. The ability of new media to easily store and retrieve information, predominantly through databases and the Internet, allows for it to be shared without difficulty. Thus, through interaction with new media, knowledge easily passes between sources resulting in a form of collective intelligence. The use of interactive new media, particularly the internet, promotes online interaction and this distribution of knowledge between users.

Francis Heylighen, Valentin Turchin, and Gottfried Mayer-Kress are among those who view collective intelligence through the lens of computer science and cybernetics. In their view, the Internet enables collective intelligence at the widest, planetary scale, thus facilitating the emergence of a global brain.

The developer of the World Wide Web, Tim Berners-Lee, aimed to promote sharing and publishing of information globally. Later his employer opened up the technology for free use. In the early '90s, the Internet's potential was still untapped, until the mid-1990s when 'critical mass', as termed by the head of the Advanced Research Project Agency (ARPA), Dr. J.C.R. Licklider, demanded more accessibility and utility. The driving force of this Internet-based collective intelligence is the digitization of information and communication. Henry Jenkins, a key theorist of new media and media convergence draws on the theory that collective intelligence can be attributed to media convergence and participatory culture. He criticizes contemporary education for failing to incorporate online trends of collective problem solving into the classroom, stating "whereas a collective intelligence community encourages ownership of work as a group, schools grade individuals". Jenkins argues that interaction within a knowledge community builds vital skills for young people, and teamwork through collective intelligence communities contribute to the development of such skills. Collective intelligence is not merely a quantitative contribution of information from all cultures, it is also qualitative.

Lévy and de Kerckhove consider CI from a mass communications perspective, focusing on the ability of networked information and communication technologies to enhance the community knowledge pool. They suggest that these communications tools enable humans to interact and to share and collaborate with both ease and speed (Flew 2008). With the development of the Internet and its widespread use, the opportunity to contribute to knowledge-building communities, such as Wikipedia, is greater than ever before. These computer networks give participating users the opportunity to store and to retrieve knowledge through the collective access to these databases and allow them to "harness the hive" Researchers at the MIT Center for Collective Intelligence research and explore collective intelligence of groups of people and computers.

In this context collective intelligence is often confused with shared knowledge. The former is the sum total of information held individually by members of a community while the latter is information that is believed to be true and known by all members of the community. Collective intelligence as represented by Web 2.0 has less user engagement than collaborative intelligence. An art project using Web 2.0 platforms is "Shared Galaxy", an experiment developed by an anonymous artist to create a collective identity that shows up as one person on several platforms like MySpace, Facebook, YouTube and Second Life. The password is written in the profiles and the accounts named "Shared Galaxy" are open to be used by anyone. In this way many take part in being one. Another art project using collective intelligence to produce artistic work is Curatron, where a large group of artists together decides on a smaller group that they think would make a good collaborative group. The process is used based on an algorithm computing the collective preferences In creating what he calls 'CI-Art', Nova Scotia based artist Mathew Aldred follows Pierry Lévy's definition of collective intelligence. Aldred's CI-Art event in March 2016 involved over four hundred people from the community of Oxford, Nova Scotia, and internationally. Later work developed by Aldred used the UNU swarm intelligence system to create digital drawings and paintings. The Oxford Riverside Gallery held a public CI-Art event in May 2016, which connected with online participants internationally.

In social bookmarking (also called collaborative tagging), users assign tags to resources shared with other users, which gives rise to a type of information organisation that emerges from this crowdsourcing process. The resulting information structure can be seen as reflecting the collective knowledge (or collective intelligence) of a community of users and is commonly called a "Folksonomy", and the process can be captured by models of collaborative tagging.

Recent research using data from the social bookmarking website Delicious, has shown that collaborative tagging systems exhibit a form of complex systems (or self-organizing) dynamics. Although there is no central controlled vocabulary to constrain the actions of individual users, the distributions of tags that describe different resources has been shown to converge over time to a stable power law distributions. Once such stable distributions form, examining the correlations between different tags can be used to construct simple folksonomy graphs, which can be efficiently partitioned to obtained a form of community or shared vocabularies. Such vocabularies can be seen as a form of collective intelligence, emerging from the decentralised actions of a community of users. The Wall-it Project is also an example of social bookmarking.

4.16 P2P BUSINESS

Research performed by Tapscott and Williams has provided a few examples of the benefits of collective intelligence to business:

4.16.1 Talent Utilization

At the rate technology is changing, no firm can fully keep up in the innovations needed to compete. Instead, smart firms are drawing on the power of mass collaboration to involve participation of the people they could not employ. This also helps generate continual interest in the firm in the form of those drawn to new idea creation as well as investment opportunities.

4.16.2 Demand Creation

Firms can create a new market for complementary goods by engaging in open source community. Firms also are able to expand into new fields that they previously would not have been able to without the addition of resources and collaboration from the community. This creates, as mentioned before, a new market for complementary goods for the products in said new fields.

4.16.3 Costs Reduction

Mass collaboration can help to reduce costs dramatically. Firms can release a specific software or product to be evaluated or debugged by online communities. The results will be more personal, robust and error-free products created in a short amount of time and costs. New ideas can also be generated and explored by collaboration of online communities creating opportunities for free R&D outside the confines of the company.

4.16.4 Open Source Software

Cultural theorist and online community developer, John Banks considered the contribution of online fan communities in the creation of the Trainz product. He argued that its commercial success was fundamentally dependent upon "the formation and growth of an active and vibrant online fan community that would both actively promote the product and create content- extensions and additions to the game software".

The increase in user created content and interactivity gives rise to issues of control over the game itself and ownership of the player-created content. This gives rise to fundamental legal issues, highlighted by Lessig and Bray and Konsynski, such as intellectual property and property ownership rights.

Gosney extends this issue of Collective Intelligence in videogames one step further in his discussion of alternate reality gaming. This genre, he describes as an "across-media game that deliberately blurs the line between the in-game and out-of-game experiences" as events that happen outside the game reality "reach out" into the player's lives in order to bring them together. Solving the game requires "the collective and collaborative efforts of multiple players"; thus the issue of collective and collaborative team play is essential to ARG. Gosney argues that the Alternate Reality genre of gaming dictates an unprecedented level of collaboration and "collective intelligence" in order to solve the mystery of the game.

4.16.5 Benefits of Co-Operation

Co-operation helps to solve most important and most interesting multi-science problems. In his book, James Surowiecki mentioned that most scientists think that benefits of co-operation have much more value when compared to potential costs. Co-operation works also because at best it guarantees number of different viewpoints. Because of the possibilities of technology global co-operation is nowadays much easier and productive than before. It is clear that, when co-operation goes from university level to global it has significant benefits.

For example, why do scientists co-operate? Science has become more and more isolated and each science field has spread even more and it is impossible for one person to be aware of all developments. This is true especially in experimental research where highly advanced equipment requires special skills. With co-operation scientists can use information from different fields and use it effectively instead of gathering all the information just by reading by themselves."

4.17 COORDINATION

4.17.1 Ad-Hoc Communities

Military, trade unions, and corporations satisfy some definitions of CI – the most rigorous definition would require a capacity to respond to very arbitrary conditions without orders or guidance from "law" or "customers" to constrain actions. Online advertising companies are using collective intelligence to bypass traditional marketing and creative agencies.

The UNU open platform for "human swarming" (or "social swarming") establishes real-time closed-loop systems around groups of networked users molded after biological swarms, enabling human participants to behave as a unified collective intelligence. When connected to UNU, groups of distributed users collectively answer questions and make predictions in real-time. Early testing shows that human swarms can out-predict individuals. In 2016, an UNU swarm was challenged by a reporter to predict the winners of the Kentucky Derby, and successfully picked the first four horses, in order, beating 540 to 1 odds.

Specialized information sites such as Digital Photography Review or Camera Labs is an example of collective intelligence. Anyone who has an access to the internet can contribute to distributing their knowledge over the world through the specialized information sites.

In learner-generated context a group of users marshal resources to create an ecology that meets their needs often (but not only) in relation to the co-configuration, co-creation and co-design of a particular learning space that allows learners to create their own context. Learner-generated contexts represent an ad hoc community that facilitates coordination of collective action in a network of trust. An example of learner-generated context is found on the Internet when collaborative users pool knowledge in a "shared intelligence space". As the Internet has developed so has the concept of CI as a shared public forum. The global accessibility and availability of the Internet has allowed more people than ever to contribute and access ideas.

Games such as The Sims Series, and Second Life are designed to be non-linear and to depend on collective intelligence for expansion. This way of sharing is gradually evolving and influencing the mindset of the current and future generations. For them, collective intelligence has become a norm. In Terry Flew's discussion of 'interactivity' in the online games environment, the ongoing interactive dialogue between users and game developers, he refers to Pierre Lévy's concept of Collective Intelligence and argues this is active in videogames as clans or guilds in MMORPG constantly work to achieve goals. Henry Jenkins proposes that the participatory cultures emerging between games producers, media companies, and the end-users mark a fundamental shift in the nature of media production and consumption. Jenkins argues that this new participatory culture arises at the intersection of three broad new media trends. Firstly, the development of new media tools/technologies enabling the creation of content. Secondly, the rise of subcultures promoting such creations, and lastly, the growth of value adding media conglomerates, which foster image, idea and narrative flow.

4.17.2 Coordinating Collective Actions

Improvisational actors also experience a type of collective intelligence which they term "group mind", as theatrical improvisation relies on mutual cooperation and agreement, leading to the unity of "group mind".

Growth of the Internet and mobile telecom has also produced "swarming" or "rendezvous" events that enable meetings or even dates on demand. The full impact has yet to be felt but the anti-globalization movement, for example, relies heavily on e-mail, cell phones, pagers, SMS and other means of organizing. The Indymedia organization does this in a more journalistic way. Such resources could combine into a form of collective intelligence accountable only to the current participants yet with some strong moral or linguistic guidance from generations of contributors – or even take on a more obviously democratic form to advance shared goal.

A further application of collective intelligence is found in the "Community Engineering for Innovations". In such an integrated framework proposed by Ebner et al., idea competitions and virtual communities are combined to better realize the potential of the collective intelligence of the participants, particularly in open-source R&D. In management theory the use of collective intelligence and crowd sourcing leads to innovations and very robust answers to quantitative issues. Therefore, collective intelligence and crowd sourcing is not necessarily leading to the best solution to economic problems, but to a stable, good solution.

4.17.3 Coordination in Different Types of Tasks

Collective actions or tasks require different amounts of coordination depending on the complexity of the task. Tasks vary from being highly independent simple tasks that require very little coordination to complex interdependent tasks that are built by many individuals and require a lot of coordination. In the article written by Kittur, Lee and Kraut the writers introduce a problem in cooperation: "When tasks require high coordination because the work is highly interdependent, having more contributors can increase process losses, reducing the effectiveness of the group below what individual members could optimally accomplish". Having a team too large the overall effectiveness may suffer even when the extra contributors increase the resources. In the end the overall costs from coordination might overwhelm other costs.

Group collective intelligence is a property that emerges through coordination from both bottom-up and top-down processes. In a bottom-up process the different characteristics of each member are involved in contributing and enhancing coordination. Top-down processes are more strict and fixed with norms, group structures and routines that in their own way enhance the group's collective work.

4.18 ALTERNATIVE VIEWS

4.18.1 A Tool for Combating Self-Preservation

Tom Atlee reflects that, although humans have an innate ability to gather and analyze data, they are affected by culture, education and social institutions. [self-published source?] A single person tends to make decisions motivated by self-preservation. Therefore, without collective intelligence, humans may drive themselves into extinction based on their selfish needs.

4.18.2 Separation from IQISM

Phillip Brown and Hugh Lauder quotes Bowles and Gintis (1976) that in order to truly define collective intelligence, it is crucial to separate 'intelligence' from IQism. They go on to argue that intelligence is an achievement and can only be developed if allowed to. For example, earlier on, groups from the lower levels of society are severely restricted from aggregating and pooling their intelligence. This is because the elites fear that the collective intelligence would convince the people to rebel. If there is no such capacity and relations, there would be no infrastructure on which collective intelligence is built. This reflects how powerful collective intelligence can be if left to develop.

4.18.3 Artificial Intelligence Views

Skeptics, especially those critical of artificial intelligence and more inclined to believe that risk of bodily harm and bodily action are the basis of all unity between people, are more likely to emphasize the capacity of a group to take action and withstand harm as one fluid mass mobilization, shrugging off harms the way a body shrugs off the loss of a few cells. This train of thought is most obvious in the anti-globalization movement and characterized by the works of John Zerzan, Carol Moore, and Starhawk, who typically shun academics. These theorists are more likely to refer to ecological and collective wisdom and to the role of consensus process in making ontological distinctions than to any form of "intelligence" as such, which they often argue does not exist, or is mere "cleverness".

Harsh critics of artificial intelligence on ethical grounds are likely to promote collective wisdom-building methods, such as the new tribalists and the Gaians. [self-published source] Whether these can be said to be collective intelligence systems is an open question. Some, e.g. Bill Joy, simply wish to avoid any form of autonomous artificial intelligence and seem willing to work on rigorous collective intelligence in order to remove any possible niche for AI.

In contrast to these views, companies such as Amazon Mechanical Turk and Crowd Flower are using collective intelligence and crowd sourcing or consensus-based assessment to collect the enormous amounts of data for machine learning algorithms.

4.19 TRANSFER OF LEARNING

Transfer of learning occurs when people apply information, strategies, and skills they have learned to a new situation or context. Transfer is not a discrete activity, but is rather an integral part of the learning process. Researchers attempt to identify when and how transfer occurs and to offer strategies to improve transfer.

The formal discipline approach to learning believed that specific mental faculties could be strengthened by particular courses of training and that these strengthened faculties transferred to other situations, based on faculty psychology which viewed the mind as a collection of separate modules or faculties assigned to various mental tasks. This approach resulted in school curricula that required students to study subjects such as mathematics and Latin in order to strengthen reasoning and memory faculties.

Disputing formal discipline, Edward Thorndike and Robert S. Woodworth in 1901 postulated that the transfer of learning was restricted or assisted by the elements in common between the original context and the next context. The notion was originally introduced as transfer of practice. They explored how individuals would transfer learning in one context to another similar context and how "improvement in one mental function" could influence a related one. Their theory implied that transfer of learning depends on how similar the learning task and transfer tasks are, or where "identical elements are concerned in the influencing and influenced function", now known as the identical element theory. Thorndike urged schools to design curricula with tasks similar to those students would encounter outside of school to facilitate the transfer of learning.

In contrast to Thorndike, Edwin Ray Guthrie's law of contiguity expected little transfer of learning. Guthrie recommended studying in the exact conditions in which one would be tested, because of his view that "we learn what we do in the presence of specific stimuli". The expectation is that training in conditions as similar as possible to those in which learners will have to perform will facilitate transfer.

The argument is also made that transfer is not distinct from learning, as people do not encounter situations as blank slates. Perkins and Salomon considered it more a continuum, with no bright line between learning and transfer.

Transfer may also be referred to as generalization, B. F. Skinner's concept of a response to a stimulus occurring to other stimuli.

Today, transfer of learning is usually described as the process and the effective extent to which past experiences affect learning and performance in a new situation (the transfer target). However, there remains controversy as to how transfer of learning should be conceptualized and explained, what its prevalence is, what its relation is to learning in general, and whether it exists at all.

4.19.1 Transfer and Learning

People store propositions, or basic units of knowledge, in long-term memory. When new information enters the working memory, long-term memory is searched for associations which combine with the new information in working memory. The associations reinforce the new information and help assign meaning to it. Learning that takes place in varying contexts can create more links and encourage generalization of the skill or knowledge. Connections between past learning and new learning can provide a context or framework for the new information, helping students to determine sense and meaning, and encouraging retention of the new information. These connections can build up a framework of associative networks that students can call upon for future problem-solving. Information stored in memory is "flexible, interpretive, generically altered, and its recall and transfer are largely context-dependent".

When Thorndike refers to similarity of elements between learning and transfer, the elements can be conditions or procedures. Conditions can be environmental, physical, mental, or emotional, and the possible combinations of conditions are countless. Procedures include sequences of events or information. Although the theory is that the similarity of elements facilitates transfer, there is a challenge in identifying which specific elements had an effect on the learner at the time of learning.

Factors that can affect transfer include:

- **Context and degree of original learning:** how well the learner acquired the knowledge.
- **Similarity:** commonalities between original learning and new, such as environment and other memory cues.
- **Critical attributes:** characteristics that make something unique.
- **Association:** connections between multiple events, actions, bits of information, and so on; as well as the conditions and emotions connected to it by the learner.

Learners can increase transfer through effective practice and by mindfully abstracting knowledge. Abstraction is the process of examining our experiences for similarities. Methods for abstracting knowledge include seeking the underlying principles in what is learned, creating models, and identifying analogies and metaphors, all of which assist with creating associations and encouraging transfer.

4.19.2 Teaching for Transfer

Transfer is less a deliberate activity by the learner than it is a result of the environment at the time of learning. Teachers, being part of the learning environment, can be an instrument of transfer (both positive and negative). Recommendations for teaching for transfer include the hugging and bridging strategies; providing authentic environment and activities within a conceptual framework; encouraging problem-based learning; community of practice; cognitive apprenticeship; and game-based learning.

4.19.3 Hugging and Bridging

Hugging and bridging as techniques for positive transfer were suggested by the research of Perkins and Salomon.

Hugging is when the teacher encourages transfer by incorporating similarities between the learning situation and the future situations in which the learning might be used. Some methods for hugging include simulation games, mental practice, and contingency learning.

Bridging is when the teacher encourages transfer by helping students to find connections between learning and to abstract their existing knowledge to new concepts. Some methods for bridging include brainstorming, developing analogies, and metacognition.

CHAPTER

INFORMATION AND COMMUNICATIONS TECHNOLOGY AND E-LEARNING

5

5.1 INTRODUCTION

Information and Communications Technology (ICT) is often used as an extended synonym for Information Technology (IT), It is a more extensive term that stresses the role of unified communications and the integration of telecommunications, computers as well as necessary enterprise software, middleware, storage, and audio-visual systems, which enable users to access, store, transmit, and manipulate information.

The term ICT is also used to refer to the convergence of audio-visual and telephone networks with computer networks through a single cabling or link system. There are large economic incentives to merge the telephone network with the computer network system using a single unified system of cabling, signal distribution and management.

However, ICT has no universal definition, as "the concepts, methods and applications involved in ICT are constantly evolving on an almost daily basis." The broadness of ICT covers any product that will store, retrieve, manipulate, transmit or receive information electronically in a digital form, e.g. personal computers, digital television, email, robots.

5.2 MEANING AND CONCEPT

The phrase "information and communication technology" has been used by academic researchers since the 1980s, and the abbreviation ICT became popular after it was used in a report to the UK government by Dennis Stevenson in 1997, and in the revised National Curriculum for England, Wales and Northern Ireland in 2000. But in 2012, the Royal Society recommended that ICT should no longer be used in British schools "as it has attracted too many negative connotations", and with this being in effect since 2014 the National Curriculum began to utilize the word computing, which reflects the addition of computer programming into the curriculum. A leading group of universities consider

ICT to be a soft subject and thus advise students against studying A-level ICT, preferring A-level Computer Science instead.

5.2.1 Monetization of ICT

The money spent on IT worldwide has been most recently estimated as US $3.5 trillion and is currently growing at 6% per year – doubling every 15 years. The 2014 IT budget of US federal government is nearly $82 billion. IT costs, as a percentage of corporate revenue, have grown 50% since 2002, putting a strain on IT budgets. When looking at current companies' IT budgets, 75% are recurrent costs, used to "keep the lights on" in the IT department, and 25% are cost of new initiatives for technology development.

The average IT budget has the following breakdown:

- 31% personnel costs (internal)
- 29% software costs (external/purchasing category)
- 26% hardware costs (external/purchasing category)
- 14% costs of external service providers (external/services).

5.3 ICT DEVELOPMENT INDEX

The ICT Development Index ranks and compares the level of ICT use and access across the various countries around the world. In 2014 ITU (International Communications Union) released the latest rankings of the IDI, with Denmark attaining the top spot, followed by South Korea. The top 30 countries in the rankings include most high-income countries where quality of life is higher than average, which includes countries from Europe and other regions such as "Australia, Bahrain, Canada, Japan, Macao (China), New Zealand, Singapore and the United States; almost all countries surveyed improved their IDI ranking this year."

5.3.1 The WSIS Process and ICT Development Goals

On 21 December 2001, the United Nations General Assembly approved Resolution 56/183, endorsing the holding of the World Summit on the Information Society (WSIS) to discuss the opportunities and challenges facing today's information society. According to this resolution, the General Assembly related the Summit to the United Nations Millennium Declaration's goal of implementing ICT to achieve Millennium Development Goals. It also emphasized a multi-stakeholder approach to achieve these goals, using all stakeholders including civil society and the private sector, in addition to governments.

To help anchor and expand ICT to every habitable part of the world, "2015 is the deadline for achievements of the UN Millennium Development Goals (MDGs), which global leaders agreed upon in the year 2000."

5.3.2 ICT in Education

Information and Communication Technology can contribute to universal access to education, equity in education, the delivery of quality learning and teaching, teachers' professional development and more efficient education management, governance and administration. UNESCO takes a holistic and comprehensive approach to promoting ICT in education. Access, inclusion and quality are among the main challenges they can address. The Organization's Intersectral Platform for ICT in education focuses on these issues through the joint work of three of its sectors: Communication & Information, Education and Science.

What is the relevance of Information and Communication Technology (ICT) in Education? There are two issues we need to understand. The first one is the very meaning of ICT. Why is the expression ICT used instead of computers? The second one is how we can incorporate ICT for enhancing learning.

The very expression Information and Communication Technology has lots of ideas in it. It is not just using gadgets. The focus is on what is being transacted through this medium. We have information technology and communication technology. Managing of large quantities of information and communicating the same to the concerned people is the need of the hour. Hence the name ICT. It is a very comprehensive expression. It is not limited to the computers or the internet. It ranges from the use of FM radio to the use of satellite for communication. It includes both the form and essence of communication. ICT has the potential to make learning more experiential. Moreover the large amount of data, visuals available on any topic can be brought to the classroom from all over the world. That is why ICT has been considered an emerging area with lots of potential for making educational process more meaningful.

The developments in the use of the electronic media have influenced all walks of life. Education is no exception to this. The use of computers and the internet for enhancing the quality of education by making learning more relevant to life has been seen as an ideal by educational institutions. The citizens of tomorrow who are our students now are going to live in the age of the electronic media. How are we preparing them for the same? Are we giving them technology based Education? Are we giving them exposure to the use of computers and the itnernet? Have we integrated the ICT into classroom processes? What are the efforts made by the department in this direction? What does policy say about ICT in Education? There are several such questions which we need to probe into. An understanding of these issues will enable us to use the ICT more meaningfully in Education.

5.4 ICT TODAY

In modern society ICT is ever-present, with over three billion people having access to the Internet. With approximately 8 out of 10 Internet users owning a smartphone, information and data are increasing by leaps and bounds. This rapid growth, especially in developing countries, has led ICT to become a keystone of everyday life, in which life without some facet of technology renders most of clerical, work and routine tasks dysfunctional. The most recent authoritative data, released, shows "that Internet use continues to grow steadily, at 6.6% globally in 2014; the number of Internet users in developing countries has doubled in five years, with two thirds of all people online now living in the developing world."

However, hurdles are still at large. "Of the 4.3 billion people not yet using the Internet, 90% live in developing countries. In the world's 42 Least Connected Countries (LCCs), which are home to 2.5 billion people, access to ICTs remains largely out of reach, particularly for these countries' large rural populations." ICT has yet to penetrate the remote areas of some countries, with many developing countries dearth of any type of Internet. This also includes the availability of telephone lines, particularly the availability of cellular coverage, and other forms of electronic transmission of data. The latest "Measuring the Information Society Report" cautiously stated that the increase in the aforementioned cellular data coverage is ostensible, as "many users have multiple subscriptions, with global growth figures sometimes translating into little real improvement in the level of connectivity of those at the very bottom of the pyramid; an estimated 450 million people worldwide live in places which are still out of reach of mobile cellular service."

Favorably, the gap between the access to the Internet and mobile coverage has decreased substantially in the last fifteen years, in which "2015 is the deadline for achievements of the UN Millennium Development Goals (MDGs), which global leaders agreed upon in the year 2000, and the new data show ICT progress and highlight remaining gaps deadline for achievements of the UN Millennium Development Goals (MDGs), which global leaders agreed upon in the year 2000, and the new data show ICT progress and highlight remaining gaps." ICT continues to take on new form, with nanotechnology set to usher in a new wave of ICT electronics and gadgets. ICT newest editions into the modern electronic world include smart watches, such as the Apple Watch, smart wristbands such as the Nike+ FuelBand, and smart TVs such as Google TV. With desktops soon becoming part of a bygone era, and laptops becoming the preferred method of computing, ICT continues to insinuate and alter itself in the ever-changing globe.

5.4.1 Role of ICT in Indian Educational Sector

Importance of education in almost all walks of life has increased with the support of Information and Communication Technologies (ICT). During the past 20 years, the use of ICT has fundamentally changed the working of education. In the current environment-conscious world, the importance of education and acceptability of ICT as a social necessity has been increasing. Social acceptability of information and communication tools is necessary to improve the mobility in the society and increase the pitch for equity and social justice. Education as a qualitative development is not confined within the classroom structure. The modern tools of ICT such as eLearning and online practice of learning and getting information are much sought after by the students as well as by the institutions.

The government is spending a lot of money on ICT. In the higher education sector, the National Mission on Education is emphasising on the role of ICT in increasing the enrolment ratio in higher education. School education in India has a problem of high dropout rate and we need to work on how to decrease this rate. Similarly, in the field of higher education, we need to increase the number of students. Therefore, if we make our learning more engaging with the use of ICT, it can completely change how our education system works. Also, we should examine the challenges of cost-factor and availability of trained teachers in the process of dissemination of education with the help of ICT.

India is developing as a knowledge economy and it cannot function without the support of ICT. The gap between demand and supply of higher education has necessitated the governments and institutions to formulate the policies for the better use of ICT. And, in order to bridge the gap, it is necessary to evolve the cooperation between the public and private sectors. The education ICT policy should identify specific ways in which the application of ICT will enhance the educational capacity and the capability of higher education institutions. According to a recent study, innovations such as using Twitter to send messages are really helpful in disseminating education. In a similar fashion, the use of YouTube in sharing video information will go a long way in disseminating education. During the last decade, higher education has gained importance in India's changing policy landscape as the government realises that India's strength lies in education.

5.5 ICT IN EDUCATION/DEFINITION OF TERMS

5.5.1 What are ICTs and What Types of ICTs are Commonly Used in Education?

ICTs stand for information and communication technologies and are defined, for the purposes of this primer, as a "diverse set of technological tools and resources used to communicate, and to create, disseminate, store, and manage information." These technologies include computers, the Internet, broadcasting technologies (radio and television), and telephony.

In recent years there has been a groundswell of interest in how computers and the Internet can best be harnessed to improve the efficiency and effectiveness of education at all levels and in both formal and non-formal settings. But ICTs are more than just these technologies; older technologies such as the telephone, radio and television, although now given less attention, have a longer and richer history as instructional tools. For instance, radio and television have for over forty years been used for open and distance learning, although print remains the cheapest,most accessible and therefore most dominant delivery mechanism in both developed and developing countries. The use of computers and the Internet is still in its infancy in developing countries, if these are used at all, due to limited infrastructure and the attendant high costs of access.

Moreover, different technologies are typically used in combination rather than as the sole delivery mechanism. For instance, the Kothmale Community Radio Internet uses both radio broadcasts and computer and Internet technologies to facilitate the sharing of information and provide educational opportunities in a rural community in Sri Lanka.Similarly, the Indira Gandhi National Open University in India combines the use of print, recorded audio and video, broadcast radio and television, and audioconferencing technologies.

5.5.2 What is E-Learning?

Although most commonly associated with higher education and corporate training, e-learning encompasses learning at all levels, both formal and non-formal, that uses an information network—the Internet, an intranet (LAN) or extranet (WAN)—whether wholly or in part, for course delivery, interaction, evaluation and/or facilitation. Others prefer the term online learning. Web-based learning is a subset of e-learning and refers to learning using an Internet mainly using a browser (such as Chrome or Firefox or Internet Explorer).It can also be viewed as learning through the use of electronic devices.

5.5.3 What is Blended Learning?

Another term that is gaining currency is blended learning.This refers to learning models that combine traditional classroom practice with e-learning solutions.For example, students in a traditional class can be assigned both print-based and online materials, have online mentoring sessions with their teacher through chat, and are subscribed to a class email list. Or a Web-based training course can be enhanced by periodic face-to-face instruction."Blending"was prompted by the recognition that not all learning is best achieved in an electronically-mediated environment, particularly one that dispenses with a live instructor altogether. Instead, consideration must be given to the subject matter, the learning objectives and outcomes, the characteristics of the learners, and the learning context in order to arrive at the optimum mix of instructional and delivery methods.This method is very useful in education

5.5.4 What is Open and Distance Learning?

Open and distance learning is defined by the Commonwealth of Learning as "a way of providing learning opportunities that is characterized by the separation of teacher and learner in time or place, or both time and place; learning that is certified in some way by an institution or agency; the use of a variety of media, including print and electronic; two-way communications that allow learners and tutors to interact; the possibility of occasional face-to-face meetings; and a specialized division of labour in the production and delivery of courses."

5.5.5 What is Meant by a Learner-Centered Environment?

National Research Council of the U.S. defines learner-centered environments as those that "pay careful attention to the knowledge, skills, attitudes, and beliefs that learners bring with them to the classroom." The impetus for learner-centredness derives from a theory of learning called constructivism, which views learning as a process in which individuals "construct" meaning based on prior knowledge and experience. Experience enables individuals to build mental models or schemas, which in turn provide meaning and organization to subsequent experience. Thus knowledge is not "out there",independent of the learner and which the learner passively receives; rather, knowledge is created through an active process in which the learner transforms information, constructs hypothesis, and makes decisions using his/her mental models. A form of constructivism called social constructivism also emphasizes the role of the teacher, parents, peers and other community members in helping learners to master concepts that they would not be able to understand on their own. For social constructivists, learning must be active, contextual and social. It is best done in a group setting with the teacher as facilitator or guide.

5.6 MODELS OF COMMUNICATION

Models of communication are conceptual models used to explain the human communication process. The first major model for communication came in 1949 and was conceived by Claude Elwood Shannon and Warren Weaver for Bell Laboratories. Following the basic concept, communication is the process of sending and receiving messages or transferring information from one part (sender) to another (receiver).

5.6.1 Shannon and Weaver

The new model was designed to mirror the functioning of radio and telephone technologies. Their initial model consisted of three primary parts: sender, channel, and receiver. The sender was the part of a telephone a person spoke into, the channel was the telephone itself, and the receiver was the part of the phone where one could hear the other person. Shannon and Weaver also recognized that often there is static that interferes with one listening to a telephone conversation, which they deemed noise. The noise could also mean the absence of signal.

In a simple model, often referred to as the transmission model or standard view of communication, information or content (e.g. a message in natural language) is sent in some form (as spoken language) from an emissdor/ sender/ encoder to a destination/ receiver/ decoder. This common conception of communication views communication as a means of sending and receiving information. The strengths of this model are simplicity, generality, and quantifiability. Mathematicians Claude Shannon and Warren Weaver structured this model based on the following elements:

- An information source, which produces a message.
- A transmitter, which encodes the message into signals

- A channel, to which signals are adapted for transmission
- A receiver, which 'decodes' (reconstructs) the message from the signal.
- A destination, where the message arrives.
- Shannon and Weaver argued that there were three levels of problems for communication within this concept
- The technical problem: how accurately can the message be transmitted?
- The semantic problem: how precisely is the meaning 'conveyed'?
- The effectiveness problem: how effectively does the received meaning affect behavior?
- Daniel Chandler critiques the transmission model by stating:
- It assumes communicators are isolated individuals.
- No allowance for differing purposes.
- No allowance for differing interpretations.
- No allowance for unequal power relations.

5.6.2 Berlo

In 1960, David Berlo expanded Shannon and Weaver's 1949 linear model of communication and created the Sender-Message-Channel-Receiver (SMCR) Model of Communication. The SMCR Model of Communication separated the model into clear parts and has been expanded upon by other scholars.

5.6.3 Schramm

Communication is usually described along a few major dimensions: Message (what type of things are communicated), source / emissor / sender / encoder (by whom), form (in which form), channel (through which medium), destination / receiver / target / decoder (to whom), and Receiver. Wilbur Schramm (1954) also indicated that we should also examine the impact that a message has on the target of the message. Between parties, communication includes acts that confer knowledge and experiences, give advice and commands, and ask questions. These acts may take many forms, in one of the various manners of communication. The form depends on the abilities of the group communicating. Together, communication content and form make messages that are sent towards a destination. The target can be oneself, another person or being, another entity.

Communication can be seen as processes of information transmission governed by three levels of semiotic rules:

1. Syntactic (formal properties of signs and symbols),
2. Pragmatic (concerned with the relations between signs/expressions and their users) and

3. Semantic (study of relationships between signs and symbols and what they represent).

Therefore, communication is social interaction where at least two interacting agents share a common set of signs and a common set of semiotic rules. This commonly held rule in some sense ignores autocommunication, including intrapersonal communication via diaries or self-talk, both secondary phenomena that followed the primary acquisition of communicative competences within social interactions.

5.6.4 Barnlund

In light of these weaknesses, Barnlund (1970) proposed a transactional model of communication. The basic premise of the transactional model of communication is that are simultaneously engaging in the sending and receiving of messages.

In a slightly more complex form, a sender and a receiver are linked reciprocally. This second attitude of communication, referred to as the constitutive model or constructionist view, focuses on how an individual communicates as the determining factor of the way the message will be interpreted. Communication is viewed as a conduit; a passage in which information travels from one individual to another and this information becomes separate from the communication itself. A particular instance of communication is called a speech act. The sender's personal filters and the receiver's personal filters may vary depending upon different regional traditions, cultures, or gender; which may alter the intended meaning of message contents.

In the presence of "communication noise" on the transmission channel (air, in this case), reception and decoding of content may be faulty, and thus the speech act may not achieve the desired effect. One problem with this encode-transmit-receive-decode model is that the processes of encoding and decoding imply that the sender and receiver each possess something that functions as a code-book, and that these two code books are, at the very least, similar if not identical. Although something like code books is implied by the model, they are nowhere represented in the model, which creates many conceptual difficulties.

Theories of co-regulation describe communication as a creative and dynamic continuous process, rather than a discrete exchange of information. Canadian media scholar Harold Innis had the theory that people use different types of media to communicate and which one they choose to use will offer different possibilities for the shape and durability of society (Wark, McKenzie 1997). His famous example of this is using ancient Egypt and looking at the ways they built themselves out of media with very different properties stone and papyrus.

Papyrus is what he called 'Space Binding'. it made possible the transmission of written orders across space, empires and enables the waging of distant military campaigns and colonial administration. The other is stone and 'Time Binding', through the construction of temples and the pyramids can sustain their authority generation to generation, through this media they can change and shape communication in their society.

5.7 PSYCHOLOGY OF COMMUNICATION

Bernard Luskin, UCLA, 1970, advanced computer assisted instruction and began to connect media and psychology into what is now the field of media psychology. In 1998, the American Association of Psychology, Media Psychology Division 46 Task Force report on psychology and new technologies combined media and communication as pictures, graphics and sound increasingly dominate modern communication. The Social Psychology of Communication is the first comprehensive introduction to social psychological perspectives on communication. This accessible guide provides an overview of key theoretical approaches from a variety of different disciplines (including cognitive, developmental and evolutionary psychology) as well as practical guidance on how to implement communication interventions in differing contexts.

Divided into three parts covering theoretical perspectives, special topics in communication and applied areas and practice, the book features:

- Navigational tools providing a "how to" guide to using the book most effectively
- A list of key words at the beginning of each chapter which are highlighted throughout the chapter for easy reference
- A thorough glossary of keywords and definitions
- A section on Special Topics in Communication including identity and resistance, rumour and gossip, evolution and communication

This book is considered a resource for students, academics and practitioners in psychology and communication.

5.7.1 Constructionist Model

There is an additional working definition of communication to consider that authors like Richard A. Lanham (2003) and as far back as Erving Goffman (1959) have highlighted. This is a progression from Lasswell's attempt to define human communication through to this century and revolutionized into the constructionist model. Constructionists believe that the process of communication is in itself the only messages that exist. The packaging can not be separated from the social and historical context from which it arose, therefore the substance to look at in communication theory is style for Richard Lanham and the performance of self for Erving Goffman.

Lanham chose to view communication as the rival to the over encompassing use of CBS model. CBS model argues that clarity, brevity, and sincerity are the only purpose to prose discourse, therefore communication. Lanham wrote: "If words matter too, if the whole range of human motive is seen as animating prose discourse, then rhetoric analysis leads us to the essential questions about prose style". This is saying that rhetoric and style are fundamentally important; they are not errors to what we actually intend to transmit. The process which we construct and deconstruct meaning deserves analysis.

Erving Goffman sees the performance of self as the most important frame to understand communication. Goffman wrote: "What does seem to be required of the individual is that he learn enough pieces of expression to be able to 'fill in' and manage, more or less, any part that he is likely to be given", highlighting the significance of expression.

The truth in both cases is the articulation of the message and the package as one. The construction of the message from social and historical context is the seed as is the pre-existing message is for the transmission model. Therefore, any look into communication theory should include the possibilities drafted by such great scholars as Richard A. Lanham and Goffman that style and performance is the whole process.

Communication stands so deeply rooted in human behaviors and the structures of society that scholars have difficulty thinking of it while excluding social or behavioral events. Because communication theory remains a relatively young field of inquiry and integrates itself with other disciplines such as philosophy, psychology, and sociology, one probably cannot yet expect a consensus conceptualization of communication across disciplines.

Communication Model Terms as provided by Rothwell:

- Noise; interference with effective transmission and reception of a message.

For example;

- Physical noise or external noise which are environmental distractions such as poorly heated rooms, startling sounds, appearances of things, music playing some where else, and someone talking really loudly near you.
- Physiological noise are biological influences that distract you from communicating competently such as sweaty palms, pounding heart, butterfly in the stomach, induced by speech anxiety, or feeling sick, exhausted at work, the ringing noise in your ear, being really hungry, and if you have a runny nose or a cough.
- Psychological noise are the preconception bias and assumptions such as thinking someone who speaks like a valley girl is dumb, or someone from a foreign country can't speak English well so you speak loudly and slowly to them.
- Semantic noise are word choices that are confusing and distracting such as using the word tri-syllabic instead of three syllables.
- Sender; the initiator and encoder of a message
- Receiver; the one that receives the message (the listener) and the decoder of a message

- Decode; translates the sender's spoken idea/message into something the receiver understands by using their knowledge of language from personal experience.
- Encode; puts the idea into spoken language while putting their own meaning into the word/message.
- Channel; the medium through which the message travels such as through oral communication or written communication.
- Feedback; the receiver's verbal and nonverbal responses to a message such as a nod for understanding, a raised eyebrow for being confused, or asking a question to clarify the message.
- Message; the verbal and nonverbal components of language that is sent to the receiver by the sender which conveys an idea.

Humans act toward people or things on the basis of the meanings they assign to those people or things. -"Language is the source of meaning". -Meaning arises out of the social interaction people have with each other.

Meaning is not inherent in objects but it is negotiated through the use of language, hence the term symbolic interactionism. As human beings, we have the ability to name things.

Symbols, including names, are arbitrary signs. By talking with others, we ascribe meaning to words and develop a universe of discourse A symbol is a stimulus that has a learned/shared meaning and a value for people Significant symbols can be nonverbal as well as linguistic.

-Negative responses can consequently reduce a person to nothing. -Our expectations evoke responses that confirm what we originally anticipated, resulting in a self-fulfilling prophecy.

5.7.2 Linear Model

It is a one way model to communicate with others. It consists of the sender encoding a message and channeling it to the receiver in the presence of noise. In this model there is no feedback which may allow for a continuous exchange of information. This form of communication is a one-way form of communication that does not involve any feedback or response, and noise.

5.7.3 Interactive/Convergence Model

It is two linear models stacked on top of each other. The sender channels a message to the receiver and the receiver then becomes the sender and channels a message to the original sender. This model has added feedback, indicating that communication is not a one way but a two way process. It also has "field of experience" which includes our cultural background, ethnicity geographic location, extent of travel, and general personal experiences accumulated over the course of your lifetime. Draw backs – there is feedback but it is not simultaneous.

- For example, – instant messaging. The sender sends an IM to the receiver, then the original sender has to wait for the IM from the original receiver to react. Or a question/answer session where you just ask a question then you get an answer.

5.7.4 Transactional Model

It assumes that people are connected through communication; they engage in transaction. First, it recognizes that each of us is a sender-receiver, not merely a sender or a receiver. Secondly, it recognizes that communication affects all parties involved. So communication is fluid/simultaneous. This is what most conversations are like. The transactional model also contains ellipses that symbolize the communication environment. Where the ellipses meet is the most effective communication area because both communicators share the same meaning of the message.

5.7.5 Communication Theory Framework

It is helpful to examine communication theory through one of the following viewpoints

- **Mechanistic:** This view considers communication as a perfect transaction of a message from the sender to the receiver.
- **Psychological:** This view considers communication as the act of sending a message to a receiver, and the feelings and thoughts of the receiver upon interpreting the message.
- **Social Constructionist (Symbolic Interactionist):** This view considers communication to be the product of the interactants sharing and creating meaning. The Constructionist View can also be defined as, how you say something determines what the message is. The Constructionist View assumes that "truth" and "ideas" are constructed or invented through the social process of communication. Robert T. Craig saw the Constructionist View or the constitutive view as it's called in his article, as "...an ongoing process that symbolically forms and re-forms our personal identities." The other view of communication, the Transmission Model, sees communication as robotic and computer-like. The Transmission Model sees communication as a way of sending or receiving messages and the perfection of that. But, the Constructionist View sees communications as, "...in human life, info does not behave as simply as bits in an electronic stream. In human life, information flow is far more like an electric current running from one landmine to another". The Constructionist View is a more realistic view of communication because it involves the interacting of human beings and the free sharing of thoughts and ideas. Daniel Chandler looks to prove that the Transmission Model is a lesser way of communicating by saying "The transmission model is not merely a gross

over-simplification but a dangerously misleading representation of the nature of human communication". Humans do not communicate simply as computers or robots so that's why it's essential to truly understand the Constructionist View of Communication well. We do not simply send facts and data to one another, but we take facts and data and they acquire meaning through the process of communication, or through interaction with others.

- **Systemic:** This view considers communication to be the new messages created via "through-put", or what happens as the message is being interpreted and re-interpreted as it travels through people.
- **Critical:** This view considers communication as a source of power and oppression of individuals and social groups.

Inspection of a particular theory on this level will provide a framework on the nature of communication as seen within the confines of that theory.

Theories can also be studied and organized according to the ontological, epistemological, and axiological framework imposed by the theorist.

5.7.6 Ontology

Ontology essentially poses the question of what, exactly, it is the theorist is examining. One must consider the very nature of reality. The answer usually falls in one of three realms depending on whether the theorist sees the phenomena through the lens of a realist, nominalist, or social constructionist. Realist perspective views the world objectively, believing that there is a world outside of our own experience and cognitions. Nominalists see the world subjectively, claiming that everything outside of one's cognitions is simply names and labels. Social constructionists straddle the fence between objective and subjective reality, claiming that reality is what we create together.

5.7.7 Epistemology

Epistemology is an examination of how the theorist studies the chosen phenomena. In studying epistemology, particularly from a positivist perspective, objective knowledge is said to be the result of a systematic look at the causal relationships of phenomena. This knowledge is usually attained through use of the scientific method. Scholars often think that empirical evidence collected in an objective manner is most likely to reflect truth in the findings. Theories of this ilk are usually created to predict a phenomenon. Subjective theory holds that understanding is based on situated knowledge, typically found using interpretative methodology such as ethnography and also interviews. Subjective theories are typically developed to explain or understand phenomena in the social world.

5.7.8 Axiology

Axiology is concerned with how values inform research and theory development. Most communication theory is guided by one of three axiological approaches. The first approach recognizes that values will influence theorists' interests but suggests that those values must be set aside once actual research begins. Outside replication of research findings is particularly important in this approach to prevent individual researchers' values from contaminating their findings and interpretations. The second approach rejects the idea that values can be eliminated from any stage of theory development. Within this approach, theorists do not try to divorce their values from inquiry. Instead, they remain mindful of their values so that they understand how those values contextualize, influence or skew their findings. The third approach not only rejects the idea that values can be separated from research and theory, but rejects the idea that they should be separated. This approach is often adopted by critical theorists who believe that the role of communication theory is to identify oppression and produce social change. In this axiological approach, theorists embrace their values and work to reproduce those values in their research and theory development.

5.8 MAPPING THE THEORETICAL LANDSCAPE

A discipline gets defined in large part by its theoretical structure. Communication studies often borrow theories from other social sciences. This theoretical variation makes it difficult to come to terms with the field as a whole. That said, some common taxonomies exist that serve to divide up the range of communication research. Two common mappings involve contexts and assumptions.

5.8.1 Contexts

Many authors and researchers divide communication by what they sometimes called "contexts" or "levels", but which more often represent institutional histories. The study of communication in the US, while occurring within departments of psychology, sociology, linguistics, and anthropology, generally developed from schools of rhetoric and from schools of journalism. While many of these have become "departments of communication", they often retain their historical roots, adhering largely to theories from speech communication in the former case, and from mass media in the latter. The great divide between speech communication and mass communication becomes complicated by a number of smaller sub-areas of communication research, including intercultural and international communication, small group communication, communication technology, policy and legal studies of communication, telecommunication, and work done under a variety of other labels. Some of these departments take a largely social-scientific perspective, others tend more heavily toward the humanities, and still others gear themselves more toward production and professional preparation.

These "levels" of communication provide some way of grouping communication theories, but inevitably, some theories and concepts leak from one area to another, or fail to find a home at all.

5.9 THE CONSTITUTIVE METAMODEL

Another way of dividing up the communication field emphasizes the assumptions that undergird particular theories, models, and approaches. Robert T. Craig suggests that the field of communication as a whole can be understood as several different traditions who have a specific view on communication. By showing the similarities and differences between these traditions, Craig argues that the different traditions will be able to engage each other in dialogue rather than ignore each other. Craig proposes seven different traditions which are:

1. **Rhetorical:** views communication as the practical art of discourse.
2. **Semiotic:** views communication as the mediation by signs.
3. **Phenomenological:** communication is the experience of dialogue with others.
4. **Cybernetic:** communication is the flow of information.
5. **Socio-psychological:** communication is the interaction of individuals.
6. **Socio-cultural:** communication is the production and reproduction of the social order.
7. **Critical:** communication is the process in which all assumptions can be challenged.

Craig finds each of these clearly defined against the others, and remaining cohesive approaches to describing communicative behavior. As a taxonomic aid, these labels help to organize theory by its assumptions, and help researchers to understand why some theories may seem incommensurable.

While communication theorists very commonly use these two approaches, theorists decentralize the place of language and machines as communicative technologies. The idea (as argued by Vygotsky) of communication as the primary tool of a species defined by its tools remains on the outskirts of communication theory. It finds some representation in the Toronto School of communication theory as represented by the work of Innis, McLuhan, and others. It seems that the ways in which individuals and groups use the technologies of communication — and in some cases are used by them — remain central to what communication researchers do. The ideas that surround this, and in particular the place of persuasion, remain constants across both the "traditions" and "levels" of communication theory.

Some realms of communication and their theories

- **Universal communication Law:** Universal Theory, Dynamic-transactional Ansatz
- **Message production:** Constructivist Theory, Action Assembly Theory
- **Message processing:** Elaboration Likelihood Model, Inoculation theory
- **Discourse and interaction:** Speech Acts Theory, Coordinated Management of Meaning
- **developing relationships:** Uncertainty Reduction Theory, Social Penetration Theory, Predicted Outcome Value Theory

- **ongoing relationships:** Relational Systems Theory, Relational Dialectics
- organizational: Structuration Theory, Unobtrusive and Concertive Control Theory
- **small group:** Functional Theory, Symbolic Convergence Theory
- media processing and effects: Social Cognitive Theory, Uses and Gratifications Theory
- **media and society:** Agenda Setting, Information deficit model, Spiral of silence, Symbolic Convergence Theory
- **culture:** Speech Codes Theory, Face-saving Theory
- **making social worlds:** Coordinated Management of Meaning, Symbolic Interactionism

5.10 CLASSROOM COMMUNICATION

The communication process is vital to effective learning within a classroom environment. Classroom instruction that produces positive results acknowledges the need for a liberal use of nonverbal cues, student involvement and team communication.

5.10.1 Delivering Instruction

Whether by means of direct or indirect communication, instructors must convey instruction to students within a classroom. When lecturing or describing assignments, a teacher must gauge the comfort level of each of his students with his communication style. For example, if he explicitly defines rules and regulations associated with classwork, he may help students to be clearly aware of their boundaries, but may also lead them to feel micromanaged. In actual practice, communication within the classroom tends to be a happy compromise between both extremes, being neither exclusively direct or indirect in nature.

5.10.2 Soliciting Participation

Student involvement during classroom discussions typically fosters a healthy communication process. Students should be coaxed to participate in the classroom, despite the fact that many students are reticent to voice their opinions. The solicitation of participation serves multiple purposes. Students observe that their questions are worthy of being answered, can freely exchange ideas with one another and can build confidence as they express themselves in public. Often, instructors can quickly identify weak areas of student understanding when they are invited to speak up during a class session.

5.11 VERBAL AND NONVERBAL COMMUNICATION

Communication within a classroom context relies just as heavily on written instruction, body language and implicit expectancies as it does on verbal cues. Two-thirds of an instructor's message is contained in his nonverbal language. Educators should devote attention to the use of appropriate gestures, facial expressions and constructive use of physical space when teaching a class of students.

5.11.1 Team Building

Acquisition of essential learning concepts is reinforced when students are encouraged to incorporate team communication skills within the classroom. Group work allows students to advance a division of responsibilities as well as to provide one another with peer support. Educators should monitor teams as they operate within a classroom, helping students to establish consensus regarding their approach to the material being studied.

5.11.2 Assessments

In order to assess student mastery of concepts touched upon during classroom instruction, an educator should compel his students to demonstrate their knowledge through written or oral tests.

5.12 CONCEPT OF TELE-COMMUNICATION

Telecommunication occurs when the exchange of information between two or more entities (communication) includes the use of technology. Communication technology uses channels to transmit information, either over a physical medium, or in the form of electromagnetic waves. The word is often used in its plural form, telecommunications, because it involves many different technologies.

Early means of communicating over a distance included visual signals, such as beacons, smoke signals, semaphore telegraphs, signal flags, and optical heliographs. Other examples of pre-modern long-distance communication included audio messages such as coded drumbeats, lung-blown horns, and loud whistles. Modern technologies for long-distance communication usually involve electrical and electromagnetic technologies, such as telegraph, telephone, and teleprinter, networks, radio, microwave transmission, fiber optics, and communications satellites.

A revolution in wireless communication began in the first decade of the 20th century with the pioneering developments in radio communications by Guglielmo Marconi, who won the Nobel Prize in Physics in 1909. Other highly notable pioneering inventors and developers in the field of electrical and electronic telecommunications include Charles Wheatstone and Samuel Morse (telegraph), Alexander Graham Bell (telephone), Edwin Armstrong, and Lee de Forest (radio), as well as Vladimir K. Zworykin, John Logie Baird and Philo Farnsworth (television).

5.12.1 Etymology

The word telecommunication was adapted from the French. It is a compound of the Greek prefix tele-, meaning "distant", and the Latin communicare, meaning "to share"in 1904 by the French engineer and novelist Édouard Estaunié.

5.13 HISTORY OF TELE-COMMUNICATIONS

5.13.1 Early Tele-Communications

In the Middle Ages, chains of beacons were commonly used on hilltops as a means of relaying a signal. Beacon chains suffered the drawback that they could only pass a single bit of information, so the meaning of the message such as "the enemy has been sighted" had to be agreed upon in advance. One notable instance of their use was during the Spanish Armada, when a beacon chain relayed a signal from Plymouth to London.

In 1792, Claude Chappe, a French engineer, built the first fixed visual telegraphy system (or semaphore line) between Lille and Paris. However semaphore suffered from the need for skilled operators and expensive towers at intervals of ten to thirty kilometres. As a result of competition from the electrical telegraph, the last commercial line was abandoned in 1880.

Homing pigeons have occasionally been used through history by different cultures. Pigeon post is thought to have Persians roots and was used by the Romans to aid their military. Frontinus said that Julius Caesar used pigeons as messengers in his conquest of Gaul. The Greeks also conveyed the names of the victors at the Olympic Games to various cities using homing pigeons. In the early 19th century, the Dutch government used the system in Java and Sumatra. And in 1849, Paul Julius Reuter started a pigeon service to fly stock prices between Aachen and Brussels, a service that operated for a year until the gap in the telegraph link was closed.

5.13.2 Telegraph and Telephone

Sir Charles Wheatstone and Sir William Fothergill Cooke invented the electric telegraph in 1837. Also, the first commercial electrical telegraph is purported to have been constructed by Wheatstone and Cooke and opened on 9 April 1839. Both inventors viewed their device as "an improvement to the [existing] electromagnetic telegraph" not as a new device.

Samuel Morse independently developed a version of the electrical telegraph that he unsuccessfully demonstrated on 2 September 1837. His code was an important advance over Wheatstone's signaling method. The first transatlantic telegraph cable was successfully completed on 27 July 1866, allowing transatlantic telecommunication for the first time.

The conventional telephone was invented independently by Alexander Bell and Elisha Gray in 1876. Antonio Meucci invented the first device that allowed the electrical transmission of voice over a line in 1849. However Meucci's device was of little practical value because it relied upon the electrophonic effect and thus required users to place the receiver in their mouth to "hear" what was being said. The first commercial telephone services were set-up in 1878 and 1879 on both sides of the Atlantic in the cities of New Haven and London.

5.13.3 Radio and Television

In 1832, James Lindsay gave a classroom demonstration of wireless telegraphy to his students. By 1854, he was able to demonstrate a transmission across the Firth of Tay from Dundee, Scotland to Woodhaven, a distance of two miles (3 km), using water as the transmission medium. In December 1901, Guglielmo Marconi established wireless communication between St. John's, Newfoundland (Canada) and Poldhu, Cornwall (England), earning him the 1909 Nobel Prize in physics (which he shared with Karl Braun). However small-scale radio communication had already been demonstrated in 1893 by Nikola Tesla in a presentation to the National Electric Light Association.

On 25 March 1925, John Logie Baird was able to demonstrate the transmission of moving pictures at the London department store Selfridges. Baird's device relied upon the Nipkow disk and thus became known as the mechanical television. It formed the basis of experimental broadcasts done by the British Broadcasting Corporation beginning 30 September 1929. However, for most of the twentieth century televisions depended upon the cathode ray tube invented by Karl Braun. The first version of such a television to show promise was produced by Philo Farnsworth and demonstrated to his family on 7 September 1927.

5.13.4 Computer Networks and the Internet

On 11 September 1940, George Stibitz was able to transmit problems using teletype to his Complex Number Calculator in New York and receive the computed results back at Dartmouth College in New Hampshire. This configuration of a centralized computer or mainframe with remote dumb terminals remained popular throughout the 1950s. However, it was not until the 1960s that researchers started to investigate packet switching — a technology that would allow chunks of data to be sent to different computers without first passing through a centralized mainframe. A four-node network emerged on 5 December 1969; this network would become ARPANET, which by 1981 would consist of 213 nodes.

ARPANET's development centred around the Request for Comment process and on 7 April 1969, RFC 1 was published. This process is important because ARPANET would eventually merge with other networks to form the Internet and many of the protocols the Internet relies upon today were specified through the Request for Comment process. In September 1981, RFC 791 introduced the Internet Protocol v4 (IPv4) and RFC 793 introduced the Transmission Control Protocol (TCP) — thus creating the TCP/IP protocol that much of the Internet relies upon today.

However, not all important developments were made through the Request for Comment process. Two popular link protocols for Local Area Networks (LANs) also appeared in the 1970s. A patent for the token ring protocol was filed by Olof Soderblom on 29 October 1974 and a paper on the Ethernet protocol was published by Robert Metcalfe and David Boggs in the July 1976 issue of Communications of the ACM.

5.13.5 Key Concepts

A number of key concepts reoccur throughout the literature on modern telecommunication theory and systems. Some of these concepts are discussed below.

Basic Elements

A basic telecommunication system consists of three primary units that are always present in some form:

- A transmitter that takes information and converts it to a signal.
- A transmission medium, also called the "physical channel" that carries the signal. An example of this is the "free space channel".
- A receiver that takes the signal from the channel and converts it back into usable information.

For example, in a radio broadcasting station the station's large power amplifier is the transmitter; and the broadcasting antenna is the interface between the power amplifier and the "free space channel". The free space channel is the transmission medium; and the receiver's antenna is the interface between the free space channel and the receiver. Next, the radio receiver is the destination of the radio signal, and this is where it is converted from electricity to sound for people to listen to.

Sometimes, telecommunication systems are "duplex" (two-way systems) with a single box of electronics working as both a transmitter and a receiver, or a transceiver. For example, a cellular telephone is a transceiver. The transmission electronics and the receiver electronics in a transceiver are actually quite independent of each other. This can be readily explained by the fact that radio transmitters contain power amplifiers that operate with electrical powers measured in the watts or kilowatts, but radio receivers deal with radio powers that are measured in the microwatts or nanowatts. Hence, transceivers have to be carefully designed and built to isolate their high-power circuitry and their low-power circuitry from each other.

Telecommunication over fixed lines is called point-to-point communication because it is between one transmitter and one receiver. Telecommunication through radio broadcasts is called broadcast communication because it is between one powerful transmitter and numerous low-power but sensitive radio receivers.

Telecommunications in which multiple transmitters and multiple receivers have been designed to cooperate and to share the same physical channel are called multiplex systems. The sharing of physical channels using multiplexing often gives very large reductions in costs. Multiplexed systems are laid out in telecommunication networks, and the multiplexed signals are switched at nodes through to the correct destination terminal receiver.

5.14 ANALOG VERSUS DIGITAL COMMUNICATIONS

Communications signals can be either by analog signals or digital signals. There are analog communication systems and digital communication systems. For an analog signal, the signal is varied continuously with respect to the information. In a digital signal, the information is encoded as a set of discrete values. During the propagation and reception, the information contained in analog signals will inevitably be degraded by undesirable physical noise. Commonly, the noise in a communication system can be expressed as adding or subtracting from the desirable signal in a completely random way. This form of noise is called additive noise, with the understanding that the noise can be negative or positive at different instants of time. Noise that is not additive noise is a much more difficult situation to describe or analyze, and these other kinds of noise will be omitted here.

On the other hand, unless the additive noise disturbance exceeds a certain threshold, the information contained in digital signals will remain intact. Their resistance to noise represents a key advantage of digital signals over analog signals.

5.14.1 Telecommunication Networks

A communications network is a collection of transmitters, receivers, and communications channels that send messages to one another. Some digital communications networks contain one or more routers that work together to transmit information to the correct user. An analog communications network consists of one or more switches that establish a connection between two or more users. For both types of network, repeaters may be necessary to amplify or recreate the signal when it is being transmitted over long distances. This is to combat attenuation that can render the signal indistinguishable from the noise. Another advantage of digital systems over analog is that their output is easier to store in memory, i.e. two voltage states (high and low) are easier to store than a continuous range of states.

5.14.2 Communication Channels

The term "channel" has two different meanings. In one meaning, a channel is the physical medium that carries a signal between the transmitter and the receiver. Examples of this include the atmosphere for sound communications, glass optical fibers for some kinds of optical communications, coaxial cables for communications by way of the voltages and electric currents in them, and free space for communications using visible light, infrared waves, ultraviolet light, and radio waves. This last channel is called the "free space channel". The sending of radio waves from one place to another has nothing to do with the presence or absence of an atmosphere between the two. Radio waves travel through a perfect vacuum just as easily as they travel through air, fog, clouds, or any other kind of gas besides air.

The other meaning of the term "channel" in telecommunications is seen in the phrase communications channel, which is a subdivision of a transmission medium so that it can be used to send multiple streams of information simultaneously. For example, one radio station can broadcast radio waves into free space at frequencies in the neighborhood of 94.5 MHz (megahertz) while another radio station can simultaneously broadcast radio waves at frequencies in the neighborhood of 96.1 MHz. Each radio station would transmit radio waves over a frequency bandwidth of about 180 kHz (kilohertz), centered at frequencies such as the above, which are called the "carrier frequencies". Each station in this example is separated from its adjacent stations by 200 kHz, and the difference between 200 kHz and 180 kHz (20 kHz) is an engineering allowance for the imperfections in the communication system.

In the example above, the "free space channel" has been divided into communications channels according to frequencies, and each channel is assigned a separate frequency bandwidth in which to broadcast radio waves. This system of dividing the medium into channels according to frequency is called "frequency-division multiplexing"

Another way of dividing a communications medium into channels is to allocate each sender a recurring segment of time, and to allow each sender to send messages only within its own time slot. This method of dividing the medium into communication channels is called "time-division multiplexing" (TDM), and is used in optical fiber communication. Some radio communication systems use TDM within an allocated FDM channel. Hence, these systems use a hybrid of TDM and FDM.

5.14.3 Modulation

The shaping of a signal to convey information is known as modulation. Modulation can be used to represent a digital message as an analog waveform. This is commonly called "keying" – a term derived from the older use of Morse Code in telecommunications – and several keying techniques exist. The "Bluetooth" system, for example, uses phase-shift keying to exchange information between various devices. In addition, there are combinations of phase-shift keying and amplitude-shift keying which is called "Quadrature Amplitude Modulation" (QAM) that are used in high-capacity digital radio communication systems.

Modulation can also be used to transmit the information of low-frequency analog signals at higher frequencies. This is helpful because low-frequency analog signals cannot be effectively transmitted over free space. Hence the information from a low-frequency analog signal must be impressed into a higher-frequency signal before transmission. There are several different modulation schemes available to achieve this [two of the most basic being Amplitude Modulation (AM) and Frequency Modulation (FM)]. An example of this process is a disc jockey's voice being impressed into a 96 MHz carrier wave using frequency modulation (the voice would then be received on a radio as the channel "96 FM"). In addition, modulation has the advantage that it may use Frequency Division Multiplexing (FDM).

5.14.4 Society

Telecommunication has a significant social, cultural and economic impact on modern society. In 2008, estimates placed the telecommunication industry's revenue at $4.7 trillion or just under 3 percent of the gross world product. Several following sections discuss the impact of telecommunication on society.

5.15 ECONOMIC IMPACT

5.15.1 Microeconomics

On the microeconomic scale, companies have used telecommunications to help build global business empires. This is self-evident in the case of online retailer Amazon.com but, according to academic Edward Lenert, even the conventional retailer Walmart has benefited from better telecommunication infrastructure compared to its competitors. In cities throughout the world, home owners use their telephones to order and arrange a variety of home services ranging from pizza deliveries to electricians. Even relatively poor communities have been noted to use telecommunication to their advantage. In Bangladesh's Narshingdi district, isolated villagers use cellular phones to speak directly to wholesalers and arrange a better price for their goods. In Côte d'Ivoire, coffee growers share mobile phones to follow hourly variations in coffee prices and sell at the best price.

5.15.2 Macroeconomics

On the macroeconomic scale, Lars-Hendrik Röller and Leonard Waverman suggested a causal link between good telecommunication infrastructure and economic growth. Few dispute the existence of a correlation although some argue it is wrong to view the relationship as causal.

Because of the economic benefits of good telecommunication infrastructure, there is increasing worry about the inequitable access to telecommunication services amongst various countries of the world—this is known as the digital divide. A 2003 survey by the International Telecommunication Union (ITU) revealed that roughly a third of countries have fewer than one mobile subscription for every 20 people and one-third of countries have fewer than one land-line telephone subscription for every 20 people. In terms of Internet access, roughly half of all countries have fewer than one out of 20 people with Internet access. From this information, as well as educational data, the ITU was able to compile an index that measures the overall ability of citizens to access and use information and communication technologies. Using this measure, Sweden, Denmark and Iceland received the highest ranking while the African countries Nigeria, Burkina Faso and Mali received the lowest.

5.15.3 Social Impact

Telecommunication has played a significant role in social relationships. Nevertheless, devices like the telephone system were originally advertised with an emphasis on the practical dimensions of the device as opposed to the social dimensions. It was not until the late 1920s and 1930s that the social dimensions of the device became a prominent theme in telephone advertisements. New promotions started appealing to consumers' emotions, stressing the importance of social conversations and staying connected to family and friends.

Since then the role that telecommunications has played in social relations has become increasingly important. In recent years, the popularity of social networking sites has increased dramatically. These sites allow users to communicate with each other as well as post photographs, events and profiles for others to see. The profiles can list a person's age, interests, sexual preference and relationship status. In this way, these sites can play important role in everything from organising social engagements to courtship. Prior to social networking sites, technologies like Short Message Service (SMS) and the telephone also had a significant impact on social interactions. In 2000, market research group Ipsos MORI reported that 81% of 15- to 24-year-old SMS users in the United Kingdom had used the service to coordinate social arrangements and 42% to flirt.

5.15.4 Other Impacts

In cultural terms, telecommunication has increased the public's ability to access music and film. With television, people can watch films they have not seen before in their own home without having to travel to the video store or cinema. With radio and the Internet, people can listen to music they have not heard before without having to travel to the music store.

Telecommunication has also transformed the way people receive their news. A survey led in 2006 by the non-profit Pew Internet and American Life Project found that when just over 3,000 people living in the United States were asked where they got their news "yesterday", more people said television or radio than newspapers. The results are summarised in the following table (the percentages add up to more than 100% because people were able to specify more than one source).

Local TV	National TV	Radio	Local paper	Internet	National paper
59%	47%	44%	38%	23%	12%

Telecommunication has had an equally significant impact on advertising. TNS Media Intelligence reported that in 2007, 58% of advertising expenditure in the United States was spent on mediums that depend upon telecommunication. The results are summarised in the following table.

5.15.5 Government

Many countries have enacted legislation which conforms to the International Telecommunication Regulations established by the International Telecommunication

Union (ITU), which is the "leading UN agency for information and communication technology issues." In 1947, at the Atlantic City Conference, the ITU decided to "afford international protection to all frequencies registered in a new international frequency list and used in conformity with the Radio Regulation." According to the ITU's Radio Regulations adopted in Atlantic City, all frequencies referenced in the International Frequency Registration Board, examined by the board and registered on the International Frequency List "shall have the right to international protection from harmful interference."

From a global perspective, there have been political debates and legislation regarding the management of telecommunication and broadcasting. The history of broadcasting discusses some debates in relation to balancing conventional communication such as printing and telecommunication such as radio broadcasting. The onset of World War II brought on the first explosion of international broadcasting propaganda. Countries, their governments, insurgents, terrorists, and militiamen have all used telecommunication and broadcasting techniques to promote propaganda. Patriotic propaganda for political movements and colonization started the mid-1930s. In 1936, the BBC broadcast propaganda to the Arab World to partly counter similar broadcasts from Italy, which also had colonial interests in North Africa.

Modern insurgents, such as those in the latest Iraq war, often use intimidating telephone calls, SMSs and the distribution of sophisticated videos of an attack on coalition troops within hours of the operation. "The Sunni insurgents even have their own television station, Al-Zawraa, which while banned by the Iraqi government, still broadcasts from Erbil, Iraqi Kurdistan, even as coalition pressure has forced it to switch satellite hosts several times."

On 10 November 2014, President Obama recommended the Federal Communications Commission reclassify broadband Internet service as a telecommunications service in order to preserve net neutrality.

5.16 MODERN MEDIA

5.16.1 Telephone

In a telephone network, the caller is connected to the person they want to talk to by switches at various telephone exchanges. The switches form an electrical connection between the two users and the setting of these switches is determined electronically when the caller dials the number. Once the connection is made, the caller's voice is transformed to an electrical signal using a small microphone in the caller's handset. This electrical signal is then sent through the network to the user at the other end where it is transformed back into sound by a small speaker in that person's handset.

The landline telephones in most residential homes are analog—that is, the speaker's voice directly determines the signal's voltage. Although short-distance calls may be handled from end-to-end as analog signals, increasingly telephone service providers are transparently converting the signals to digital signals for transmission. The advantage of this is that digitized voice data can travel side-by-side with data from the Internet and can be perfectly reproduced in long distance communication.

Mobile phones have had a significant impact on telephone networks. Mobile phone subscriptions now outnumber fixed-line subscriptions in many markets. Sales of mobile phones in 2005 totalled 816.6 million with that figure being almost equally shared amongst the markets of Asia/Pacific (204 m), Western Europe (164 m), CEMEA (Central Europe, the Middle East and Africa) (153.5 m), North America (148 m) and Latin America (102 m). In terms of new subscriptions over the five years from 1999, Africa has outpaced other markets with 58.2% growth. Increasingly these phones are being serviced by systems where the voice content is transmitted digitally such as GSM or W-CDMA with many markets choosing to depreciate analog systems such as AMPS.

There have also been dramatic changes in telephone communication behind the scenes. Starting with the operation of TAT-8 in 1988, the 1990s saw the widespread adoption of systems based on optical fibers. The benefit of communicating with optic fibers is that they offer a drastic increase in data capacity. TAT-8 itself was able to carry 10 times as many telephone calls as the last copper cable laid at that time and today's optic fibre cables are able to carry 25 times as many telephone calls as TAT-8. This increase in data capacity is due to several factors: First, optic fibres are physically much smaller than competing technologies. Second, they do not suffer from crosstalk which means several hundred of them can be easily bundled together in a single cable. Lastly, improvements in multiplexing have led to an exponential growth in the data capacity of a single fibre.

Assisting communication across many modern optic fibre networks is a protocol known as Asynchronous Transfer Mode (ATM). The ATM protocol allows for the side-by-side data transmission mentioned in the second paragraph. It is suitable for public telephone networks because it establishes a pathway for data through the network and associates a traffic contract with that pathway. The traffic contract is essentially an agreement between the client and the network about how the network is to handle the data; if the network cannot meet the conditions of the traffic contract it does not accept the connection. This is important because telephone calls can negotiate a contract so as to guarantee themselves a constant bit rate, something that will ensure a caller's voice is not delayed in parts or cut off completely. There are competitors to ATM, such as Multiprotocol Label Switching (MPLS), that perform a similar task and are expected to supplant ATM in the future.

5.16.2 Radio and Television

In a broadcast system, the central high-powered broadcast tower transmits a high-frequency electromagnetic wave to numerous low-powered receivers. The high-frequency wave sent by the tower is modulated with a signal containing visual or audio information.

The receiver is then tuned so as to pick up the high-frequency wave and a demodulator is used to retrieve the signal containing the visual or audio information. The broadcast signal can be either analog.

The broadcast media industry is at a critical turning point in its development, with many countries moving from analog to digital broadcasts. This move is made possible by the production of cheaper, faster and more capable integrated circuits. The chief advantage of digital broadcasts is that they prevent a number of complaints common to traditional analog broadcasts. For television, this includes the elimination of problems such as snowy pictures, ghosting and other distortion. These occur because of the nature of analog transmission, which means that perturbations due to noise will be evident in the final output. Digital transmission overcomes this problem because digital signals are reduced to discrete values upon reception and hence small perturbations do not affect the final output. In a simplified example, if a binary message was transmitted with signal amplitudes and received with signal amplitudes it would still decode to the binary message — a perfect reproduction of what was sent. From this example, a problem with digital transmissions can also be seen in that if the noise is great enough it can significantly alter the decoded message. Using forward error correction a receiver can correct a handful of bit errors in the resulting message but too much noise will lead to incomprehensible output and hence a breakdown of the transmission.

In digital television broadcasting, there are three competing standards that are likely to be adopted worldwide. These are the ATSC, DVB and ISDB standards; the adoption of these standards thus far is presented in the captioned map. All three standards use MPEG-2 for video compression. ATSC uses Dolby Digital AC-3 for audio compression, ISDB uses Advanced Audio Coding (MPEG-2 Part 7) and DVB has no standard for audio compression but typically uses MPEG-1 Part 3 Layer 2. The choice of modulation also varies between the schemes. In digital audio broadcasting, standards are much more unified with practically all countries choosing to adopt the Digital Audio Broadcasting standard (also known as the Eureka 147 standard). The exception is the United States which has chosen to adopt HD Radio. HD Radio, unlike Eureka 147, is based upon a transmission method known as in-band on-channel transmission that allows digital information to "piggyback" on normal AM or FM analog transmissions.

However, despite the pending switch to digital, analog television remains being transmitted in most countries. An exception is the United States that ended analog television transmission (by all but the very low-power TV stations) on 12 June 2009 after twice delaying the switchover deadline,Kenya also ended analog television transmission in December 2014 after multiple delays. For analog television, there are three standards in use for broadcasting color TV. These are known as PAL (German designed), NTSC (North American designed), and SECAM (French designed). (It is important to understand that these are the ways of sending color TV, and they do not have anything to do with the standards for black & white TV, which also vary from country to country.) For analog radio, the switch to digital radio is made more difficult by the fact that analog receivers are sold at a small fraction of the price of digital receivers. The choice of modulation for analog radio is typically between amplitude (AM) or frequency modulation (FM). To achieve stereo playback, an amplitude modulated subcarrier is used for stereo FM.

5.16.3 Internet

The Internet is a worldwide network of computers and computer networks that communicate with each other using the Internet Protocol. Any computer on the Internet has a unique IP address that can be used by other computers to route information to it. Hence, any computer on the Internet can send a message to any other computer using its IP address. These messages carry with them the originating computer's IP address allowing for two-way communication. The Internet is thus an exchange of messages between computers.

It is estimated that the 51% of the information flowing through two-way telecommunications networks in the year 2000 were flowing through the Internet (most of the rest (42%) through the landline telephone). By the year 2007 the Internet clearly dominated and captured 97% of all the information in telecommunication networks (most of the rest (2%) through mobile phones). As of 2008, an estimated 21.9% of the world population has access to the Internet with the highest access rates (measured as a percentage of the population) in North America (73.6%), Oceania/Australia (59.5%) and Europe (48.1%). In terms of broadband access, Iceland (26.7%), South Korea (25.4%) and the Netherlands (25.3%) led the world.

The Internet works in part because of protocols that govern how the computers and routers communicate with each other. The nature of computer network communication lends itself to a layered approach where individual protocols in the protocol stack run more-or-less independently of other protocols. This allows lower-level protocols to be customized for the network situation while not changing the way higher-level protocols operate. A practical example of why this is important is because it allows an Internet browser to run the same code regardless of whether the computer it is running on is connected to the Internet through an Ethernet or Wi-Fi connection. Protocols are often talked about in terms of their place in the OSI reference model, which emerged in 1983 as the first step in an unsuccessful attempt to build a universally adopted networking protocol suite.

For the Internet, the physical medium and data link protocol can vary several times as packets traverse the globe. This is because the Internet places no constraints on what physical medium or data link protocol is used. This leads to the adoption of media and protocols that best suit the local network situation. In practice, most intercontinental communication will use the Asynchronous Transfer Mode (ATM) protocol on top of optic fiber. This is because for most intercontinental communication the Internet shares the same infrastructure as the public switched telephone network.

At the network layer, things become standardized with the Internet Protocol (IP) being adopted for logical addressing. For the World Wide Web, these "IP addresses" are derived from the human readable form using the Domain Name System. At the moment, the most widely used version of the Internet Protocol is version four but a move to version six is imminent.

At the transport layer, most communication adopts either the Transmission Control Protocol (TCP) or the User Datagram Protocol (UDP). TCP is used when it is essential every message sent is received by the other computer whereas UDP is used when it is merely desirable. With TCP, packets are retransmitted if they are lost and placed in order before they are presented to higher layers. With UDP, packets are not ordered or retransmitted if lost. Both TCP and UDP packets carry port numbers with them to specify what application or process the packet should be handled by. Because certain application-level protocols use certain ports, network administrators can manipulate traffic to suit particular requirements. Examples are to restrict Internet access by blocking the traffic destined for a particular port or to affect the performance of certain applications by assigning priority.

Above the transport layer, there are certain protocols that are sometimes used and loosely fit in the session and presentation layers, most notably the Secure Sockets Layer (SSL) and Transport Layer Security (TLS) protocols. These protocols ensure that data transferred between two parties remains completely confidential. Finally, at the application layer, are many of the protocols Internet users would be familiar with such as HTTP (web browsing), POP3 (e-mail), FTP (file transfer), IRC (Internet chat), BitTorrent (file sharing) and XMPP (instant messaging).

Voice over Internet Protocol (VoIP) allows data packets to be used for synchronous voice communications. The data packets are marked as voice type packets and can be prioritized by the network administrators so that the real-time, synchronous conversation is less subject to contention with other types of data traffic which can be delayed (i.e. file transfer or email) or buffered in advance (i.e. audio and video) without detriment. That prioritization is fine when the network has sufficient capacity for all the VoIP calls taking place at the same time and the network is enabled for prioritization i.e. a private corporate style network, but the Internet is not generally managed in this way and so there can be a big difference in the quality of VoIP calls over a private network and over the public Internet.

5.16.4 Local Area Networks and Wide Area Networks

Despite the growth of the Internet, the characteristics of local area networks (LANs)—computer networks that do not extend beyond a few kilometers—remain distinct. This is because networks on this scale do not require all the features associated with larger networks and are often more cost-effective and efficient without them. When they are not connected with the Internet, they also have the advantages of privacy and security. However, purposefully lacking a direct connection to the Internet does not provide assured protection from hackers, military forces, or economic powers. These threats exist if there are any methods for connecting remotely to the LAN.

Wide Area Networks (WANs) are private computer networks that may extend for thousands of kilometers. Once again, some of their advantages include privacy and security. Prime users of private LANs and WANs include armed forces and intelligence agencies that must keep their information secure and secret.

In the mid-1980s, several sets of communication protocols emerged to fill the gaps between the data-link layer and the application layer of the OSI reference model. These included Appletalk, IPX, and NetBIOS with the dominant protocol set during the early 1990s being IPX due to its popularity with MS-DOS users. TCP/IP existed at this point, but it was typically only used by large government and research facilities.

As the Internet grew in popularity and its traffic was required to be routed into private networks, the TCP/IP protocols replaced existing local area network technologies. Additional technologies, such as DHCP, allowed TCP/IP-based computers to self-configure in the network. Such functions also existed in the AppleTalk/ IPX/ NetBIOS protocol sets.

Whereas Asynchronous Transfer Mode (ATM) or Multiprotocol Label Switching (MPLS) are typical data-link protocols for larger networks such as WANs; Ethernet and Token Ring are typical data-link protocols for LANs. These protocols differ from the former protocols in that they are simpler, e.g., they omit features such as quality of service guarantees, and offer collision prevention. Both of these differences allow for more economical systems.

Despite the modest popularity of IBM Token Ring in the 1980s and 1990s, virtually all LANs now use either wired or wireless Ethernet facilities. At the physical layer, most wired Ethernet implementations use copper twisted-pair cables (including the common 10BASE-T networks). However, some early implementations used heavier coaxial cables and some recent implementations (especially high-speed ones) use optical fibers. When optic fibers are used, the distinction must be made between multimode fibers and single-mode fibers. Multimode fibers can be thought of as thicker optical fibers that are cheaper to manufacture devices for, but that suffers from less usable bandwidth and worse attenuation – implying poorer long-distance performance.

5.16.5 Transmission Capacity

The effective capacity to exchange information worldwide through two-way telecommunication networks grew from 281 petabytes of (optimally compressed) information in 1986, to 471 petabytes in 1993, to 2.2 (optimally compressed) exabytes in 2000, and to 65 (optimally compressed) exabytes in 2007. This is the informational equivalent of two newspaper pages per person per day in 1986, and six entire newspapers per person per day by 2007. Given this growth, telecommunications play an increasingly important role in the world economy and the global telecommunications industry was about a $4.7 trillion sector in 2012. The service revenue of the global telecommunications industry was estimated to be $1.5 trillion in 2010, corresponding to 2.4% of the world's Gross Domestic Product (GDP).

5.17 SATELLITE COMMUNICATIONS

In satellite communication, signal transferring between the sender and receiver is done with the help of satellite. In this process, the signal which is basically a beam of modulated microwaves is sent towards the satellite. Then the satellite amplifies the signal and sent it back to the receiver's antenna present on the earth's surface. So, all the signal transferring is happening in space. Thus this type of communication is known as space communication. Two satellites which are commonly used in satellite communication are Active and passive satellites.

Passive satellites: It is just a plastic balloon having a metal coated over it. This sphere reflects the coming microwave signals coming from one part of the earth to other part. This is also known as passive sphere. Our earth also has a passive satellite i.e. moon.

Active satellites: It basically does the work of amplifying the microwave signals coming. In active satellites an antenna system, transmitter, power supply and a receiver is used. These satellites are also called as transponders. The transmitters fitted on the earth generate the microwaves. These rays are received by the transponders attached to the satellite. Then after amplifying, these signals are transmitted back to earth. This sending can be done at the same time or after some delay. These amplified signals are stored in the memory of the satellites, when earth properly faces the satellite. Then the satellite starts sending the signals to earth. Some active satellites also have programming and recording features. Then these recording can be easily played and watched. The first active satellite was launched by Russia in 1957. The signals coming from the satellite when reach the earth, are of very low intensity. Their amplification is done by the receivers themselves. After amplification these become available for further use.

Microwave communication is possible only if the position of satellite becomes stationary with respect to the position of earth. So, these types of satellites are known as geostationary satellites.

5.17.1 What are the Requirements for a Satellite to be Geostationary?

1. Its revolutionary direction must be same as that of the earth, i.e. from west to east.
2. The time period of satellite's revolution must be same to the time period of the rotation of earth along its polar axis, which is equal to 24 hours.

3. The equatorial plane of earth must be coplanar with the orbital plane of the satellites revolution.

The name given to the orbit of the geo-stationary satellites is synchronous orbit. Due to this geo-stationary satellites are also called as geo-synchronous satellites. Geo-synchronous orbit is at a height of nearly 36000km from the surface of earth.

These orbits are capable of giving a successful communication link between two stations present on the earth. These satellites can handle communication up to large distances. But it is impossible for a single geo-stationary satellite to cover the whole earth and provide a communication link. Due to curvature of earth the stations will be out of sight after covering some distance. If we want to cover the whole earth then we have to put three satellites onto the geosynchronous orbit. These satellites can cover the earth if all are inclined at an angle of 120o to each other.

A communications satellite is an artificial satellite that relays and amplifies through the use of a transponder, radio telecommunications signals, between a source transmitter and a receiver at different locations on Earth. Communications satellites are used for television, telephone, radio, internet, and military applications. There are over 2,000 communications satellites in Earth's orbit, used by both private and government organizations.

Wireless communication uses electromagnetic waves to carry signals. These waves require line-of-sight, and are thus obstructed by the curvature of the Earth. The purpose of communications satellites is to relay the signal around the curve of the Earth allowing communication between widely separated points.

There are two major classes of communications satellites, passive and active. Passive satellites only reflect the signal coming from the source, toward the direction of the receiver. With passive satellites, the reflected signal is not amplified at the satellite, and only a very small amount of the transmitted energy reflects toward the receiver. Since the satellite is so far above Earth the radio signal is attenuated on its long journey due to free-space path loss, so the signal received on Earth is very weak. Active satellites, on the other hand, amplify the received signal before re-transmitting it to the receiver on the ground Passive satellites were the first communications satellites, but are little used now.

Communications satellites usually have one of three types of orbit (although several other types of orbits are sometimes used). Geostationary satellites have a geostationary orbit (GEO), which is 35,786 kilometres (22,236 mi) from Earth's surface. This orbit has the special characteristic that the apparent position of the satellite in the sky when viewed by a ground observer does not change, the satellite appears to "stand still" in the sky. This is because the satellite's orbital period is the same as the rotation rate of the Earth. The advantage of this orbit is that ground antennas do not have to track the satellite across the sky, they can be fixed to point at the location in the sky the satellite appears.

Closer to the Earth is the medium Earth orbit (MEO). It ranges from 2,000–35,786 kilometres (1,243–22,236 mi) above Earth. Below MEO is low Earth orbit (LEO) and is about 160 to 2,000 kilometres (99 to 1,243 mi) above Earth. As satellites in MEO and LEO orbit the Earth faster, they cannot stay visible in the sky continually like a geostationary satellite, but appear to a ground observer to cross the sky and "set" while they go behind the Earth. Therefore, to provide continuous communications capability with these lower orbits requires more satellites, so one will always be in the sky when needed. However, due to their relatively small distance to the Earth their signals are stronger.

The electromagnetic signals that communication satellites work with, have a large spectrum of wavelengths and frequencies. To keep these waves from interfering with one another, international organizations have certain rules and regulations describing which wavelength a certain company or group can use. By separating out wavelengths, communication satellites will have minimal interference and be able to communicate effectively.

5.18 TELECONFERENCING

A teleconference or teleseminar is the live exchange and mass articulation of information among several persons and machines remote from one another but linked by a telecommunications system. Terms such as audio conferencing, telephone conferencing and phone conferencing are also sometimes used to refer to teleconferencing.

The telecommunications system may support the teleconference by providing one or more of the following: audio, video, and/or data services by one or more means, such as telephone, computer, telegraph, teletypewriter, radio, and television.

5.18.1 Internet Teleconferencing

Internet teleconferencing includes internet telephone conferencing, Video conferencing, web conferencing, and Augmented Reality conferencing.

Internet telephony involves conducting a teleconference over the Internet or a Wide Area Network. One key technology in this area is Voice over Internet Protocol (VOIP). Popular software for personal use includes Skype, Google Talk, Windows Live Messenger and Yahoo! Messenger.

A working example of an Augmented Reality conferencing was demonstrated at the Salone di Mobile in Milano by AR+RFID Lab. is another AR teleconferencing tool.

5.18.2 Software and Service Providers

Notable Vendors with Articles

- ACT Conferencing
- Adobe Acrobat Connect

- AT Conference, Inc.
- Elluminate
- Glance
- Google Hangouts
- GoToMeeting
- InterCall
- LifeSize
- Microsoft Office Live Meeting
- Polycom
- Premiere Global Services
- Skype
- TrueConf
- Voxeet
- WebEx

5.19 VIDEO CONFERENCING

Video Conferencing (VC) is the conduct of a video conference (also known as a video conference or video teleconference) by a set of telecommunication technologies which allow two or more locations to communicate by simultaneous two-way video and audio transmissions. It has also been called 'visual collaboration' and is a type of groupware.

Video conferencing differs from videophone calls in that it's designed to serve a conference or multiple locations rather than individuals. It is an intermediate form of video telephony, first used commercially in Germany during the late-1930s and later in the United States during the early 1970s as part of AT&T's development of Picturephone technology.

With the introduction of relatively low cost, high capacity broadband telecommunication services in the late 1990s, coupled with powerful computing processors and video compression techniques, video conferencing has made significant inroads in business, education, medicine and media.

5.19.1 History Video Conferencing

Video conferencing uses audio and video telecommunications to bring people at different sites together. This can be as simple as a conversation between people in private offices (point-to-point) or involve several (multipoint) sites in large rooms at multiple locations. Besides the audio and visual transmission of meeting activities, allied Video conferencing technologies can be used to share documents and display information on whiteboards.

Simple analog videophone communication could be established as early as the invention of the television. Such an antecedent usually consisted of two closed-circuit television systems connected via coax cable or radio. An example of that was the German Reich Postzentralamt (post office) video telephone network serving Berlin and several German cities via coaxial cables between 1936 and 1940.

During the first manned space flights, NASA used two radio-frequency (UHF or VHF) video links, one in each direction. TV channels routinely use this type of videotelephony when reporting from distant locations. The news media were to become regular users of mobile links to satellites using specially equipped trucks, and much later via special satellite videophones in a briefcase.

This technique was very expensive, though, and could not be used for applications such as telemedicine, distance education, and business meetings. Attempts at using normal telephony networks to transmit slow-scan video, such as the first systems developed by AT&T Corporation, first researched in the 1950s, failed mostly due to the poor picture quality and the lack of efficient video compression techniques. The greater 1 MHz bandwidth and 6 Mbit/s bit rate of the Picturephone in the 1970s also did not achieve commercial success, mostly due to its high cost, but also due to a lack of network effect —with only a few hundred Picturephones in the world, users had extremely few contacts they could actually call to, and interoperability with other videophone systems would not exist for decades.

It was only in the 1980s that digital telephony transmission networks became possible, such as with ISDN networks, assuring a minimum bit rate (usually 128 kilobits/s) for compressed video and audio transmission. During this time, there was also research into other forms of digital video and audio communication. Many of these technologies, such as the Media space, are not as widely used today as Video conferencing but were still an important area of research. The first dedicated systems started to appear in the market as ISDN networks were expanding throughout the world. One of the first commercial Video conferencing systems sold to companies came from PictureTel Corp., which had an Initial Public Offering in November, 1984.

In 1984 Concept Communication in the United States replaced the then-100 pound, US$100,000 computers necessary for teleconferencing, with a $12,000 circuit board that doubled the video frame rate from 15 up to 30 frames per second, and which reduced the equipment to the size of a circuit board fitting into standard personal computers. The company also secured a patent for a codec for full-motion Video conferencing, first demonstrated at AT&T Bell Labs in 1986.

Video conferencing systems throughout the 1990s rapidly evolved from very expensive proprietary equipment, software and network requirements to a standards-based technology readily available to the general public at a reasonable cost.

Finally, in the 1990s, Internet Protocol-based Video conferencing became possible, and more efficient video compression technologies were developed, permitting desktop, or Personal Computer (PC)-based Video conferencing. In 1992 CU-SeeMe was developed at Cornell by Tim Dorcey et al. In 1995 the first public videoconference between North America and Africa took place, linking a technofair in San Francisco with a techno-rave and cyberdeli in Cape Town. At the Winter Olympics opening ceremony in Nagano, Japan, Seiji Ozawa conducted the Ode to Joy from Beethoven's Ninth Symphony simultaneously across five continents in near-real time.

While Video conferencing technology was initially used primarily within internal corporate communication networks, one of the first community service usages of the technology started in 1992 through a unique partnership with PictureTel and IBM Corporations which at the time were promoting a jointly developed desktop based Video conferencing product known as the PCS/1. Over the next 15 years, Project DIANE (Diversified Information and Assistance Network) grew to utilize a variety of Video conferencing platforms to create a multi-state cooperative public service and distance education network consisting of several hundred schools, neighborhood centers, libraries, science museums, zoos and parks, public assistance centers, and other community oriented organizations.

In the 2000s, videotelephony was popularized via free Internet services such as Skype and iChat, web plugins and on-line telecommunication programs that promoted low cost, albeit lower-quality, Video conferencing to virtually every location with an Internet connection.

In May 2005, the first high definition video conferencing systems, produced by LifeSize Communications, were displayed at the Interop trade show in Las Vegas, Nevada, able to provide video at 30 frames per second with a 1280 by 720 display resolution. Polycom introduced its first high definition video conferencing system to the market in 2006. As of the 2010s, high definition resolution for Video conferencing became a popular feature, with most major suppliers in the Video conferencing market offering it.

Technological developments by Video conferencing developers in the 2010s have extended the capabilities of video conferencing systems beyond the boardroom for use with hand-held mobile devices that combine the use of video, audio and on-screen drawing capabilities broadcasting in real-time over secure networks, independent of location. Mobile collaboration systems now allow multiple people in previously unreachable locations, such as workers on an off-shore oil rig, the ability to view and discuss issues with colleagues thousands of miles away. Traditional Video conferencing system manufacturers have begun providing mobile applications as well, such as those that allow for live and still image streaming.

5.19.2 Technology

The core technology used in a Video conferencing system is digital compression of audio and video streams in real time. The hardware or software that performs compression is called a codec (coder/decoder). Compression rates of up to 1:500 can be achieved. The resulting digital stream of 1s and 0s is subdivided into labeled packets, which are then transmitted through a digital network of some kind (usually ISDN or IP). The use of audio modems in the transmission line allow for the use of POTS, or the Plain Old Telephone System, in some low-speed applications, such as videotelephony, because they convert the digital pulses to/from analog waves in the audio spectrum range.

The other components required for a Video conferencing system include:

- **Video input:** video camera or webcam
- **Video output:** computer monitor, television or projector
- **Audio input:** microphones, CD/DVD player, cassette player, or any other source of PreAmp audio outlet.
- **Audio output:** usually loudspeakers associated with the display device or telephone
- **Data transfer:** analog or digital telephone network, LAN or Internet
- **Computer:** a data processing unit that ties together the other components, does the compressing and decompressing, and initiates and maintains the data linkage via the network.

There are basically two kinds of Video conferencing systems:

1. Dedicated systems have all required components packaged into a single piece of equipment, usually a console with a high quality remote controlled video camera. These cameras can be controlled at a distance to pan left and right, tilt up and down, and zoom. They became known as PTZ cameras. The console contains all electrical interfaces, the control computer, and the software or hardware-based codec. Omnidirectional microphones are connected to the console, as well as a TV monitor with loudspeakers and/or a video projector. There are several types of dedicated Video conferencing devices:

1. Large group Video conferencing are non-portable, large, more expensive devices used for large rooms and auditoriums.
2. Small group Video conferencing are non-portable or portable, smaller, less expensive devices used for small meeting rooms.
3. Individual Video conferencing are usually portable devices, meant for single users, have fixed cameras, microphones and loudspeakers integrated into the console.

2. Desktop systems are add-ons (hardware boards or software codes) to normal PCs and laptops, transforming them into Video conferencing devices. A range of different cameras and microphones can be used with the codec, which contains

the necessary codec and transmission interfaces. Most of the desktops systems work with the H.323 standard. Videoconferences carried out via dispersed PCs are also known as e-meetings. These can also be nonstandard, Microsoft Lync, Skype for Business, Google Hangouts, or Yahoo Messenger or standards based, Cisco Jabber.

3. WebRTC Platforms are video conferencing solutions that are not resident by using a software application but is available through the standard web browser. Solutions such as Adobe Connect and Cisco WebEX can be accessed by going to a URL sent by the meeting organizer and various degrees of security can be attached to the virtual "room". Often the user will be required to download a piece of software, called an "Add In" to enable the browser to access the local camera, microphone and establish a connection to the meeting.

5.19.3 Conferencing Layers

The components within a Conferencing System can be divided up into several different layers: User Interface, Conference Control, Control or Signal Plane, and Media Plane.

Video conferencing User Interfaces (VUI) can be either graphical or voice responsive. Many in the industry have encountered both types of interfaces, and normally graphical interfaces are encountered on a computer. User interfaces for conferencing have a number of different uses; they can be used for scheduling, setup, and making a videocall. Through the user interface the administrator is able to control the other three layers of the system.

Conference Control performs resource allocation, management and routing. This layer along with the User Interface creates meetings (scheduled or unscheduled) or adds and removes participants from a conference.

Control (Signaling) Plane contains the stacks that signal different endpoints to create a call and/or a conference. Signals can be, but aren't limited to, H.323 and Session Initiation Protocol (SIP) Protocols. These signals control incoming and outgoing connections as well as session parameters.

The Media Plane controls the audio and video mixing and streaming. This layer manages Real-Time Transport Protocols, User Datagram Packets (UDP) and Real-Time Transport Control Protocol (RTCP). The RTP and UDP normally carry information such the payload type which is the type of codec, frame rate, video size and many others. RTCP on the other hand acts as a quality control Protocol for detecting errors during streaming.

5.20 MULTIPOINT VIDEO CONFERENCING

Simultaneous Video conferencing among three or more remote points is possible by means of a Multipoint Control Unit (MCU). This is a bridge that interconnects calls from several sources (in a similar way to the audio conference call). All parties call the MCU, or the MCU can also call the parties which are going to participate, in sequence. There are MCU bridges for IP and ISDN-based Video conferencing. There are MCUs which are pure software, and others which are a combination of hardware and software. An MCU is characterised according to the number of simultaneous calls it can handle, its ability to conduct transposing of data rates and protocols, and features such as Continuous Presence, in which multiple parties can be seen on-screen at once. MCUs can be stand-alone hardware devices, or they can be embedded into dedicated Video conferencing units.

The MCU consists of two logical components:

1. A single Multipoint Controller (MC), and
2. Multipoint Processors (MP), sometimes referred to as the mixer.

The MC controls the conferencing while it is active on the signaling plane, which is simply where the system manages conferencing creation, endpoint signaling and in-conferencing controls. This component negotiates parameters with every endpoint in the network and controls conferencing resources. While the MC controls resources and signaling negotiations, the MP operates on the media plane and receives media from each endpoint. The MP generates output streams from each endpoint and redirects the information to other endpoints in the conference.

Some systems are capable of multipoint conferencing with no MCU, stand-alone, embedded or otherwise. These use a standards-based H.323 technique known as "decentralized multipoint", where each station in a multipoint call exchanges video and audio directly with the other stations with no central "manager" or other bottleneck. The advantages of this technique are that the video and audio will generally be of higher quality because they don't have to be relayed through a central point. Also, users can make ad-hoc multipoint calls without any concern for the availability or control of an MCU. This added convenience and quality comes at the expense of some increased network bandwidth, because every station must transmit to every other station directly.

5.20.1 Video Conferencing Modes

Video conferencing systems use several common operating modes:

1. Voice-Activated Switch (VAS);
2. Continuous Presence.

In VAS mode, the MCU switches which endpoint can be seen by the other endpoints by the levels of one's voice. If there are four people in a conference, the only one that will be seen in the conference is the site which is talking; the location with the loudest voice will be seen by the other participants.

Continuous Presence mode, displays multiple participants at the same time. The MP in this mode takes the streams from the different endpoints and puts them all together into a single video image. In this mode, the MCU normally sends the same type of images to all participants. Typically these types of images are called "layouts" and can vary depending on the number of participants in a conference.

5.20.2 Echo Cancellation

A fundamental feature of professional Video conferencing systems is Acoustic Echo Cancellation (AEC). Echo can be defined as the reflected source wave interference with new wave created by source.

AEC is an algorithm which is able to detect when sounds or utterances reenter the audio input of the Video conferencing codec, which came from the audio output of the same system, after some time delay. If unchecked, this can lead to several problems including:

1. The remote party hearing their own voice coming back at them (usually significantly delayed)
2. Strong reverberation, which makes the voice channel useless, and
3. Howling created by feedback.

Echo cancellation is a processor-intensive task that usually works over a narrow range of sound delays.

5.20.3 Cloud-Based Video Conferencing

Cloud-based video conferencing can be used without the hardware generally required by other video conferencing systems, and can be designed for use by SMEs, or larger international companies like Facebook.

Cloud based systems can handle either 2D or 3D video broadcasting. Cloud-based systems can also implement mobile calls, VOIP, and other forms of video calling. They can also come with a video recording function to archive past meetings.

5.21 COMPUTER NETWORK

A computer network is a set of computers sharing resources located on or provided by network nodes. The computers use common communication protocols over digital interconnections to communicate with each other. These interconnections are made up of telecommunication network technologies, based on physically wired, optical, and wireless radio-frequency methods that may be arranged in a variety of network topologies.

The nodes of a computer network may include personal computers, servers, networking hardware, or other specialised or general-purpose hosts. They are identified by network addresses, and may have hostnames. Hostnames serve as memorable labels for the nodes, rarely changed after initial assignment. Network addresses serve for locating and identifying the nodes by communication protocols such as the Internet Protocol.

Computer networks may be classified by many criteria, including the transmission medium used to carry signals, bandwidth, communications protocols to organize network traffic, the network size, the topology, traffic control mechanism, and organizational intent.

Computer networks support many applications and services, such as access to the World Wide Web, digital video, digital audio, shared use of application and storage servers, printers, and fax machines, and use of email and instant messaging applications.

5.21.1 History

Computer networking may be considered a branch of computer science, computer engineering, and telecommunications, since it relies on the theoretical and practical application of the related disciplines. Computer networking was influenced by a wide array of technology developments and historical milestones.

- In the late 1950s, a network of computers was built for the U.S. military Semi-Automatic Ground Environment (SAGE) radar system using the Bell 101 modem. It was the first commercial modem for computers, released by AT&T Corporation in 1958. The modem allowed digital data to be transmitted over regular unconditioned telephone lines at a speed of 110 bits per second (bit/s).
- In 1959, Christopher Strachey filed a patent application for time-sharing and John McCarthy initiated the first project to implement time-sharing of user programs at MIT. Stratchey passed the concept on to J. C. R. Licklider at the inaugural UNESCO Information Processing Conference in Paris that year. McCarthy was instrumental in the creation of three of the earliest time-sharing systems (Compatible Time-Sharing System in 1961, BBN Time-Sharing System in 1962, and Dartmouth Time Sharing System in 1963).
- In 1959, Anatoly Kitov proposed to the Central Committee of the Communist Party of the Soviet Union a detailed plan for the re-organisation of the control of the Soviet armed forces and of the Soviet economy on the basis of a network of computing centres. Kitov's proposal was rejected, as later was the 1962 OGAS economy management network project.
- In 1960, the commercial airline reservation system semi-automatic business research environment (SABRE) went online with two connected mainframes.
- In 1963, J. C. R. Licklider sent a memorandum to office colleagues discussing the concept of the "Intergalactic Computer Network", a computer network intended to allow general communications among computer users.
- Throughout the 1960s, Paul Baran and Donald Davies independently developed the concept of packet switching to transfer information between computers over a network. Davies pioneered the implementation of the concept. The NPL network,

a local area network at the National Physical Laboratory (United Kingdom) used a line speed of 768 kbit/s and later high-speed T1 links (1.544 Mbit/s line rate).

- In 1965, Western Electric introduced the first widely used telephone switch that implemented computer control in the switching fabric.
- In 1969, the first four nodes of the ARPANET were connected using 50 kbit/s circuits between the University of California at Los Angeles, the Stanford Research Institute, the University of California at Santa Barbara, and the University of Utah. In the early 1970s, Leonard Kleinrock carried out mathematical work to model the performance of packet-switched networks, which underpinned the development of the ARPANET. His theoretical work on hierarchical routing in the late 1970s with student Farouk Kamoun remains critical to the operation of the Internet today.
- In 1972, commercial services were first deployed on public data networks in Europe, which began using X.25 in the late 1970s and spread across the globe. The underlying infrastructure was used for expanding TCP/IP networks in the 1980s.
- In 1973, the French CYCLADES network was the first to make the hosts responsible for the reliable delivery of data, rather than this being a centralized service of the network itself.
- In 1973, Robert Metcalfe wrote a formal memo at Xerox PARC describing Ethernet, a networking system that was based on the Aloha network, developed in the 1960s by Norman Abramson and colleagues at the University of Hawaii. In July 1976, Robert Metcalfe and David Boggs published their paper "Ethernet: Distributed Packet Switching for Local Computer Networks" and collaborated on several patents received in 1977 and 1978.
- In 1974, Vint Cerf, Yogen Dalal, and Carl Sunshine published the Transmission Control Protocol (TCP) specification, RFC 675, coining the term Internet as a shorthand for internetworking.
- In 1976, John Murphy of Datapoint Corporation created ARCNET, a token-passing network first used to share storage devices.
- In 1977, the first long-distance fiber network was deployed by GTE in Long Beach, California.
- In 1977, Xerox Network Systems (XNS) was developed by Robert Metcalfe and Yogen Dalal at Xerox.
- In 1979, Robert Metcalfe pursued making Ethernet an open standard.
- In 1980, Ethernet was upgraded from the original 2.94 Mbit/s protocol to the 10 Mbit/s protocol, which was developed by Ron Crane, Bob Garner, Roy Ogus, and Yogen Dalal.

- In 1995, the transmission speed capacity for Ethernet increased from 10 Mbit/s to 100 Mbit/s. By 1998, Ethernet supported transmission speeds of 1 Gbit/s. Subsequently, higher speeds of up to 400 Gbit/s were added (as of 2018). The scaling of Ethernet has been a contributing factor to its continued use.

5.21.2 Use

A computer network extends interpersonal communications by electronic means with various technologies, such as email, instant messaging, online chat, voice and video telephone calls, and video conferencing. A network allows sharing of network and computing resources. Users may access and use resources provided by devices on the network, such as printing a document on a shared network printer or use of a shared storage device. A network allows sharing of files, data, and other types of information giving authorized users the ability to access information stored on other computers on the network. Distributed computing uses computing resources across a network to accomplish tasks.

5.21.3 Network Packet

Most modern computer networks use protocols based on packet-mode transmission. A network packet is a formatted unit of data carried by a packet-switched network.

Packets consist of two types of data: control information and user data (payload). The control information provides data the network needs to deliver the user data, for example, source and destination network addresses, error detection codes, and sequencing information. Typically, control information is found in packet headers and trailers, with payload data in between.

With packets, the bandwidth of the transmission medium can be better shared among users than if the network were circuit switched. When one user is not sending packets, the link can be filled with packets from other users, and so the cost can be shared, with relatively little interference, provided the link isn't overused. Often the route a packet needs to take through a network is not immediately available. In that case, the packet is queued and waits until a link is free.

The physical link technologies of packet network typically limit the size of packets to a certain Maximum Transmission Unit (MTU). A longer message may be fragmented before it is transferred and once the packets arrive, they are reassembled to construct the original message.

5.21.4 Network Topology

The physical or geographic locations of network nodes and links generally have relatively little effect on a network, but the topology of interconnections of a network can significantly affect its throughput and reliability. With many technologies, such as bus or star networks, a single failure can cause the network to fail entirely. In general, the more interconnections there are, the more robust the network is; but the more expensive it is to install. Therefore most network diagrams are arranged by their network topology which is the map of logical interconnections of network hosts.

Common layouts are:

- **Bus network:** all nodes are connected to a common medium along this medium. This was the layout used in the original Ethernet, called 10BASE5 and 10BASE2. This is still a common topology on the data link layer, although modern physical layer variants use point-to-point links instead, forming a star or a tree.
- **Star network:** all nodes are connected to a special central node. This is the typical layout found in a small switched Ethernet LAN, where each client connects to a central network switch, and logically in a wireless LAN, where each wireless client associates with the central wireless access point.
- **Ring network:** each node is connected to its left and right neighbour node, such that all nodes are connected and that each node can reach each other node by traversing nodes left- or rightwards. Token ring networks, and the Fiber Distributed Data Interface (FDDI), made use of such a topology.
- **Mesh network:** each node is connected to an arbitrary number of neighbours in such a way that there is at least one traversal from any node to any other.
- **Fully connected network:** each node is connected to every other node in the network.
- **Tree network:** nodes are arranged hierarchically. This is the natural topology for a larger Ethernet network with multiple switches and without redundant meshing.

The physical layout of the nodes in a network may not necessarily reflect the network topology. As an example, with FDDI, the network topology is a ring, but the physical topology is often a star, because all neighboring connections can be routed via a central physical location. Physical layout is not completely irrelevant, however, as common ducting and equipment locations can represent single points of failure due to issues like fires, power failures and flooding.

5.21.5 Overlay Network

An overlay network is a virtual network that is built on top of another network. Nodes in the overlay network are connected by virtual or logical links. Each link corresponds to a path, perhaps through many physical links, in the underlying network. The topology of the overlay network may differ from that of the underlying one. For example, many peer-to-peer networks are overlay networks. They are organized as nodes of a virtual system of links that run on top of the Internet.

Overlay networks have been around since the invention of networking when computer systems were connected over telephone lines using modems before any data network existed.

The most striking example of an overlay network is the Internet itself. The Internet itself was initially built as an overlay on the telephone network. Even today, each Internet node can communicate with virtually any other through an underlying mesh of sub-networks of wildly different topologies and technologies. Address resolution and routing are the means that allow mapping of a fully connected IP overlay network to its underlying network.

Another example of an overlay network is a distributed hash table, which maps keys to nodes in the network. In this case, the underlying network is an IP network, and the overlay network is a table (actually a map) indexed by keys.

Overlay networks have also been proposed as a way to improve Internet routing, such as through quality of service guarantees achieve higher-quality streaming media. Previous proposals such as IntServ, DiffServ, and IP Multicast have not seen wide acceptance largely because they require modification of all routers in the network. On the other hand, an overlay network can be incrementally deployed on end-hosts running the overlay protocol software, without cooperation from Internet service providers. The overlay network has no control over how packets are routed in the underlying network between two overlay nodes, but it can control, for example, the sequence of overlay nodes that a message traverses before it reaches its destination.

For example, Akamai Technologies manages an overlay network that provides reliable, efficient content delivery. Academic research includes end system multicast, resilient routing and quality of service studies, among others.

5.22 NETWORK LINKS

The transmission media used to link devices to form a computer network include electrical cable, optical fiber, and free space. In the OSI model, the software to handle the media is defined at layers 1 and 2 — the physical layer and the data link layer.

A widely adopted family that uses copper and fiber media in local area network (LAN) technology are collectively known as Ethernet. The media and protocol standards that enable communication between networked devices over Ethernet are defined by IEEE 802.3. Wireless LAN standards use radio waves, others use infrared signals as a transmission medium. Power line communication uses a building's power cabling to transmit data.

5.22.1 Wired

The following classes of wired technologies are used in computer networking.

- Coaxial cable is widely used for cable television systems, office buildings, and other work-sites for local area networks. Transmission speed ranges from 200 million bits per second to more than 500 million bits per second.
- ITU-T G.hn technology uses existing home wiring (coaxial cable, phone lines and power lines) to create a high-speed local area network.

- Twisted pair cabling is used for wired Ethernet and other standards. It typically consists of 4 pairs of copper cabling that can be utilized for both voice and data transmission. The use of two wires twisted together helps to reduce crosstalk and electromagnetic induction. The transmission speed ranges from 2 Mbit/s to 10 Gbit/s. Twisted pair cabling comes in two forms: Unshielded Twisted Pair (UTP) and Shielded Twisted-Pair (STP). Each form comes in several category ratings, designed for use in various scenarios.
- An optical fiber is a glass fiber. It carries pulses of light that represent data via lasers and optical amplifiers. Some advantages of optical fibers over metal wires are very low transmission loss and immunity to electrical interference. Using dense wave division multiplexing, optical fibers can simultaneously carry multiple streams of data on different wavelengths of light, which greatly increases the rate that data can be sent to up to trillions of bits per second. Optic fibers can be used for long runs of cable carrying very high data rates, and are used for undersea cables to interconnect continents. There are two basic types of fiber optics, single-mode optical fiber (SMF) and multi-mode optical fiber (MMF). Single-mode fiber has the advantage of being able to sustain a coherent signal for dozens or even a hundred kilometers. Multimode fiber is cheaper to terminate but is limited to a few hundred or even only a few dozens of meters, depending on the data rate and cable grade.

5.22.2 Wireless

Network connections can be established wirelessly using radio or other electromagnetic means of communication.

- **Terrestrial microwave** – Terrestrial microwave communication uses Earth-based transmitters and receivers resembling satellite dishes. Terrestrial microwaves are in the low gigahertz range, which limits all communications to line-of-sight. Relay stations are spaced approximately 40 miles (64 km) apart.
- **Communications satellites** – Satellites also communicate via microwave. The satellites are stationed in space, typically in geosynchronous orbit 35,400 km (22,000 mi) above the equator. These Earth-orbiting systems are capable of receiving and relaying voice, data, and TV signals.
- **Cellular networks use several radio communications technologies** - The systems divide the region covered into multiple geographic areas. Each area is served by a low-power transceiver.
- **Radio and spread spectrum technologies** – Wireless LANs use a high-frequency radio technology similar to digital cellular. Wireless LANs use spread spectrum technology to enable communication between multiple devices in a limited area. IEEE 802.11 defines a common flavor of open-standards wireless radio-wave technology known as Wi-Fi.

- Free-space optical communication uses visible or invisible light for communications. In most cases, line-of-sight propagation is used, which limits the physical positioning of communicating devices.
- Extending the Internet to interplanetary dimensions via radio waves and optical means, the Interplanetary Internet.
- IP over Avian Carriers was a humorous April fool's Request for Comments, issued as RFC 114. It was implemented in real life in 2001.

The last two cases have a large round-trip delay time, which gives slow two-way communication but doesn't prevent sending large amounts of information.

5.23 NETWORK NODES

Apart from any physical transmission media, networks are built from additional basic system building blocks, such as network interface controllers (NICs), repeaters, hubs, bridges, switches, routers, modems, and firewalls. Any particular piece of equipment will frequently contain multiple building blocks and so may perform multiple functions.

5.23.1 Network Interfaces

A network interface controller (NIC) is computer hardware that connects the computer to the network media and has the ability to process low-level network information. For example, the NIC may have a connector for accepting a cable, or an aerial for wireless transmission and reception, and the associated circuitry.

In Ethernet networks, each network interface controller has a unique Media Access Control (MAC) address—usually stored in the controller's permanent memory. To avoid address conflicts between network devices, the Institute of Electrical and Electronics Engineers (IEEE) maintains and administers MAC address uniqueness. The size of an Ethernet MAC address is six octets. The three most significant octets are reserved to identify NIC manufacturers. These manufacturers, using only their assigned prefixes, uniquely assign the three least-significant octets of every Ethernet interface they produce.

5.23.2 Repeaters and Hubs

A repeater is an electronic device that receives a network signal, cleans it of unnecessary noise and regenerates it. The signal is retransmitted at a higher power level, or to the other side of obstruction so that the signal can cover longer distances without degradation. In most twisted pair Ethernet configurations, repeaters are required for cable that runs longer than 100 meters. With fiber optics, repeaters can be tens or even hundreds of kilometers apart.

Repeaters work on the physical layer of the OSI model but still require a small amount of time to regenerate the signal. This can cause a propagation delay that affects network performance and may affect proper function. As a result, many network architectures limit the number of repeaters used in a network, e.g., the Ethernet 5-4-3 rule.

An Ethernet repeater with multiple ports is known as an Ethernet hub. In addition to reconditioning and distributing network signals, a repeater hub assists with collision detection and fault isolation for the network. Hubs and repeaters in LANs have been largely obsoleted by modern network switches.

5.23.3 Bridges and Switches

Network bridges and network switches are distinct from a hub in that they only forward frames to the ports involved in the communication whereas a hub forwards to all ports. Bridges only have two ports but a switch can be thought of as a multi-port bridge. Switches normally have numerous ports, facilitating a star topology for devices, and for cascading additional switches.

Bridges and switches operate at the data link layer (layer 2) of the OSI model and bridge traffic between two or more network segments to form a single local network. Both are devices that forward frames of data between ports based on the destination MAC address in each frame. They learn the association of physical ports to MAC addresses by examining the source addresses of received frames and only forward the frame when necessary. If an unknown destination MAC is targeted, the device broadcasts the request to all ports except the source, and discovers the location from the reply.

Bridges and switches divide the network's collision domain but maintain a single broadcast domain. Network segmentation through bridging and switching helps break down a large, congested network into an aggregation of smaller, more efficient networks.

5.23.4 Routers

Fig.1 Routers.

A typical home or small office router showing the ADSL telephone line and Ethernet network cable connections

A router is an internetworking device that forwards packets between networks by processing the addressing or routing information included in the packet. The routing information is often processed in conjunction with the routing table. A router uses its routing table to determine where to forward packets and does not require broadcasting packets which is inefficient for very big networks.

5.23.5 Modems

Modems (modulator-demodulator) are used to connect network nodes via wire not originally designed for digital network traffic, or for wireless. To do this one or more carrier signals are modulated by the digital signal to produce an analog signal that can be tailored to give the required properties for transmission. Early modems modulated audio signals sent over a standard voice telephone line. Modems are still commonly used for telephone lines, using a digital subscriber line technology and cable television systems using DOCSIS technology.

5.23.6 Firewalls

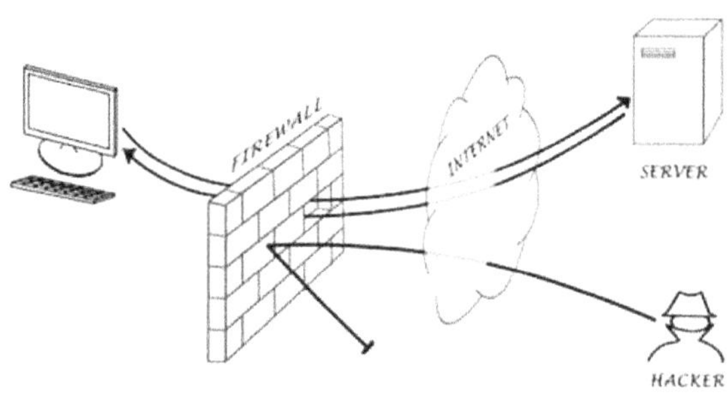

Fig. 2 Finewels

A firewall is a network device or software for controlling network security and access rules. Firewalls are inserted in connections between secure internal networks and potentially insecure external networks such as the Internet. Firewalls are typically configured to reject access requests from unrecognized sources while allowing actions from recognized ones. The vital role firewalls play in network security grows in parallel with the constant increase in cyber attacks.

5.24 COMMUNICATION PROTOCOLS

A communication protocol is a set of rules for exchanging information over a network. Communication protocols have various characteristics. They may be connection-oriented or connectionless, they may use circuit mode or packet switching, and they may use hierarchical addressing or flat addressing.

In a protocol stack, often constructed per the OSI model, communications functions are divided up into protocol layers, where each layer leverages the services of the layer below it until the lowest layer controls the hardware that sends information across the media. The use of protocol layering is ubiquitous across the field of computer networking. An important example of a protocol stack is HTTP (the World Wide Web protocol) running over TCP over IP (the Internet protocols) over IEEE 802.11 (the Wi-Fi protocol). This stack is used between the wireless router and the home user's personal computer when the user is surfing the web.

There are many communication protocols, a few of which are described below.

5.24.1 Common Protocols

Internet Protocol Suite

The Internet Protocol Suite, also called TCP/IP, is the foundation of all modern networking. It offers connection-less and connection-oriented services over an inherently unreliable network traversed by datagram transmission using Internet protocol (IP). At its core, the protocol suite defines the addressing, identification, and routing specifications for Internet Protocol Version 4 (IPv4) and for IPv6, the next generation of the protocol with a much enlarged addressing capability. The Internet Protocol Suite is the defining set of protocols for the Internet.

IEEE 802

IEEE 802 is a family of IEEE standards dealing with local area networks and metropolitan area networks. The complete IEEE 802 protocol suite provides a diverse set of networking capabilities. The protocols have a flat addressing scheme. They operate mostly at layers 1 and 2 of the OSI model.

For example, MAC bridging (IEEE 802.1D) deals with the routing of Ethernet packets using a Spanning Tree Protocol. IEEE 802.1Q describes VLANs, and IEEE 802.1X defines a port-based Network Access Control protocol, which forms the basis for the authentication mechanisms used in VLANs (but it is also found in WLANs) – it is what the home user sees when the user has to enter a "wireless access key".

Ethernet

Ethernet is a family of technologies used in wired LANs. It is described by a set of standards together called IEEE 802.3 published by the Institute of Electrical and Electronics Engineers.

Wireless LAN

Wireless LAN based on the IEEE 802.11 standards, also widely known as WLAN or WiFi, is probably the most well-known member of the IEEE 802 protocol family for home users today. IEEE 802.11 shares many properties with wired Ethernet.

Sonet/SDH

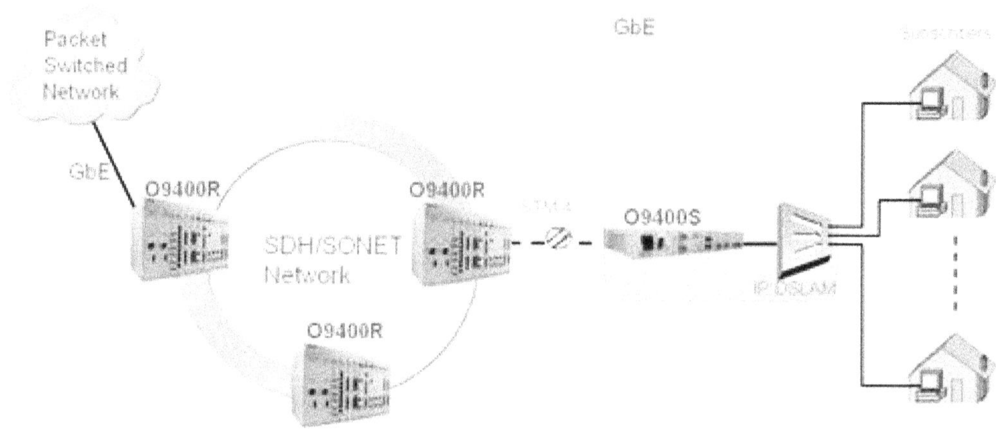

Fig. 3 Sonet & SDH.

Synchronous optical networking (SONET) and Synchronous Digital Hierarchy (SDH) are standardized multiplexing protocols that transfer multiple digital bit streams over optical fiber using lasers. They were originally designed to transport circuit mode communications from a variety of different sources, primarily to support circuit-switched digital telephony. However, due to its protocol neutrality and transport-oriented features, SONET/SDH also was the obvious choice for transporting Asynchronous Transfer Mode (ATM) frames.

5.24.2 Asynchronous Transfer Mode

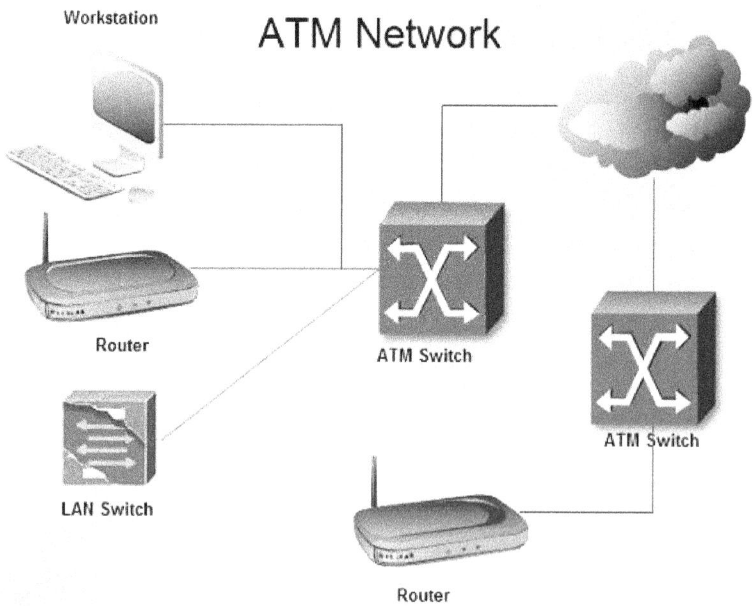

Fig.4 Asynchronous transfer mode.

Asynchronous Transfer Mode (ATM) is a switching technique for telecommunication networks. It uses asynchronous time-division multiplexing and encodes data into small, fixed-sized cells. This differs from other protocols such as the Internet Protocol Suite or Ethernet that use variable-sized packets or frames. ATM has similarities with both circuit and packet switched networking. This makes it a good choice for a network that must handle both traditional high-throughput data traffic, and real-time, low-latency content such as voice and video. ATM uses a connection-oriented model in which a virtual circuit must be established between two endpoints before the actual data exchange begins.

ATM still plays a role in the last mile, which is the connection between an Internet service provider and the home user.

5.24.3 Cellular Standards

There are a number of different digital cellular standards, including: Global System for Mobile Communications (GSM), General Packet Radio Service (GPRS), cdmaOne, CDMA2000, Evolution-Data Optimized (EV-DO), Enhanced Data Rates for GSM Evolution (EDGE), Universal Mobile Telecommunications System (UMTS), Digital Enhanced Cordless Telecommunications (DECT), Digital AMPS (IS-136/TDMA), and Integrated Digital Enhanced Network (iDEN).

5.25 ROUTING

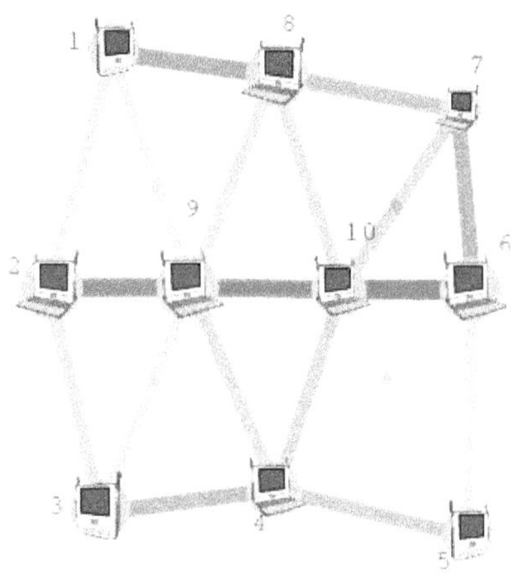

Fig. 5 Routing

Routing calculates good paths through a network for information to take. For example, from node 1 to node 6 the best routes are likely to be 1-8-7-6, 1-8-10-6 or 1-9-10-6, as these are the shortest routes.

Routing is the process of selecting network paths to carry network traffic. Routing is performed for many kinds of networks, including circuit switching networks and packet switched networks.

In packet-switched networks, routing protocols direct packet forwarding through intermediate nodes. Intermediate nodes are typically network hardware devices such as routers, bridges, gateways, firewalls, or switches. General-purpose computers can also forward packets and perform routing, though because they lack specialized hardware, may offer limited performance. The routing process directs forwarding on the basis of routing tables, which maintain a record of the routes to various network destinations. Most routing algorithms use only one network path at a time. Multipath routing techniques enable the use of multiple alternative paths.

Routing can be contrasted with bridging in its assumption that network addresses are structured and that similar addresses imply proximity within the network. Structured addresses allow a single routing table entry to represent the route to a group of devices. In large networks, the structured addressing used by routers outperforms unstructured addressing used by bridging. Structured IP addresses are used on the Internet. Unstructured MAC addresses are used for bridging on Ethernet and similar local area networks.

CHAPTER

E-LEARNING THEORY 6

6.1 INTRODUCTION

E-learning theory is built on cognitive science principles that demonstrate how the use and design of educational technology can enhance effective learning. The theory was developed from a set of principles created based on Cognitive Load Theory. According to David (2015), Cognitive Load Theory is "the amount of mental effort involved in working memory" during a task and can be categorized into germane, intrinsic, and extraneous effort. Since the working memory has limited capacity and the brain will suffer from overload if learners are presented with too much information, causing inefficient learning, it is essential to balance these three types of load to promote learning efficiency. Based on this, Mayer, Sweller and Moreno (2015) established 11 design principles that were created to reduce extraneous cognitive load and manage germane and intrinsic loads at an appropriate level for learners using technology. These types of cognitive load, along with design principles and technology, comprise e-learning theory. E-learning theory belongs to the grand theory of Connectivism because it emphasizes how technologies can be used and designed to create new learning opportunities and to promote effective learning.

6.2 PREVIOUS STUDIES

Multimedia learning is one specific principle of e-learning theory, and it contends that deeper learning can be promoted using two formats among audio, visual, and text instead of one or three. Previous studies relevant to e-learning theory have provided evidence that multimedia design principles can foster effective learning. For example, Mayer (1997) conducted several reviews of multimedia learning and found that multimedia instruction was effective. To be specific, Mayer (1997) reviewed eight studies on whether multimedia instruction was effective and found that students who were given a presentation with both verbal and visual explanations had a 75% higher median score for creative solutions on problem-solving transfer tests than students who experienced only verbal explanation.

Ten studies reviewed by Mayer (1997) found that students showed scored more than 50% over the median on creative solution transfer tests when verbal and visual descriptions were concurrently employed.

Personalization is also an essential principle of e-learning theory. This principle suggests that presenting words in a conversational and informal style can help enhance effective learning. Several studies have shown that personalization can be effective in learning. For example, Kartal's (2010) study investigated the effectiveness of the design principle of personalization with 89 college students in an Istanbul university in Turkey by testing their computerized instructional content in a personalized informal style, personalized formal style, and neutral-formal style. The results showed that the amount of learning increased when the language style was formal and conversational.

Another study conducted by Kurt (2011) showed consistent results with Kartal's (2010) study. Kurt (2011) examined the personalization effect with multimedia material in a formal style with 22 students and conversational style with 23 students. Using an achievement test, a cognitive load scale for both groups, and a questionnaire for the personalized group, Kurt found that students' cognitive load scores in the personalized group were significantly different from and better than those in the non-personalized group.

Besides, students in the personalized group said that the conversational style applied in the multimedia software inspired them to learn and they felt that a real human was talking to them. In addition, students showed a preference for multimedia materials.

Several other studies have also shown other design principles of e-learning theory to be effective. Some researchers studied the modality principle, which claims that the use of visuals accompanied by audio narration instead of on-screen text is more effective for learning. For example, Moreno (2006) conducted a meta-analysis on modality effects. The results revealed significant learning benefits due to the modality principle across different media.

As can be seen from the above discussion, applying the principles of e-learning theory with its design principles can promote effective learning. Therefore, e-learning theory can be useful for teachers to design effective courses and for researchers to understand how effective learning with and through technology can happen.

6.3 MODEL OF E-LEARNING THEORY

The model in Figure 1 demonstrates that concepts of three types of cognitive load and eleven empirical principles compose two constructs: cognitive load and design principles. These two constructs then combine to lead to the proposition of e-learning theory.

Figure 1
A model of e-learning theory based on Mayer et al (2015)

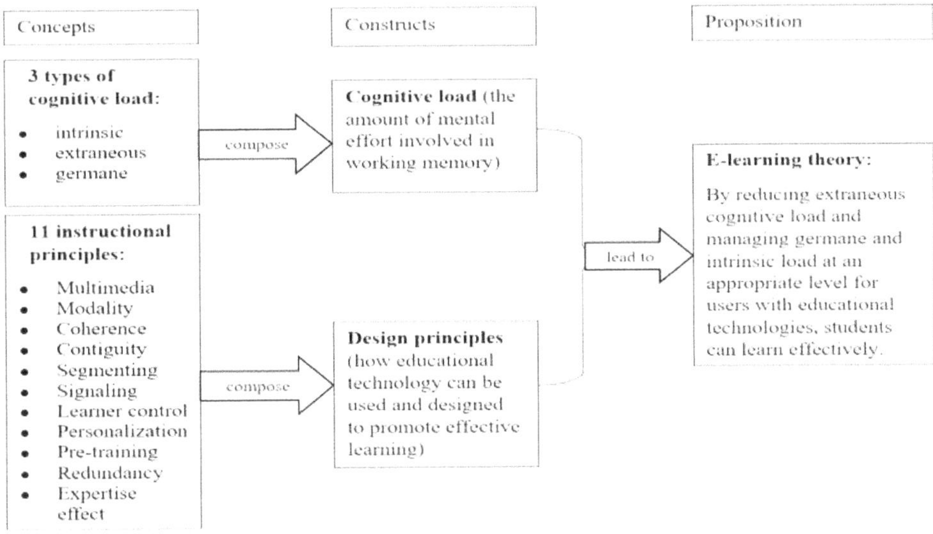

Fig.1 Model of E-learning Theory

6.3.1 Concepts and Constructs

As noted previously, the three cognitive loads are intrinsic, germane, and extraneous based on the amount of mental effort. Intrinsic load is "the mental work imposed by the complexity of the content in your lessons and is primarily determined by your instructional goals". Germane load is "mental work imposed by instructional activities that benefit the instructional goal". Extraneous load is "the mental work that is irrelevant to the learning goal and consequently wastes limited mental resources". Together these form the construct "cognitive load."

E-learning theory is also composed of principles that can be integrated into instructional design; they that demonstrate "how educational technology can be used and designed to promote effective learning" (Wang, 2012, p.346). The eleven principles of the model that can promote effective learning are:

1. **Multimedia principle:** Using two formats of audio, visual, and text instead of using one or three.
2. **Modality principle:** Explaining visual content with audio narration instead of on-screen text.
3. **Coherence principle:** Avoiding irrelevant videos and audio.
4. **Contiguity principle:** Aligning relevant information to corresponding pictures concurrently.

5. **Segmenting principle:** Managing complicated content by breaking a lesson into small parts.
6. **Signaling principle:** Offering signals for the narration, such as arrows, circles, and highlights.
7. **Learner control principle:** Allowing the learner to control their learning pace.
8. **Personalization principle:** Presenting words in a conversational and informal style.
9. **Pre-training principle:** Providing descriptions or explanations for key concepts in a lesson before the main procedure of that lesson.
10. **Redundancy principle:** Presenting visuals with audio or on-screen text but not both.
11. **Expertise effect:** Considering that design principles may have a different effect on learners with various amounts of prior knowledge.

Together, these eleven principles form the construct "design principles."

Overall, the ideas of cognitive load and design principles can be integrated to reduce extraneous cognitive load and manage germane and intrinsic loads by making it easier for learners' brains to handle the amount of information and processing that they must do during instructional tasks.

6.3.2 Proposition

Based on the concepts and constructs, the model ends with the proposition, that if teachers design principled tasks with educational technologies that reduce extraneous cognitive load and manage germane and intrinsic load at appropriate levels for students, they can learn effectively (Mayer, Sweller & Moreno, 2015).

6.3.3 Learning Theory

Learning theory is meant to explain and help us understand how people learn; however, the literature is complex and extensive enough to fill entire sections of a library. It involves multiple disciplines, including psychology, sociology, neuroscience, and of course, education. Three of the more popular learning theories – behaviorism, cognitivism, and social constructivism – will be highlighted to form the foundation for further discussion. Mention will also be made of several other learning theories that are relevant to online education. Before reviewing these theories, it will be worthwhile to have a brief discussion of the term theory itself.

Theory is defined as a set of statements, principles, or ideas that relate to a particular subject. A theory usually describes, explains, and/or predicts phenomena. The definition of theory also varies depending upon disciplines, especially when related to the term model. As noted by Graham, Henrie, and Gibbons (2013), the two terms are used interchangeably and generally refer to the same concept. However, a model is more frequently a visual representation of reality or a concept. In this discussion, the terms theory and model will be used interchangeably. The purpose of a theory or model is to propose the answers to basic questions associated with a phenomenon. Graham, Henrie and Gibbons (2013) reviewed this issue as related to instructional technology and recommended a three-part taxonomy first proposed by Gibbons and Bunderson (2005) that includes theories that:

1. **Explore:** "What exists?" and attempts to define and categorize;
2. **Explain:** "Why does this happen?" and looks for causality and correlation, and work with variables and relationships.
3. **Design:** "How do I achieve this outcome?" and describes interventions for reaching targeted outcomes and operational principles (Graham, Henrie, & Gibbons, 2013, p. 13).

This taxonomy will serve as an overall guiding principle for the discussion of learning theories and models in this article.

6.3.4 Behaviorism

As its name implies, behaviorism focuses on how people behave. It evolved from a positivist worldview related to cause and effect. In simple terms, action produces reaction. In education, behaviorism examines how students behave while learning. More specifically, behaviorism focuses on observing how students respond to certain stimuli that, when repeated, can be evaluated, quantified, and eventually controlled for each individual. The emphasis in behaviorism is on that which is observable and not on the mind or cognitive processes. In sum, if you cannot observe it, it cannot be studied.

The development of behaviorism is frequently associated with Ivan Pavlov, famous for his experiments with dogs, food, and audible stimuli, such as a bell. In his experiments, dogs learned to associate food or feeding time with the sound of the bell and began to salivate. Pavlov conducted his experiments in the early 1900s and they were replicated by many other researchers throughout the 20th century. John B. Watson, among the first Americans to follow Pavlov's work, saw it as a branch of natural science. Watson became a major proponent of Pavlov and is generally credited with coining the term behaviorism. He argued that mind and consciousness are unimportant in the learning process and that everything can be studied in terms of stimulus and response.

Other major figures associated with behaviorism are B.F. Skinner and Edward Thorndike. Skinner is particularly well known, primarily because he introduced what he referred to as operant conditioning which emphasized the use of both positive and negative reinforcement to help individuals learn new behaviors. This was quite different from Pavlov, who relied on simple reflexive responses to specific stimuli although both Pavlov and Skinner promoted repetitive behavior that leads to habit formation. Skinner had a significant influence on early computer-assisted instructional (CAI) models as developed by Pat Suppes and others. A common aspect of early CAI programs was the reliance on encouragement and repetition to promote positive learning activities.

6.3.5 Cognitivism

Cognitivism has been considered a reaction to the "rigid" emphasis by behaviorists on predictive stimulus and response. Cognitive theorists promoted the concept that the mind has an important role in learning and sought to focus on what happens in between the occurrence of environmental stimulus and student response. They saw the cognitive processes of the mind, such as motivation and imagination, as critical elements of learning that bridge environmental stimuli and student responses. For example, Noam Chomsky (1959) wrote a critical review of Skinner's behaviorist work in which he raised the importance of creative mental processes that are not observable in the physical world. Although written mainly from the perspective of a linguist, Chomsky's view gained popularity in other fields, including psychology. Interdisciplinary in nature, cognitive science draws from psychology, biology, neuroscience, computer science, and philosophy to explain the workings of the brain as well as levels of cognitive development that form the foundation of learning and knowledge acquisition. As a result, cognitivism has evolved into one of the dominant learning theories. The future of cognitivism is particularly interesting as more advanced online software evolves into adaptive and personalized learning applications that seek to integrate artificial intelligence and learning analytics into instruction.

Behaviorism led to the development of taxonomies of learning because it emphasized the study and evaluation of multiple steps in the learning process. Behaviorists repeatedly studied learning activities to deconstruct and define the elements of learning. Benjamin Bloom (1956) was among the early psychologists to establish a taxonomy of learning that related to the development of intellectual skills and to stress the importance of problem solving as a higher order skill. Bloom's (1956) Taxonomy of educational objectives handbook: Cognitive domains remains a foundational text and essential reading within the educational community. Bloom's taxonomy is based on six key elements as follows:

1. **Creating:** Putting elements together to form a coherent or functional whole, and reorganizing elements into a new pattern or structure through generating, planning, or producing.
2. **Evaluating:** Making judgments based on criteria and standards through checking and critiquing.
3. **Analyzing:** Breaking material into constituent parts, and determining how the parts relate to one another and to an overall structure or purpose through differentiating, organizing, and attributing.
4. **Applying:** Carrying out or using a procedure through executing or implementing.

5. **Understanding:** Constructing meaning from oral, written, and graphic messages through interpreting, exemplifying, classifying, summarizing, inferring, comparing, and explaining.
6. **Remembering:** Retrieving, recognizing, and recalling relevant knowledge from long-term memory.

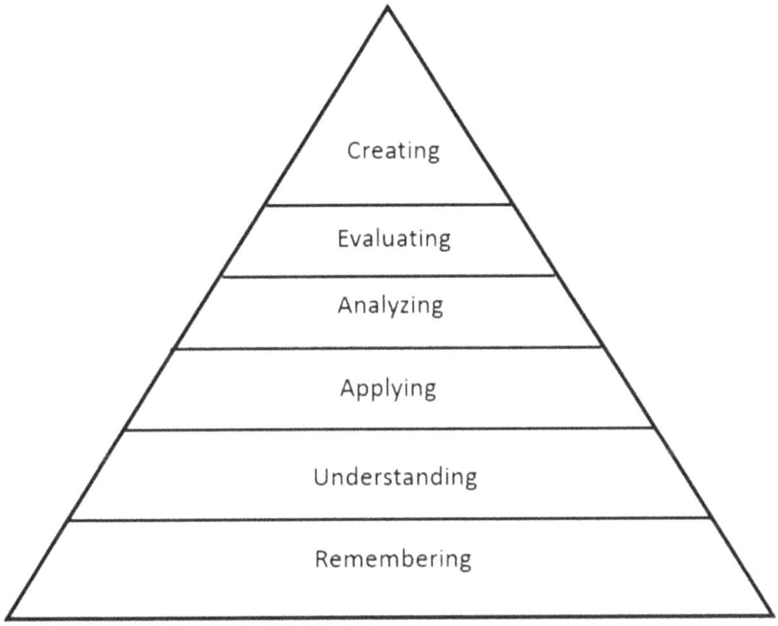

Fig.2 Bloom's taxonomy.

Bloom, in developing his taxonomy, essentially helped to move learning theory toward issues of cognition and developmental psychology. Twenty years later, Robert Gagne, an educational psychologist, developed another taxonomy (events of instruction) that built on Bloom's and became the basis for cognitivist instructional design (Harasim, 2012). Gagne emphasized nine events in instruction that drive the definitions of objectives and strategies for the design of instructional materia.

6.3.6 Social Constructivism

Parallel to behaviorism and cognitivism was the work of several education theorists, including Lev Vygotsky, John Dewey, and Jean Piaget. Their focus on social constructionism was to describe and explain teaching and learning as complex interactive social phenomena between teachers and students. Vygotsky posited that learning is problem solving and that the social construction of solutions to problems is the basis of the learning process. Vygotsky described the learning process as the establishment of a "zone of proximal development" in which the teacher, the learner, and a problem to be solved exist. The teacher provides a social environment in which the learner can assemble or construct with others the knowledge necessary to solve the problem. Likewise, John

Dewey saw learning as a series of practical social experiences in which learners learn by doing, collaborating, and reflecting with others. While developed in the early part of the 20th century, Dewey's work is very much in evidence in a good deal of present-day social constructivist instructional design. The use of reflective practice by both learner and teacher is a pedagogical cornerstone for interactive discussions that replaces straight lecturing, whether in a face-to-face or online class. Jean Piaget, whose background was in psychology and biology, based his learning theory on four stages of cognitive development that begin at birth and continue through one's teen years and beyond. Seymour Papert, in designing the Logo programming language, drew from Jean Piaget the concept of creating social, interactive microworlds or communities where children, under the guidance of a teacher, solve problems while examining social issues, mathematical and science equations, or case studies. Papert's approach of integrating computer technology into problem solving is easily applied to many facets of instructional design.

6.3.7 Derivatives of the Major Learning Theories

A number of theories and models have roots in one or more of the above frameworks. In the latter part of the 20th century, the major learning theories, especially cognitive theory and social constructivism, began to overlap. For example, Wenger and Lave (1991) and Wenger (1998) promoted concepts such as "communities of practice" and situated learning. Their position was that learning involves a deepening process situated in, and derived from, participation in a learning community of practice. Their work is very evident in many studies, including those related to online education.

Information processing learning theory is a variation of cognitivism that views the human mind as a system that processes information according to a set of logical rules. In it, the mind is frequently compared to a computer that follows a set of rules or program. Research using this perspective attempts to describe and explain changes in the mental processes and strategies that lead to greater cognitive competence as children develop. Richard Atkinson and Richard Shiffrin (1968) are generally credited with proposing the first information processing model that deals with how students acquire, encode, store (in short-term or long-term memory), and retrieve information.

One of the more popular and controversial theories relates to learning styles and posits that individuals learn differently depending upon their propensities and personalities. Carl Jung argued that individual personality types influence various elements of human behavior, including learning. Jung's theory focuses on four basic psychological dimensions:

1. Extroversion vs. Introversion
2. Sensation vs. Intuition
3. Thinking vs. Feeling
4. Judging vs. Perceiving

While each unique dimension can influence an individual learning style, it is likely that learning styles are based on a combination of these dimensions. For example, a learning style might include elements of extroversion, sensation, feeling, and perception as personality dimensions. Readers may be familiar with the Myers-Briggs Type Inventory (MBTI) which has been used for decades to assist in determining personality types, including how personality relates to student learning. The MBTI is based extensively on Jung's theories and has been used to predict and develop different teaching methods and environments and to predict individual patterns of mental functioning, such as information processing, idea development, and judgment formation. It can also be used to foretell patterns of attitudes and interests that influence an individual's preferred learning environment and to predict a person's disposition to pursue certain learning circumstances and avoid others. Lin, Cranton, and Bridglall (2005) remind us that much of the work of Carl Jung and the MBTI is applicable to learning environments, whether face-to-face or online. For example, the extrovert may prefer active, highly collaborative environments while the introvert would prefer less interaction and less collaboration. This suggests that instruction should be designed to allow both types of individuals – the outgoing social organizer as well as the introspective reflective observer – to thrive.

Howard Gardner has developed a theory of "multiple intelligences" that proposes that intelligence is not merely a singular entity but consists of multiple entities used by individuals in different proportions to understand and to learn about the world. Gardner has identified nine basic intelligences: linguistic, logical/mathematical, spatial, musical, bodily kinesthetic, interpersonal, intrapersonal, naturalistic, and existential.

Gardner's theory has received criticism from both psychologists and educators who view these "intelligences" as talents, personality traits, and abilities. His work has also been questioned by those who propose that there is, in fact, a root or base intelligence that drives the other "intelligences." Gardner does not necessarily disagree with this latter position but maintains that other intelligences can be viewed as main branches off the base root intelligence. This theory has important pedagogical implications and suggests the design of multiple learning modalities that allow learners to engage in ways they prefer, according to their interest or ability, and to challenge them to learn in other ways that are less related to their preferences, interests, or abilities. Gardner's work also addresses the common concern that too much teaching and learning is linguistically based (reading, writing, and speaking) and that the other intelligences are underutilized.

Modern neuroscience research also suggests that students learn in different ways depending upon a number of factors including age, learning stimuli, and the pace of instruction. Willingham (2008) suggests that learning is a dynamic process that may evolve and change from one classroom to another, from one subject to another, and from one day to another. This research also supports the concept that multiple intelligences and mental abilities do not exist as mere "yes/no" entities but within continua which the mind blends in a manner consistent with the way it responds and learns from the external environment and instructional stimuli. Conceptually, this suggests a framework for a multimodal instructional design that relies on a variety of pedagogical techniques, delivery approaches, and media.

Lastly, Malcom Knowles (1998) deserves mention as the individual who distinguished between andragogy (adult learning) and pedagogy (child learning). Adults, whether seeking to enhance their professional skills or to satisfy curiosity about a subject, learn differently than children. Courses designed for adults should tap into their social contexts and experiences. Knowles' insights are especially important for higher education, where online technology is used extensively for adult students in traditional and continuing education programs, competency-based learning, and career/professional development.

In sum, a number of theories have been, and will continue to be, applied to instruction, including online and blended learning. Several theories specifically related to online education will now be examined.

6.4 LEARNING THEORIES FOR ONLINE EDUCATION

Just as no single learning theory has emerged for instruction in general, the same is true for online education. A number of theories have evolved, most of which derive from the major learning theories discussed previously. In this section, several theories will be examined in terms of their appropriateness for the online environment.

6.4.1 Community of Inquiry (CoI)

The "community of inquiry" model for online learning environments developed by Garrison, Anderson, and Archer (2000) is based on the concept of three distinct "presences": cognitive, social, and teaching. While recognizing the overlap and relationship among the three components, Anderson, Rourke, Garrison, and Archer (2001) advise further research on each component. Their model supports the design of online and blended courses as active learning environments or communities dependent on instructors and students sharing ideas, information, and opinions. Of particular note is that "presence" is a social phenomenon and manifests itself through interactions among students and instructors. The community of inquiry has become one of the more popular models for online and blended courses that are designed to be highly interactive among students and faculty using discussion boards, blogs, wikis, and Video conferencing.

6.4.2 Connectivism

George Siemens (2004), one of the early MOOC pioneers, has been the main proponent of connectivism, a learning model that acknowledges major shifts in the way knowledge and information flows, grows, and changes because of vast data communications networks. Internet technology has moved learning from internal, individualistic activities to group, community, and even crowd activities. In developing the theory, Siemens acknowledged the work of Alberto Barabasi and the power of networks. He also referenced an article written by Karen Stephensen (1998) entitled "What Knowledge Tears Apart, Networks Make Whole," which accurately identified how large-scale networks become indispensable in helping people and organizations manage data and information.

Siemens describes connectivism as:

the integration of principles explored by chaos, network, and complexity and self-organization theories learning is a process that occurs within nebulous environments of shifting core elements – not entirely under the control of the individual. Learning can reside outside of ourselves (within an organization or a database), is focused on connecting specialized information sets, and the connections that enable us to learn more and are more important than our current state of knowing.

Siemens noted that connectivism as a theory is driven by the dynamic of information flow. Students need to understand, and be provided with, experiences in navigating and recognizing oceans of constantly shifting and evolving information. Siemens proposed eight principles of connectivism. Connectivism is particularly appropriate for courses with very high enrollments and where the learning goal or objective is to develop and create knowledge rather than to disseminate it.

6.4.3 Online Collaborative Learning (OCL)

Online collaborative learning (OCL) is a theory proposed by Linda Harasim that focuses on the facilities of the Internet to provide learning environments that foster collaboration and knowledge building. Harasim (2012) describes OCL as a new theory of learning that focuses on collaborative learning, knowledge building, and Internet use as a means to reshape formal, non-formal, and informal education for the Knowledge Age.

Like Siemens, Harasim sees the benefits of moving teaching and learning to the Internet and large-scale networked education. In some respects, Harasim utilizes Alberto Barabasi's position on the power of networks. In OCL, there exist three phases of knowledge construction through discourse in a group:

1. **Idea generating:** The brainstorming phase, where divergent thoughts are gathered
2. **Idea organizing:** The phase where ideas are compared, analyzed, and categorized through discussion and argument
3. **Intellectual convergence:** The phase where intellectual synthesis and consensus occurs, including agreeing to disagree, usually through an assignment, essay, or other joint piece of work.

OCL also derives from social constructivism, since students are encouraged to collaboratively solve problems through discourse and where the teacher plays the role of facilitator as well as learning community member. This is a major aspect of OCL but also of other constructivist theories where the teacher is not necessarily separate and apart but rather, an active facilitator of, knowledge building. Because of the importance of the role of the teacher, OCL is not easy to scale up. Unlike connectivism, which is suited for large-scale instruction, OCL is best situated in smaller instructional environments. This last issue becomes increasingly important when seeking commonality among online education theories.

Many other theories can be associated with online education but, rather than present more theories and in keeping with one of the major purposes of this article, it is appropriate to ask whether an integrated or unified theory of online education is possible.

6.5 A COMMON INTEGRATED THEORY OF ONLINE EDUCATION

As noted, Terry Anderson (2011) examined the possibility of building a theory of online education, starting with the assumption that it would be a difficult, and perhaps impossible, task. He approached this undertaking from a distance education perspective, having spent much of his career at Athabasca University, the major higher education distance education provider in Canada. While he acknowledged that many theorists and practitioners consider online learning as "a subset of learning in general", he also stated:

online learning as a subset of distance education has always been concerned with provision of access to educational experience that is, at least more flexible in time and in space as campus-based education.

These two perspectives complicate any attempt to build a common theory of online education. Blended learning models, for instance, do not easily fit into the distance education schema, even though they are evolving as a prevalent component of traditional face-to-face and online education environments.

Anderson considered a number of theories and models but focused on the well-respected work of Bransford, Brown, and Cocking (1999) who posited that effective learning environments are framed within the convergence of four overlapping lenses: community-centeredness, knowledge-centeredness, learner-centeredness, and assessment centeredness. These lenses provided the foundational framework for Anderson's approach to building an online education theory, as he examined in detail the characteristics and facilities that the Internet provides with regards to each of the four lenses. Second, he noted that the Internet had evolved from a text-based environment to one in which all forms of media are supported and readily available. He also accurately commented that the Internet's hyperlink capacity is most compatible with the way human knowledge is stored and accessed. In this regard, he referred to the work of Jonassen (1992) and Shank (1993) who associated hyperlinking with constructivism. Finally, Anderson extensively examined the importance of interaction in all forms of learning and referred to a number of mostly distance education theorists such as Holmberg (1989), Moore (1989), Moore and Kearsley (1996), and Garrison and Shale (1990). The essence of interaction among students, teachers, and content is well understood and is referenced in many theories of education, especially constructivism. Anderson's evaluation of interaction concludes that interactions are critical components of a theory.

With these three elements in mind, Anderson then proceeded to construct a model. He did add one important element by distinguishing community/collaborative models from self-paced instructional models, commenting that community/collaborative models and self-paced instructional models are inherently incompatible. The community/collaborative models do not scale up easily because of the extensive interactions among teachers and students. On the other hand, the self-paced instructional models are designed for independent learning with much less interaction among students and teachers.

The two major human actors, learners and teachers, and their interactions with each other and with content. Learners can of course interact directly with content that they find in multiple formats, and especially on the Web; however, many choose to have their learning sequenced, directed, and evaluated with the assistance of a teacher. This interaction can take place within a community of inquiry, using a variety of Net-based synchronous and asynchronous activities ... These environments are particularly rich, and allow for the learning of social skills, the collaborative learning of content, and the development of personal relationships among participants. However, the community binds learners in time, forcing regular sessions or at least group-paced learning. The second model of learning illustrates the structured learning tools associated with independent learning. Common tools used in this mode include computer-assisted tutorials, drills, and simulations.

Demonstrates the instructional flow within the two sides and represents the beginnings of a theory or model from the distance education perspective. Anderson concluded that his model "will help us to deepen our understanding of this complex educational context" , which he noted needs to measure more fully the direction and magnitude of each input variable on relevant outcome variables.

Anderson also commented about the potential of the Internet for education delivery, and that an online learning-based theory or model could subsume all other modes with the exception of the "rich face-to-face interaction in formal classrooms". This becomes a quandary for Anderson in trying to develop a common theory of online education in that it does not provide for in-person, face-to-face activity and is problematic for those who see online education as a subset of education in general.

6.5.1 An Integrated Model

Anderson's model assumed that none of the instruction is delivered in traditional, face-to-face mode, and so excluded blended learning models that have some face-to-face component. Is it possible, therefore, to approach the search for an integrated model for online education from the face-to-face education in general or even the blended learning perspective?

Bosch (2016), in a review of instructional technology, identified and compared four blended learning models using twenty-one different design components. These models emphasized, to one degree or another, the integration of pedagogy and technology in course design. Among the models was a Blending with Pedagogical Purpose Model, developed by this author, in which pedagogical objectives and activities drive the approaches, including the online technology that faculty members use in instruction. The model also suggests that blending the objectives, activities, and approaches within multiple modalities might be most effective for, and appeal to, a wide range of students. The model contains six basic pedagogical goals, and approaches for achieving them, to form learning modules. The model is flexible and assumes that other modules can be added as needed and where appropriate. The most important feature of this model is that pedagogy drives the approaches that will work best to support student learning. The modules are also shown as intersecting but this is optional; they may or may not intersect or overlap depending upon the approaches used. For instance, some reflection can be incorporated into collaboration or not, depending upon how the collaborative activity is designed. It might be beneficial to have the collaborative groups reflect specifically on their activities. Similar scenarios are possible for the other modules. Ultimately important is that all the modules used blend together into a coherent whole. The following paragraphs briefly review each of these modules.

Content is one of the primary drivers of instruction and there are many ways in which content can be delivered and presented. While much of what is taught is delivered linguistically (teacher speaks/students listen or teacher writes/students write), this does not have to be the case, either in face-to-face or online environments. Mayer (2009) has done extensive reviews of the research and has concluded that learning is greatly enhanced by visualization. Certain subject areas, such as science, are highly dependent upon the use of visual simulations to demonstrate processes and systems. The humanities, especially art, history, and literature, can be greatly enhanced by rich digital images as well. Course/learning management systems (CMS/LMS) such as Blackboard, Canvas, or Moodle provide basic content delivery mechanisms for blended learning and easily handle the delivery of a variety of media including text, video, and audio. Games have also evolved and now play a larger role in instructional content. In providing and presenting content, the Blending with Pedagogical Purpose model suggests that multiple technologies and media be utilized.

The Blending with Pedagogical Purpose model posits that instruction is not simply about learning content or a skill but also supports students socially and emotionally. As noted, constructivists view teaching and learning as inherently social activities. The physical presence of a teacher or tutor, in addition to providing instruction, is comforting and familiar. While perhaps more traditionally recognized as critical for K-12 students, social and emotional development must be acknowledged as important to education at all levels. Faculty members who have taught graduate courses know that students, even at this advanced level, frequently need someone with whom to speak, whether to help understand a complex concept or to provide advice about career and professional opportunities. While fully online courses and programs have evolved to the point where faculty members can provide some social and emotional support where possible and appropriate, in blended courses and programs this is more frequently provided in a face-to-face mode.

Dialectics or questioning is an important activity that allows faculty members to probe what students know and to help refine their knowledge. The Socratic Method remains one of the major techniques used in instruction, and many successful teachers are proud of their ability to stimulate discussion by asking the "right" questions to help students think critically about a topic or issue. In many cases, these questions serve to refine and narrow a discussion to very specific "points" or aspects of the topic at hand, and are not meant to be open-ended activities. For dialectic and questioning activities, a simple-to-use, threaded electronic discussion board or forum such as VoiceThread is an effective approach. A well-organized discussion board activity generally seeks to present a topic or issue and have students respond to questions and provide their own perspectives, while evaluating and responding to the opinions of others. The simple, direct visual of the "thread" also allows students to see how the entire discussion or lesson has evolved. In sum, for instructors who want to focus attention and dialogue on a specific topic, the main activity for many online courses has been, and continues to be, the electronic discussion board.

Reflection can be incorporated as a powerful pedagogical strategy under the right circumstances. There is an extensive body of scholarship on the "reflective teacher" and the "reflective learner" dating from the early 20th century (Dewey (1916), Schon (1983)). While reflection can be a deeply personal activity, the ability to share one's reflections with others can be beneficial. Pedagogical activities that require students to reflect on what they learn and to share their reflections with their teachers and fellow students extend and enrich reflection. Blogs and blogging, whether as group exercises or for individual journaling activities, have evolved into appropriate tools for student reflection and other aspects of course activities.

Collaborative learning has evolved over decades. In face-to-face classes, group work grew in popularity and became commonplace in many course activities. Many professional programs, such as business administration, education, health science, and social work, rely heavily on collaborative learning as a technique for group problem solving. In the past, the logistics and time needed for effective collaboration in face-to-face classes were sometimes problematic. Now, email, mobile technology, and other forms of electronic communication alleviate some of these logistical issues. Wikis, especially, have grown in popularity and are becoming a staple in group projects and writing assignments. They are seen as important vehicles for creating knowledge and content, as well as for generating peer-review and evaluation (Fredericksen, 2015). Unlike face-to-face group work that typically ended up on the instructor's desk when delivered in paper form, wikis allow students to generate content that can be shared with others during and beyond the end of a semester. Papers and projects developed through wikis can pass seamlessly from one group to another and from one class to another.

Evaluation of learning is perhaps the most important component of the model. CMSs/LMSs and other online tools and platforms provide a number of mechanisms to assist in this area. Papers, tests, assignments, and portfolios are among the major methods used for student learning assessment, and are easily done electronically. Essays and term projects pass back and forth between teacher and student without the need for paper. Oral classroom presentations are giving way to YouTube videos and podcasts. The portfolio is evolving into an electronic multimedia presentation of images, video, and audio that goes far beyond the three-inch, paper-filled binder. Weekly class discussions on discussion boards or blogs provide the instructor with an electronic record that can be reviewed over and over again to examine how students have participated and progressed over time. They are also most helpful to instructors to assess their own teaching and to review what worked and what did not work in a class. Increasingly, learning analytics are seen as the mechanisms for mining this trove of data to improve learning and teaching. In sum, online technology allows for a more seamless sharing of evaluation and assessment activities, and provides a permanent, accessible record for students and teachers.

The six components of the model described above form an integrated community of learning in which rich interaction, whether online or face-to-face, can be provided and blended across all modules. Furthermore, not every course must incorporate all of the activities and approaches of the model. The pedagogical objectives of a course should drive the activities and, hence, the approaches. For example, not every course needs to require collaborative learning or dialectic questioning. In addition to individual courses, faculty and instructional designers might consider examining an entire academic program to determine which components of the model best fit with overall programmatic goals and objectives. Here, the concept of learning extends beyond the course to the larger academic program where activities might integrate across courses. For example, some MBA programs enroll a cohort of students into three courses in the same semester but require that one or more assignments or projects be common to all three courses.

The critical question for our discussion, however, is whether this Blending with Pedagogical Purpose model can be modified or enlarged to be considered a model for online education in general. By incorporating several of the components from other theories and models discussed earlier in this article, this is a possibility. Presents a

Multimodal Model for Online Education that expands on the Blending with Purpose approach and adds several new components from Anderson and others, namely, community, interaction, and self-paced, independent instruction.

First, the concept of a learning community as promoted by Garrison, Anderson, and Archer (2000) and Wenger and Lave (1991) is emphasized. A course is conceived of as a learning community. This community can be extended to a larger academic program. Second, it is understood that interaction is a basic characteristic of the community and permeates the model to the extent needed. Third, and perhaps the most important revision, is the addition of the self-study/independent learning module that Anderson emphasized as incompatible with any of the community-based models. In this model, self-study/independent learning can be integrated with other modules as needed or as the primary mode of instructional delivery. Adaptive learning software, an increasingly popular form of self-study, can stand alone or be integrated into other components of the model. The latter is commonly done at the secondary school level where adaptive software programs are used primarily in stand-alone mode with teachers available to act as tutors when needed. Adaptive software is also integrated into traditional, face-to-face classes, such as science, where it is possible to have the instructor assign a lab activity that uses adaptive learning simulation software.

This Multimodal Model of Online Education attempts to address the issues that others, particularly Terry Anderson, have raised regarding elements that might be needed for an integrated or unified theory or model for online education. Whether or not this model finds acceptance is not yet clear. It is hoped that this article might serve as a vehicle for a critical examination of the model.

6.5.2 Applying the Integrated Model

To provide a clearer understanding of the integrated model, several examples of its application follow. Provides an example of the model as a representation of a self-paced, fully online course. The three major components [in green] for this course are: content as provided on an LMS/CMS, a self-paced study module, and assessment/evaluation. Other components of the model, such as a blog or discussion board to allow interaction among students, could be included but are not necessarily needed. This example is most appropriate for online programs that have rolling admissions and students are not limited by a semester schedule. Students proceed at their own pace to complete the course as is typical in some distance education programs. This example is scalable and can be used for large numbers of students.

A discussion board is also included to allow for ongoing interaction among students and teacher. This course would follow a semester schedule and would have a standard class size although most of the instruction would be provided by the self-paced study module. A standard course organization would be used, with a teacher or tutor assigned to guide and assist with instruction. The teacher or tutor could help students struggling with any of the self-paced material. This type of course is increasingly common in secondary schools, such as in credit-recovery courses.

Presentation of the course content is provided by a LMS or CMS along with other media and is used as needed by the teacher. The discussion board, blog, and wiki provide facilities for interaction among teachers and students, students and students, and students and content. In this course, the teacher could direct students to watch a fifteen-minute lecture available in the LMS database and then ask students to respond to a series of questions on the discussion board. Student responses can then be used as the basis for an interactive discussion board activity among students, guided by the teacher. The model also provides for reflection and collaborative activities.

The other modules are used to extend and enrich instruction. The teacher is the major guide for instruction and would be supplemented by content as needed by a LMS/CMS. The course would meet in a face-to-face classroom although some instructional activity would also be conducted online, either on a discussion board, a blog, or a collaborative wiki. The teacher would establish beforehand portions of the course that would meet in the face-to-face and online modes.

6.5.3 Attributes and Limitations of the Multimodal Model

The proposed Multimodal Model for Online Education includes many of the major attributes of other learning and online education theories and models. For example, behaviorists will find elements of self-study and independent learning in adaptive software. Cognitivists might appreciate reflection and dialectic questioning as important elements of the model. Social constructivists will welcome the emphasis on community and interaction throughout the model. Connectivists might value the collaboration and the possibility of student-generated content. Perhaps the most significant element of the model is its flexibility and ability to expand as new learning approaches, perhaps spurred by advances in technology, evolve.

The model is not without limitations. Learning theories can be approached through a number of perspectives and disciplines. Behavioral psychologists, cognitive psychologists, sociologists, and teacher educators might emphasize the need for deeper considerations of their perspectives for an online learning theory. The multimodal model here represents an integrated composite of several such perspectives but is essentially a pedagogical model and, therefore, may have greater appeal to instructional designers, faculty, and others who focus on learning objectives.

6.6 POSSIBLE WAYS TO USE THE MODEL

Several possible ways exist for using this model in research and practice. For example, researchers can use this model to better understand how design principles can be integrated in instruction to promote effective learning. Researchers can also conduct studies using the e-learning theory model to describe the design principles in learning contexts. In addition, this model can also help researchers address the following topics:

- How research-based e-learning methodologies can be used to create an effective e-learning course.
- How teachers can minimize extraneous load and manage intrinsic load to help effective learning.
- Which design principles could contribute most to effective student learning.

Furthermore, teachers could apply the e-learning theory model in their classrooms to create effective e-learning courses. For example, teachers can help students manage their intrinsic cognitive load by splitting the content so that students can acquire knowledge step by step. Teachers can also scaffold students with small portions of new content gradually so that students can control their learning in a self-paced e-learning environment. Further, teachers can use basic digital communication tools with visuals, text, and audio to demonstrate learning content in ways that can help to reduce students' intrinsic cognitive loads. In addition, teachers can apply effective graphics, audio, and text to minimize redundant content, concentrate on important content, and offer performance assistance to increase external memory. More examples of how teachers can apply e-learning theory in classrooms include:

- Reducing extraneous cognitive load by avoiding irrelevant audio or complex visuals to describe complicated text.
- Managing intrinsic cognitive load by segmenting content into small parts and using pretraining to teach concepts and facts separately.
- Fostering germane cognitive load by adding practice activities and relevant visuals.

There is no need to use all eleven principles to enhance students' learning. Specific design principles can be used in different situations, depending on teachers' instructional objectives and students' learning objectives.

Different theories of learning reflect different positions on the nature of knowledge. With the possible exception of connectivism, there is some form of empirical evidence to support each of the theories of learning outlined here.

However, while the theories suggest different ways in which all people learn, they do not automatically tell teachers or instructors how to teach. Indeed, theories of behaviourism, cognitivism and constructivism were all developed outside of education, in experimental labs, psychology, neuroscience, and psychotherapy respectively. Educators have had to work out how to move from the theoretical position to the practical one of applying these theories within an educational experience. In other words, they have had to develop teaching methods that build on such learning theories. The next section of the book examines a range of teaching methods that have been developed, their epistemological roots, and their implications for teaching in a digital age.

E-learning theory is about designing educational technology use to promote effective learning by reducing extraneous cognitive load and managing germane and intrinsic loads at students' appropriate levels. It can be challenging for teachers to design tasks at an appropriate level for students; the e-learning theory model can help teachers understand how cognitive load can be categorized and combined with design principles to make effective learning with technology happen.

CHAPTER

ONLINE TEACHING AND LEARNING 7

7.1 INTRODUCTION

Due to the threat of COVID-19, colleges and universities are facing decisions about how to continue teaching and learning while keeping their faculty, staff, and students safe from a public health emergency that is moving fast and not well understood. Many institutions have opted to cancel all face-to-face classes, including labs and other learning experiences, and have mandated that faculty move their courses online to help prevent the spread of the virus that causes COVID-19. The list of institutions of higher education making this decision has been growing each day. Institutions of all sizes and types—state colleges and universities, Ivy League institutions, community colleges, and others—are moving their classes online. Bryan Alexander has curated the status of hundreds of institutions.

Moving instruction online can enable the flexibility of teaching and learning anywhere, anytime, but the speed with which this move to online instruction is expected to happen is unprecedented and staggering. Although campus support personnel and teams are usually available to help faculty members learn about and implement online learning, these teams typically support a small pool of faculty interested in teaching online. In the present situation, these individuals and teams will not be able to offer the same level of support to all faculty in such a narrow preparation window. Faculty might feel like instructional MacGyvers, having to improvise quick solutions in less-than-ideal circumstances. No matter how clever a solution might be—and some very clever solutions are emerging—many instructors will understandably find this process stressful.

The temptation to compare online learning to face-to-face instruction in these circumstances will be great. In fact, an article in the Chronicle of Higher Education has already called for a "grand experiment" doing exactly that. This is a highly problematic suggestion, however. First and foremost, the politics of any such debate must be acknowledged. "Online learning" will become a politicized term that can take on any number of meanings depending on the argument someone wants to advance. In talking about lessons learned when institutions moved classes online during a shutdown in South Africa, Laura Czerniewicz starts with this very lesson and what happened around the construct of "blended learning" at the time. The idea of blended learning was drawn into political agendas without paying sufficient attention to the fact that institutions would make different decisions and invest differently, resulting in widely varying solutions and results from one institution to another. With some of that hindsight as wisdom, we seek to advance some careful distinctions that we hope can inform the evaluations and reflections that will surely result from this mass move by colleges and universities.

Online learning carries a stigma of being lower quality than face-to-face learning, despite research showing otherwise. These hurried moves online by so many institutions at once could seal the perception of online learning as a weak option, when in truth nobody making the transition to online teaching under these circumstances will truly be designing to take full advantage of the affordances and possibilities of the online format.

Researchers in educational technology, specifically in the subdiscipline of online and distance learning, have carefully defined terms over the years to distinguish between the highly variable design solutions that have been developed and implemented: distance learning, distributed learning, blended learning, online learning, mobile learning, and others. Yet an understanding of the important differences has mostly not diffused beyond the insular world of educational technology and instructional design researchers and professionals. Here, we want to offer an important discussion around the terminology and formally propose a specific term for the type of instruction being delivered in these pressing circumstances: emergency remote teaching.

Many active members of the academic community, including some of us, have been hotly debating the terminology in social media, and "emergency remote teaching" has emerged as a common alternative term used by online education researchers and professional practitioners to draw a clear contrast with what many of us know as high-quality online education. Some readers may take issue with the use of the term "teaching" over choices such as "learning" or "instruction." Rather than debating all of the details of those concepts, we selected "teaching" because of its simple definitions—"the act, practice, or profession of a teacher" and "the concerted sharing of knowledge and experience,"—along with the fact that the first tasks undertaken during emergency changes in delivery mode are those of a teacher/instructor/professor.

A recent survey of higher education in the United States reported that more than 2.35 million students enrolled in online courses in fall 2004. This report also noted that online education is becoming an important long-term strategy for many postsecondary institutions. Given the rapid growth of online education and its importance for postsecondary institutions, it is imperative that institutions of higher education provide quality online programs.

The literature addresses student achievement and satisfaction as two means to assess the quality of online education. Studies focused on academic achievement have shown mixed reviews, but some researchers point out that online education can be at least as effective as traditional classroom instruction. Several research studies on student satisfaction in online courses or programs reported both satisfied and dissatisfied students.

Faculty training and support is another critical component of quality online education. Many researchers posit that instructors play a different role from that of traditional classroom instructors when they teach online courses, as well as when they teach residential courses with Web enhancements. Such new roles for online instructors require training and support. Some case studies of faculty development programs indicate that such programs can have positive impacts on instructor transitions from teaching in a face-to-face to an online setting.

7.2 EFFECTIVE ONLINE EDUCATION

Online education, including online teaching and learning, has been studied for decades. Numerous research studies, theories, models, standards, and evaluation criteria focus on quality online learning, online teaching, and online course design. What we know from research is that effective online learning results from careful instructional design and planning, using a systematic model for design and development.

The design process and the careful consideration of different design decisions have an impact on the quality of the instruction. And it is this careful design process that will be absent in most cases in these emergency shifts.

One of the most comprehensive summaries of research on online learning comes from the book Learning Online: What Research Tells us about Whether, When and How. The authors identify nine dimensions, each of which has numerous options, highlighting the complexity of the design and decision-making process. The nine dimensions are modality, pacing, student-instructor ratio, pedagogy, instructor role online, student role online, online communication synchrony, role of online assessments, and source of feedback.

7.2.1 Online Learning Design Options (Moderating Variables)

Modality

- Fully online
- Blended (over 50% online)
- Blended (25–50% online)
- Web-enabled F2F

Pacing

- Self-paced (open entry, open exit)
- Class-paced
- Class-paced with some self-paced

Student-Instructor Ratio

- < 35 to 1
- 36–99 to 1
- 100–999 to 1
- > 1,000 to 1

Pedagogy

- Expository
- Practice
- Exploratory
- Collaborative

Role of Online Assessments

- Determine if student is ready for new content
- Tell system how to support the student (adaptive instruction)
- Provide student or teacher with information about learning state
- Input to grade
- Identify students at risk of failure
- Instructor Role Online
- Active instruction online
- Small presence online
- None

Student Role Online

- Listen or read
- Complete problems or answer questions
- Explore simulation and resources
- Collaborate with peers

Online Communication Synchrony

- Asynchronous only

- Synchronous only
- Some blend of both

Source of Feedback

- Automated
- Teacher
- Peers

Within each of these dimensions, there are options. Complicating matters, not all of the options are equally effective. For example, decisions around class size will greatly constrain what strategies you can use. Practice and feedback, for example, are well established in the literature, but it's harder to implement this as class size grows, eventually reaching a point where it's just not possible for an instructor to provide quality feedback. In the case of synchrony, what you choose will really depend on your learners' characteristics and what best meets their needs (adult learners require more flexibility, so asynchronous is usually best, perhaps with optional synchronous sessions, whereas younger learners benefit from the structure of required synchronous sessions).

Research on types of interaction—which includes student–content, student–student, and student–instructor—is one of the more robust bodies of research in online learning. In short, it shows that the presence of each of these types of interaction, when meaningfully integrated, increases the learning outcomes. Thus, careful planning for online learning includes not just identifying the content to cover but also carefully tending to how you're going to support different types of interactions that are important to the learning process. This approach recognizes learning as both a social and a cognitive process, not merely a matter of information transmission.

Those who have built online programs over the years will attest that effective online learning aims to be a learning community and supports learners not just instructionally but with co-curricular engagement and other social supports. Consider how much infrastructure exists around face-to-face education that supports student success: library resources, housing, career services, health services, and so on. Face-to-face education isn't successful because lecturing is good. Lectures are one instructional aspect of an overall ecosystem specifically designed to support learners with formal, informal, and social resources. Ultimately, effective online education requires an investment in an ecosystem of learner supports, which take time to identify and build. Relative to other options, simple online content delivery can be quick and inexpensive, but confusing that with robust online education is akin to confusing lectures with the totality of residential education.

Typical planning, preparation, and development time for a fully online university course is six to nine months before the course is delivered. Faculty are usually more comfortable teaching online by the second or third iteration of their online courses. It will be impossible for every faculty member to suddenly become an expert in online teaching and learning in this current situation, in which lead times range from a single day to a few weeks. While there are resources to which faculty can turn for assistance, the scale of change currently being required on many campuses will stress the systems that provide those resources and most likely will surpass their capacities. Let's face it: many of the online learning experiences that instructors will be able to offer their students will not be fully featured or necessarily well planned, and there's a high probability for suboptimal implementation. We need to recognize that everyone will be doing the best they can, trying to take just the essentials with them as they make a mad dash during the emergency. Thus, the distinction is important between the normal, everyday type of effective online instruction and that which we are doing in a hurry with bare minimum resources and scant time: emergency remote teaching.

7.2.2 Excellence in Online Teaching and Learning

The content for delivery via the World Wide Web is pre-determined and must be in place before students actually access online courses.

Fig. 1 World wide web.

The Web for Web-Based Courses

The process for designing and delivering web-based courses involves you as the content expert/instructor and the instructional design specialist. You will design the content of the course and identify what type(s) of multimedia would be most appropriate. The instructional design specialist assists you with the preparation of the multimedia and infuses the content with it; preparation of the course for electronic delivery; and in placing the content in the course management system. The process is illustrated in the following flowchart.

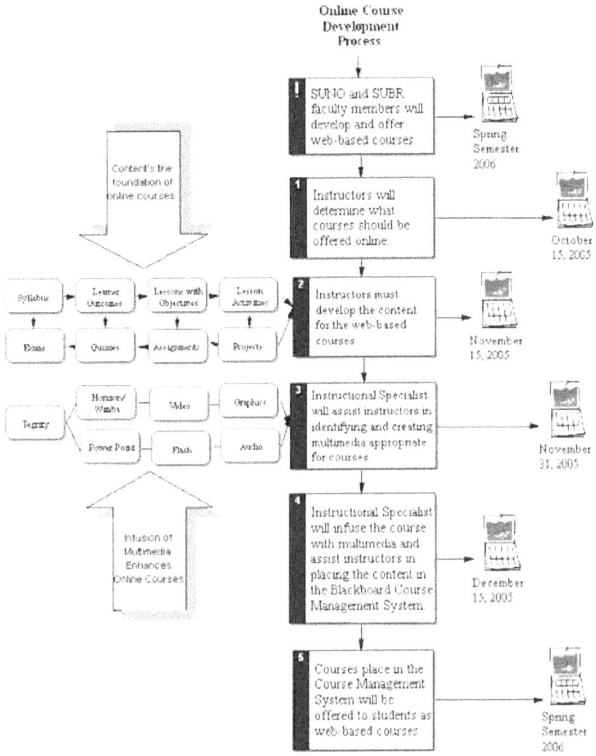

Fig. 2 The web for web-based courses.

As mentioned above, the content of an online course is the syllabus, lessons, activities, lessons, and assessments. The content is the "meat" of the course as opposed to its format or appearance and includes all of the words, images, and links which a user can read and interact with. A course management system is a tool that allows instructors and universities to develop and support online education. Often Internet based, a content management system is software that allows instructors to manage materials distribution, assignments, communications and other aspects of instruction for their courses. The content is placed within a course management system so that it can be delivered electronically via the internet.

7.3 THE FUTURE OF ONLINE TEACHING AND LEARNING IN HIGHER EDUCATION

Institutions of higher education have increasingly embraced online education, and the number of students enrolled in distance programs is rapidly rising in colleges and universities throughout the United States. In response to these changes in enrollment demands, many states, institutions, and organizations have been working on strategic plans to implement online education. At the same time, misconceptions and myths related to the difficulty of teaching and learning online, technologies available to support online instruction, the support and compensation needed for high-quality instructors, and the needs of online students create challenges for such vision statements and planning documents.

In part, this confusion swells as higher education explores dozens of e-learning technologies (for example, electronic books, simulations, text messaging, podcasting, wikis, blogs), with new ones seeming to emerge each week. Such technologies confront instructors and administrators at a time of continued budget retrenchments and rethinking. Adding to this dilemma, bored students are dropping out of online classes while pleading for richer and more engaging online learning experiences. Given the demand for online learning, the plethora of online technologies to incorporate into teaching, the budgetary problems, and the opportunities for innovation, we argue that online learning environments are facing a "perfect e-storm," linking pedagogy, technology, and learner needs.

Considering the extensive turbulence created by the perfect storm surrounding e-learning, it is not surprising that opinions are mixed about the benefits of online teaching and learning in higher education. As illustrated in numerous issues of the Chronicle of Higher Education during the past decade, excitement and enthusiasm for e-learning alternate with a pervasive sense of e-learning gloom, disappointment, bankruptcy and lawsuits, and myriad other contentions. Appropriately, the question arises as to where online learning is headed. Navigating online education requires an understanding of the current state and the future direction of online teaching and learning.

The study described here surveyed instructors and administrators in postsecondary institutions, mainly in the United States, to explore future trends of online education. In particular, the study makes predictions regarding the changing roles of online instructors, student expectations and needs related to online learning, pedagogical innovation, and projected technology use in online teaching and learning.

7.3.1 Review of Literature

We began this project with a review of past studies of the issues and trends in online teaching and learning in higher education.

7.4 PEDAGOGY AND TECHNOLOGY FOR ONLINE EDUCATION

Several research studies have covered effective pedagogical strategies for online teaching. Partlow and Gibbs, for instance, found from a Delphi study of experts in instructional technology and constructivism that online courses designed from constructivist principles should be relevant, interactive, project-based, and collaborative, while providing learners with some choice or control over their learning. Additionally, Keeton investigated effective online instructional practices based on a framework of effective teaching practices in face-to-face instruction in higher education. In this study, Keeton interviewed faculty in postsecondary institutions, who rated the effectiveness of online instructional strategies. These instructors gave higher ratings to online instructional strategies that "create an environment that supports and encourages inquiry," "broaden the learner's experience of the subject matter," and "elicit active and critical reflection by learners on their growing experience base."

In another study of pedagogical practices, Bonk found that only 23–45 percent of online instructors surveyed actually used online activities related to critical and creative thinking, hands-on performances, interactive labs, data analysis, and scientific simulations, although 40 percent of the participants said those activities were highly important in online learning environments. In effect, a significant gap separated preferred and actual online instructional practices.

Technology has played and continues to play an important role in the development and expansion of online education. Accordingly, many universities have reported an increase in the use of online tools. Over the past decade, countless efforts have sought to integrate emerging Internet technologies into the teaching and learning process in higher education. Several studies have reported cases related to the use of blogs to promote student collaboration and reflection. Some researchers also have promoted the plausibility of using wikis for online student collaboration, and podcasting is beginning to garner attention from educators for its instructional use. Although some discussions in the literature relate to effective practices in the use of emerging technologies for online education, empirical evidence to support or refute the effectiveness of such technologies, or, perhaps more importantly, guidance on how to use such tools effectively based on empirical evidence, is lacking.

7.4.1 Method

This study was based on a survey of individuals believed to have relevant experience with and insights into the factors affecting the present and future state of online education.

7.4.2 Participants

An online survey was conducted of college instructors and administrators who were members of either the Multimedia Educational Resource for Learning and Online Teaching (MERLOT) or the Western Cooperative for Educational Telecommunications (WCET), both premier associations for online education. MERLOT is a free and open resource for higher education with membership that, at the time of this study, included more than 12,000 college professors, instructional designers, and administrators who share and peer-evaluate their Web resources and materials (today, MERLOT has more than 35,000 members). WCET is an organization with 500–600 members that provides resources and information regarding the effective use of telecommunications technology in learning. Also surveyed were those who had posted one or more course syllabi at the

World Lecture Hall (WLH), which has approximately 2,000 members and was developed by the University of Texas for faculty to share syllabi.

This study is a part of a longitudinal effort to understand the use of technology in teaching, within both higher education and corporate training settings. The second author had previously surveyed MERLOT and WLH members on the state of online learning as well as corporate trainers on online training and blended learning.

7.4.3 Instrument

Using an online survey service, SurveyShare, we developed an online questionnaire as an instrument for this survey study. The questionnaire consisted of 42 questions grouped into three sections related to the current status and future trends of online education in higher education. The first section included 10 questions regarding respondents' demographic information. The second section included seven questions about the current status of online learning at the respondents' organizations. The third section included items regarding predictions about online teaching and learning. The survey used various types of questions, including Likert-type, multiple-choice, and open-ended questions.

7.5 DATA COLLECTION AND ANALYSIS

The survey took place from late November 2003 to early January 2004. An invitation was sent by e-mail to the sample of instructors, instructional designers, and administrators described earlier. The e-mail included information about the study as well as the URL to the survey site. Of more than 12,000 who received the e-mail request, 562 completed the survey. The participants responded to the survey anonymously, and the data were stored in the hosted online survey service. Descriptive data analyses (such as frequencies) were conducted using the data analysis tool provided in the online survey site.

7.5.1 Results

Our study confirmed some commonly held beliefs about online education, refuted others, and provided a range of predictions about the future of technology-enabled education.

7.6 DEMOGRAPHICS OF ONLINE INSTRUCTORS

Sixty-six percent of the survey respondents held teaching positions (professors, instructors, or lecturers), while nearly one-fourth were administrators or instructional designers. Respondents represented institutions of various types: approximately half were employed by public, four-year colleges or universities; 23 percent by community colleges or vocational institutes; and 16 percent by private postsecondary institutions. A large majority (87 percent) said their institutions offer online courses, and about 70 percent of them had taught online courses.

As shown in Figure 3, respondents' experience with online teaching varied from none to more than 10 years. Although not every respondent had online teaching experience, more than 95 percent had experience integrating computer or Web technology into their face-to-face teaching.

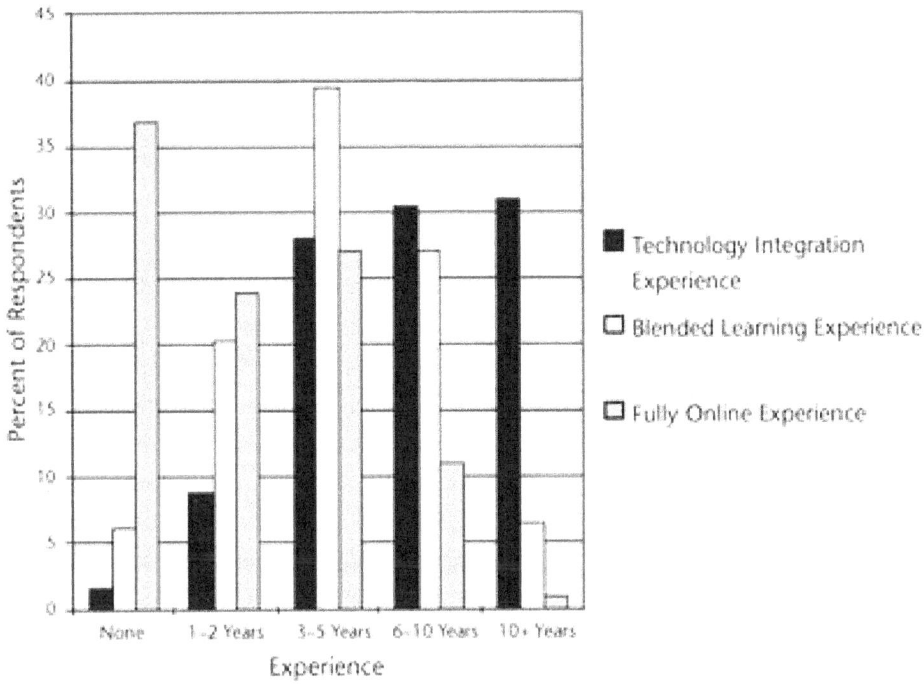

Fig. 3. Demographic of online respondents.

Survey results show that women appear to be teaching online in far greater numbers than just a few years ago. In fact, more than half of the respondents (53 percent) were women. Such findings were surprising because a similar study conducted a few years earlier was dominated by male instructors who were full professors at tier-one universities. Perhaps female instructors had become more comfortable teaching and sharing activities online during the few years that elapsed between surveys, or perhaps support for instructors had improved on college campuses, or both.

7.6.1 Emerging Technology

When asked about several emerging technologies for online education, 27 percent of respondents predicted that use of Course Management Systems (CMSs) would increase most drastically in the next five years. Those surveyed also said that video streaming, online testing and exam tools, and learning object libraries would find significantly greater use on campus during this time. Between 5 and 10 percent of respondents expected to see increases in asynchronous discussion tools, Video conferencing, synchronous presentation tools, and online testing.

The survey also asked what technology would most impact the delivery of online learning during the next five years. Respondents could select one of 14 key technologies.

About 18 percent of respondents predicted that reusable content objects and wireless technologies would have the most significant impact. Smaller percentages (from 7 to almost 14 percent) selected peer-to-peer collaboration, digital libraries, simulations and games, assistive technologies, and digital portfolios. In contrast, less than 5 percent predicted that e-books, intelligent agents, Tablet PCs, virtual worlds, language support, and wearable technologies would have significant impact on the delivery of online learning. These findings seem to reflect the perceived importance of online technologies for sharing and using preexisting content.

Additionally, respondents predicted that advances in Internet technology are likely to increase the use of multimedia and interactive simulations or games in online learning during the next five to 10 years. Only about one in 10, however, predicted that advances in Internet technology would enhance Video conferencing or international collaboration, and just one in 16 thought it might offer greater chances to interact with field experts or practitioners. Again, the focus was on enhancing content and associated content delivery, not on the social interactions, cross-cultural exchanges, or new feedback channels that wider bandwidth could offer. Such responses indicate that respondents still see learning as content-driven, not based on social interactions and distributed intelligence. The emphasis remains on a knowledge-transmission approach to education, not one rich in peer feedback, online mentoring, or cognitive apprenticeship.

7.6.2 Enormous Learner Demands

Our study revealed a number of trends related to areas of growth in online education, future needs for online instructors, and the dominance of online versus face-to-face instruction.

Growth of Online Programs/Degrees: Comparing current online offerings and projected future online offerings at respondents' institutions yields predictions about the areas of growth in online programs and degrees. Most respondents expected considerable growth in online certification and recertification programs in the next few years, as well as in associate's degrees. Yet, our survey respondents predicted little growth in the number of institutions that offer online master's or doctoral programs in the future.

Although more than half of the respondents (54 percent) expected that their institutions would offer online master's or doctoral programs in the coming years, almost the same number of respondents (53 percent) reported that their institutions were presently offering online master's or doctoral programs. In contrast, respondents predicted that certification and recertification programs would see 10–20 percent growth from present offerings. Such responses indicate that higher education institutions might be wise to explore certificate and short-program offerings rather than full degree programs.

Online Instructors' Readiness: Will online instructors be ready to meet the challenges brought by the projected increases in learner demands for online education? About half of the respondents predicted that monetary support for and pedagogical competency of online instructors would most significantly affect the success of their online programs (see Table 1). In addition, instructors' technical competency was the third most pressing factor.

Nevertheless, as illustrated in Table 2, pedagogical skill was deemed more important than technological skill for effective online teaching. With regard to the needs for pedagogical competency of online instructors, a majority of the respondents expected that online instructors would typically have received some sort of training in online teaching either internally or externally by the year 2010.

Table 1: Factors that will most significantly affect the sucess of online programs.

Response Option	Number of Respondents	Response Rate (%)
Monetary support	131	24.7
Pedagogical competency of online instructors	121	22.9
Technical competency of online instructors	81	15.3
Improvements in online technologies	57	10.8
Marketing	47	8.9
Rigorous quality management in the accreditation process	42	7.9
Other	38	7.2
Joining a consortium	12	2.3
Subtotal	529	95.3
No response	33	4.7
Total	562	100.0

The Rise of Blended Learning. The survey asked respondents for their predictions related to the growth of online education in the next few years. Respondents indicated that more emphasis is expected on blended learning—instruction that combines face-to-face with online offerings—than on fully online courses. Those surveyed predicted a distinct shift from about one-quarter of classes being blended today to perhaps the vast majority of courses having some Web component by the end of the decade.

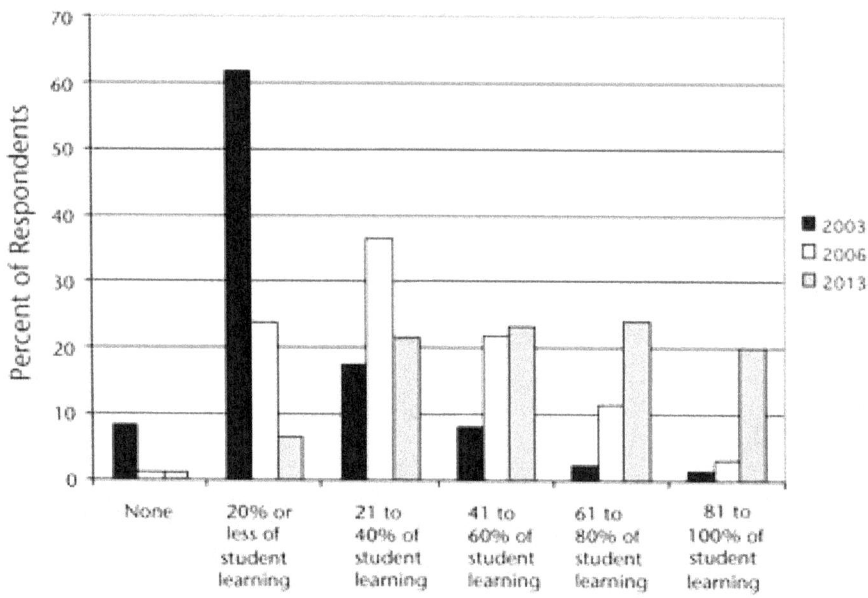

Fig. 4. Expected growth of blended learing.

7.6.3 Enhanced Pedagogy

Although the use of CMSs in higher education has increased rapidly and is likely the foundation for the rapid increase in the number of online learners during the past decade, some researchers argue that CMSs are promoted as ways to manage learners rather than to promote rich, interactive experiences.

As a result, enhancing pedagogy is perhaps the most important factor in navigating the perfect e-storm. In the present study, respondents made predictions about the quality of online education in the near future and about how online courses would be taught and evaluated.

The Quality of Future Online Education. Survey respondents generally agreed with recent Sloan reports that the quality of online education will improve in the future. Sixty percent of respondents expected that the quality of online courses would be identical to traditional instruction by the year 2006 (see Figure 5).

Also, a majority of the respondents predicted that the quality of online courses would be superior to (47 percent) or the same as (39 percent) that of traditional instruction by 2013. Only 8 percent predicted that the quality of online courses would be inferior in 2013.

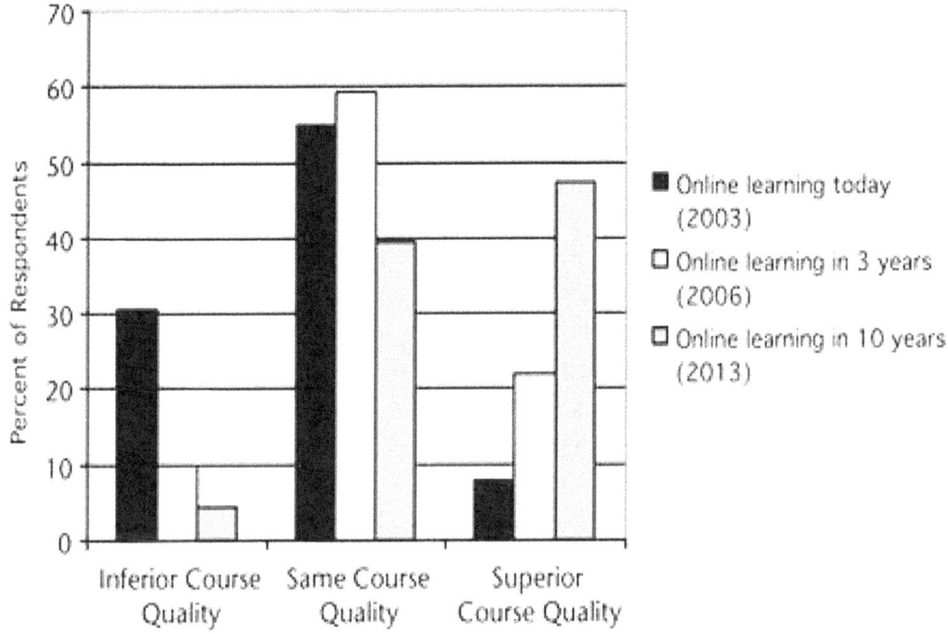

Fig. 5. Expected quality of online versus traditional education.

Similarly, a large majority of respondents predicted that learning outcomes of online students would be either the same as (39 percent) or superior to (42 percent) those of traditionally taught students by 2013. In effect, the trend is for course quality and learner outcomes to steadily and significantly improve during the coming decade. Although we did not ask about reasons for the increase in quality, such numbers should be interesting and valuable to administrators, instructors, students, and other online learning stakeholders.

In terms of factors that can improve online learners' success, respondents said that training students to self-regulate their learning (22 percent) was needed most, followed by better measures of student readiness (17 percent), better evaluation of student achievement (17 percent), and better CMSs to track student learning. Nine percent said additional technology training is needed. This concern about learner self-regulation is ironic in a world dominated and driven by learning management systems that are primarily used to manage students, as alluded to earlier. Follow-up surveys might address whether learners perceive this mixed message and whether they prefer to be managed online or engage in more self-directed online environments.

As Carmean and Haefner argued, there is a need for CMS environments that foster deeper student learning and engagement. They noted that such environments might foster student choice among various activities, reflection, apprenticeship, synthesis, real-world problem solving, and rich, timely feedback. More recently, Weigel added to this argument by suggesting that the next-generation CMS should foster a more learner-centered environment that rich in critical thinking, student exploration, peer learning and knowledge construction, interdisciplinary experiences incorporating a community of educators (practitioners, business leaders, alumni, and others), and educational opportunities.

Online Teaching Skills. Instructors' abilities to teach online are critical to the quality of online education. Unlike our earlier study related to the state of online learning in 2001, which included many questions about online learning tools and features, the present study focused more on learning outcomes and pedagogical skills. For instance, this study found that the most important skills for an online instructor during the next few years will be how to moderate or facilitate learning and how to develop or plan for high-quality online courses (see Table 2). Being a subject-matter expert was the next most important skill. In effect, the results indicate that planning and moderating skills are perhaps more important than actual "teaching" or lecturing skills in online courses. As Salmon pointed out, online instructors are moderators or facilitators of student learning.

Table 2: Skills needed to teach online in 2010.

Response Options	Number of Respondents	Response Rate (%)
Course developer	355	66.4
Facilitator or moderator	352	65.8
Subject-matter expert	298	55.7
Instructor or lecturer	273	51.0
Student counselor or advisor	193	36.1
Technology Trainer	162	30.3
Program coordinator or developer	153	28.6
Other	17	3.2
Subtotal	535	96.4
No response	27	3.6
Total	562	100.0

Pedagogical Techniques. Over half of the survey respondents predicted that online collaboration, case-based learning, and Problem-Based Learning (PBL) would be the preferred instructional methods for online instructors in the coming decade. In contrast, few respondents expected that instructors would rely on lectures, modeling, or Socratic instruction for their online teaching in the future (see Table 3). In other words, survey respondents predicted that more learner-centered techniques would be used in the future, indicating a marked shift from traditional teacher-directed approaches.

Table 3: Pedagogical techniques to be used more widely online in the coming decade.

Response Options	Number of Respondents	Response Rate (%)
Group problem-solving and collaborative tasks	356	65.4
Problem-based learning	316	58.1
Discussion	237	43.6
Case-based strategies	228	41.2
Simulations or role play	198	36.4
Student-generated content	190	34.9
Coaching or mentoring	162	29.8
Guided learning	155	28.5
Exploratory or discovery	147	27.0
Lecturing or teacher-directed activities	60	11.0
Modeling of the solution process	49	9.0
Socratic questioning	47	8.6
Subtotal	544	98.0
No response	18	2.0
Total	562	100.0

Existing research indicates that online instructors tend to use easy-to-implement tools, resources, and strategies rather than complex PBL, virtual teaming, cross-cultural collaboration, simulations, and other forms of rich interactive media If the prediction for more learner-centered pedagogies online is realized, it would be interesting to study whether those teaching online transfer such pedagogical skills to their face-to-face instructional activities.

Our findings also indicated that, in general, respondents envisioned the Web in the next few years more as a tool for virtual teaming or collaboration, critical thinking, and enhanced student engagement than as an opportunity for student idea generation and expression of creativity. This is not surprising, given that most instruction in higher education is focused on consumption and evaluation of knowledge, not on the generation of it. Perhaps online training departments and units need to offer more examples of how to successfully embed creative and generative online tasks and activities.

Evaluation and Assessment of Online Courses. Evaluation is an important part of ensuring the quality of online courses and programs. Table 4 summarizes respondents' predictions about future trends concerning the evaluation of online learning. When asked how the quality of online education will be most effectively measured during the coming decade, 44 percent answered that a comparison of online student achievement with that of students in face-to-face classroom settings would be the most effective, followed by student performance in simulated tasks of real-world activities (15 percent), calculations of return on investment (10 percent), and student course evaluations (9 percent). Clearly, respondents believe that face-to-face instruction provides a valid benchmark for teaching and learning outcomes and that online performance should at least equal its effectiveness. Such views, while politically important, seem to forget that much of the learning that occurs online could not take place in a face-to-face delivery mode (for example, asynchronous online discussions or online mentoring). It also assumes that face-to-face instruction is superior. What if institutions took the opposite stance and measured face-to-face courses based on whether they could accomplish all that online instruction can?

Table 4: Prediction about how the quality of online learning will be measured.

Response Options	Number of Respondents	Response Rate (%)
Comparison of student achievement with those in live or face-to-face classroom settings	237	43.8
Student performance in simulated tasks of real-world activities	80	14.8
Student course evaluations	47	8.7
Course completion rates	36	6.6
Course interactivity ratings and evaluations	24	4.4
Other	24	4.4
Student placement into jobs	23	4.3
Student satisfaction questionnaires	17	3.1
Computer log data of student usage and activity	1	0.2
Subtotal	541	97.5
No response	21	2.5
Total	562	100.0

As for the forms of evaluation that will be used during the next few years, respondents predicted that online practice quizzes and exams would be most highly used, followed by online surveying and polling, course evaluations, and online quizzes and exams. In particular, more than 90 percent of the respondents predicted that online surveys would be used as an important student research tool or as a teaching device in addition to student assessment and course evaluation. This finding affirms our belief that online surveys offer the chance to be learner-centered because they allow students to collect, analyze, and report on real-world data and projects.

7.7 DISCUSSION AND CONCLUSION

As institutions of higher education continue to embrace and debate online learning, it is important to envision where the field is headed. What might the next generation of online learning environments look like? Will they move from warehousing students in online environments to engaging them in interactive and motivational activities? What technological and pedagogical advantages will they offer? Current studies provide a glimpse of the pedagogical and technological possibilities. Clearly, we are entering a unique and exciting era in online teaching and learning. And perhaps the perfect e-storm is becoming less cloudy and ominous.

7.7.1 Implications of the Findings

Institutions of higher education need to consider whether they are ready to meet growing learner demands in the coming years. First of all, most respondents agreed that blended learning would have greater significance in higher education in the future. Although some institutions have already embraced blended learning, many others are slower at adopting it for various reasons. Perhaps leadership from the institution is crucial for faculty to receive adequate support to implement changes in the teaching process.

If the quality of online education is to improve as projected from this study, campuses must also look at the pedagogical issues in online learning. Collaboration, case learning, and PBL are likely to be the preferred methods of online instructors, with few relying solely on traditional methods. The data presented here also indicate that the continued explosion in online learning will bring increased attention to workshops, courses, and degree programs in how to moderate or mentor with online learning. Given that many respondents expect to receive some sort of training and support from their institutions to be ready for online teaching, colleges and universities need to consider how they will respond to these needs.

In addition, our study indicates that postsecondary institutions are finally focusing on how online learning can develop student collaboration and evaluation skills. In fact, most now see the potential of the Web in the coming years as a tool for virtual teaming or collaboration, critical thinking, and enhanced student engagement, though not necessarily as a tool for creative and individual expression. Do current CMSs provide tools to realize the potentials of the Web for innovative teaching and learning? Perhaps recent developments in open source courseware will force CMS vendors to develop and market more pedagogically engaging tools and resources.

This survey also forecasts enormous growth in online certification and recertification programs, as well as some growth in associate's and master's degree programs during the coming decade. In terms of technology, the study reveals interest among online instructors in wireless technologies, simulations, digital libraries, and reusable content objects. Perhaps we are entering a world where learning objects will be at our fingertips. Learning objects on different topics will likely be something you can grab like magazines and newspapers on the way into a plane, bus, or train. In addition, as bandwidth increases with the next-generation Internet technologies and capabilities, simulation and gaming tasks that online students engage in will be more realistic and authentic.

7.8 STUDY LIMITATIONS AND RECOMMENDATIONS FOR RESEARCH

More than two years have passed since we conducted the survey. This time gave us the opportunity to see how the predictions our survey respondents made have played out. We have continued to witness accelerating growth of learner demands for online learning as well as the potential for enhanced online pedagogy due, in part, to the recent open source movement. Predictions related to emerging technologies seem to have been inaccurate, given that only 1 percent said that the use of blogs would increase dramatically by 2008. Given the thousands of new blogs each day, it is safe to say that this prediction did not hold.

This study did not explore actual online teaching and learning practices. It is likely that some responses were related to recent fads that may or may not be sustainable. In addition, we did not survey students for their perceptions of online learning trends and possibilities.

A study of students might indicate that they deem different technologies to be important and on the cusp of significant growth. In a learner-centered world, who can better predict technology trends today—instructors or students? This study also indicated that blended learning will perhaps be a more significant growth area than fully online learning.

Follow-up studies might focus on aspects of blended learning that institutions need to address, such as types of blended learning, activities that lead to blended-learning success, and instructor training for blended-learning situations.

CHAPTER

ONLINE TEACHING TECHNIQUES 8

8.1 INTRODUCTION

Traditional forms of teaching around the world are changing rapidly with the advancement of technology. Even in physical classrooms, technology has taken on a bigger role, changing how lessons are delivered and received.

While there are numerous teaching methods, most of the traditional methods used in class can be applied equally efficiently online.

However the teaching method you select will change based on your teaching philosophy, objectives, subject area, and classroom demographics.

In this post, we'll list down x effective online teaching methods that'll help simplify the delivery of your virtual lessons.

8.2 ONLINE TEACHING METHODS

Listed below are some of the most effective methods of online teaching.

8.2.1 Presentations

Presentations, like in the physical classroom, are one of the most common methods of online teaching.

This technique helps make a more significant impact on students – most of whom are visual learners – than a teacher simply relaying information out of a textbook.

Most importantly, presentations allow you to incorporate visuals (images, GIFs, videos, etc.) which makes it easier to deliver and comprehend complex information and data while making the lesson more engaging.

Plus you can also share your presentation with the students after the lesson for revision and studying.

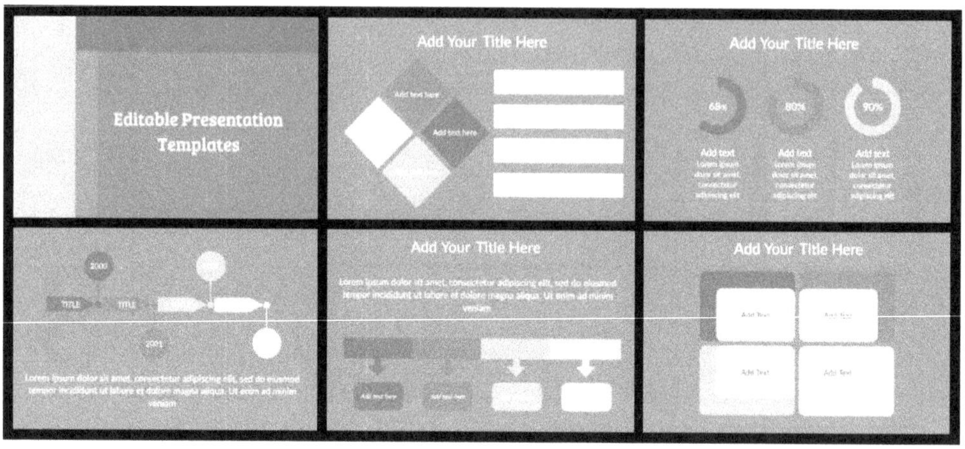

Fig. 1. Presentation template.

Here are a few presentation tools to get started with

- Google Slides
- Microsoft PowerPoint
- Prezi
- SlideShare

Online, presentations are more effective when delivered over video conferencing with a tool like Zoom or Google Meet.

8.2.2 Online Whiteboard

Online whiteboards have risen as a popular choice to virtually emulate the in-person classroom experience shared between teachers and students. They offer an infinite canvas, shape libraries to create different diagrams and charts, pre-made templates, sketching, typing, image import options, etc.

Unlike the traditional whiteboards, they also let you digitize the content created, hence allowing you to re-share them and refer to them at a later time. You can also collaborate with students on the same canvas in real-time which paves the way to

- Carry out assignments
- Brainstorm around lessons
- Mind mapping
- Do interactive exercises such as quizzes
- Review homework and leave feedback

8.2.3 Live Online Classes

Technology has made it straightforward to deliver lectures online even if you are not in the same room as the students, replicating many of the elements of face-to-face interaction.

Using video conferencing tools you can connect and communicate with students across the globe to deliver lessons. Incorporating an online whiteboard, you can make the classes even more engaging.

Lectures tend to put students in a passive role. Therefore to keep students engaged throughout the class online;

- Be prepared by outlining the content of the lesson
- Ask questions during and after the lesson and leave time for students to answer
- Carry out discussions around the topic and encourage students to participate actively
- Make use of graphic organizers, images, posters, videos, visuals, etc.
- Break down the main topic into sub-parts which will allow you to deliver the lecture in smaller chunks making it more effective in terms of keeping the students focused and engaged
- Set clear guidelines for online class etiquette for students to maintain

8.3 PRE-RECORDED VIDEO LECTURES

The benefit of pre-recorded lectures, as opposed to the live ones, is that the former allows the students to learn at their own pace at any time without the presence of the teacher. It also gives them material to go over during revision.

The teacher or instructor, on the other hand, can use the videos to avoid repetitive teaching between different classes.

To create effective pre-recorded lectures;

- Start with a script. Outline the talking points and what should go on each slide.
- Practice as necessary. Unless you are confident enough to do it in one go, rehearse what you will be saying prior to recording.
- Keep it short. If the video is longer than 20 minutes, consider breaking it up into smaller videos. This will not only come in handy when uploading them online but in case you need to replace the content with new information, it'll be easier to re-do a few minutes video than an hour-long one.
- Have everything ready before recording. Make sure that you are in a place devoid of distracting noises and backgrounds, and that your script and props are in place.
- If you are recording your screen, make sure to have closed unnecessary tabs and apps that may send you notifications.
- Maintain good eye contact with the camera and a tone you would use in a normal one-on-one conversation

8.3.1 Flipped Classroom

The flipped classroom has become one of the most popular teaching methods in education during the past few years.

It entails a strategy opposite to the traditional class format; here the students are required to review class material prior to the actual lesson, hence reserving actual in-class time to put what they have learned into test with teacher-guided activities such as debates, problem-solving, in-depth discussions, quizzes, etc.

Videos have become a core element in the flipped classroom model. While many teachers create videos of their own, some also use videos created by other teachers. Video-sharing platforms such as YouTube can be utilized to share these among students.

Some of the other effective techniques for the flipped classroom include,

- Online quizzes – help students self-regulate what they have learnt and further improve their comprehension of the subject
- Polls – help students reflect and analyze what they have learned by polling their own choices
- Infographics – increase student engagement and enhances memory
- Mind maps or word clouds – allow students to brainstorm around topic areas and develop their thinking skills

8.3.2 Game-Based Teaching

Game-based learning is a popular technique used to improve student engagement and retain attention. This approach helps reduce student anxiety and increase their involvement, especially when teaching complex concepts. It also paves the way for weaker students to develop their competences by interacting actively with their classmates.

And in online teaching, games help close the gaps in the interaction between face-to-face learning and online learning. Depending on the game you select, here are a few tips to keep in mind when carrying it out online,

- Ensure that all students in the virtual classroom have access to the same set of data. You can share your screen or communicate them to your audience using a video conferencing tool
- Use the chat option to take down concerns and questions of students and clarify and you can answer them live
- Allow students time to reflect their answers and discuss them with other group members by breaking down the game into subsequent periods
- Allow students to carry out discussions using chat platforms such as WhatsApp, Skype, Slack, Facebook, Zoom breakout rooms, etc.

Class Blog

A blog can be a great place for students to share what they have learned in the form of in-depth articles. Students can work on blog posts individually or in groups. It's a great strategy to improve students' research skills and encourage them to explore self-learning.

The teacher can also use the blog as a platform to share learning material for the lessons.

Live Chatting

Live chatting is another great way to replicate the real-time discussions that take place in the classroom. Platforms such as Slack, WhatsApp, Facebook Messenger, Skype, etc. allow students and teachers to communicate and brainstorm around lessons. The chat itself will provide the students with information for revising before exams or assignments.

Make sure to set clear guidelines to ensure that all students get an equal chance to communicate their ideas and pose their questions.

Discussion Boards and Forums

These tools provide students the space to share what they have learned or what they want to know more about with others in the classroom including the teacher.

You can maintain different discussion boards for individual lesson topics, so it'll be more organized. You can create one easily with an online visual workspace like Creately and share it with all students with one public edit link giving everyone quick access.

You can also create separate Slack channels, Facebook groups, or Whatsapp groups for forum discussions.

8.4 ONLINE COURSES AND MULTIPLE INSTRUCTIONAL STRATEGIES

Traditionally, in a teacher-centered classroom, instructors control their environment because they have a monopoly on information. In an online course, with instant access to vast resources of data and information, students are no longer totally dependent on faculty for knowledge. As faculty are beginning to teach online, learning is becoming more collaborative, contextual and active. Educators must first design their curriculum, goals and objectives and then consider how the online environment can best serve the instructional objectives and activities of that curriculum.This requires changes in pedagogy, with instructors taking the role of facilitators of information while guiding students toward solutions. In order for online learning to be successful, teachers as well as learners must take on new roles in the teaching-learning relationship, and faculty must be willing to release control of learning to the students.

Online learning environments permit a full range of interactive methodologies, and instructors have found that in adapting their courses to online models, they are paying more attention to the instructional design of their courses. As a result, the quality, quantity, and patterns of communication students practice during learning are improved.

Of the many instructional strategies available for use in the online learning environment, most have not been developed specifically for online instruction, but are currently used in traditional classrooms, and can be successfully adapted for facilitating online learning. Educators should choose instructional strategies that are most effective for accomplishing a particular educational objective. From this perspective, instructional strategies are tools available to educators for designing and facilitate learning. Below are ten instructional strategies which have been effectively used in the traditional classroom and can likewise be used in the online learning environment:

8.4.1 Learning Contracts

Learning contracts connect educational needs to individual student needs and are useful when there is diversity in learner needs and interests in a class. A learning contract is a formal agreement written by a learner which details what will be learned, how the learning will be accomplished, the period of time involved, and the specific evaluation criteria to be used in judging the completion of the learning. Learning contracts help the educator and learner share the responsibility for learning.

Contract learning can bring about many practical benefits, including deeper involvement of the learner in the learning activities which they themselves have been involved in planning. Once a learner passes through the stage of confusion and anxiety associated with developing a contract, he/she will get excited about carrying out their own plans. Another benefit of utilizing contract learning is an increase of accountability, since the learning contract provides more functional and validated evidence of the learning outcomes. The contract also provides a means for the learner to receive continuous feedback regarding progress toward accomplishing learning objectives.

Learning contracts can be extremely effective in the online environment. Because physically meeting with the class to discuss learning goals, objectives, and expectations is not possible online, instructors must be very clear and concise in what is expected from the learner. Likewise, the learner must also be clear about what he/she expects from the instructor and the course. A learning contract can facilitate negotiation and clarity of learning goals and outcomes. Sample learning contracts can be placed on a web page for the student to use as examples, and students can be encouraged to brainstorm ideas for learning contracts with their online peers as well as negotiate the final contract with the instructor through utilizing email or online conferencing.

8.4.2 Lecture

The lecture is one of the most frequently used instructional methods in adult education. It assumes the educator to be the expert and is an efficient way of disseminating information.

Most educators agree that the purpose of lectures is to lay foundations as the student works through the subject, and good lecturers know their students and develop their lectures according to the students' needs. Most importantly, lectures are most effective when used in combination with other instructional strategies.

Online lectures can be presented in a variety of ways. Lecture notes can be placed on a web page for the learner to review. Notes can be put together in a packet and either downloaded from the Internet or sent via snail mail. Lectures can also be presented via audio or video over the Internet. Also, links to related resources and other Web sites can be embedded in online lectures. Online lectures are likely to be shorter and more to the point than lectures in live classrooms which often extend far beyond the attention span of the audience. Short lectures provide enough information to serve as a basis for further reading, research, or other learning activities. Another obvious advantage of online lectures is that they are readily available for students to revisit again and again as needed.

8.5 DISCUSSION

Discussion is the instructional strategy most favored by adult learners because it is interactive and encourages active, participatory learning. The discussion format encourages learners to analyze alternative ways of thinking and acting and assists learners in exploring their own experiences so they can become better critical thinkers. The discussion is often the heart of an online course.

The Internet offers several modes for discussion including mailing lists which focus on particular topics and online conferencing programs. Both of these options utilize asynchronous communication. Synchronous (real time) communication can be offered by utilizing chat rooms or text-based virtual reality environments, better known as Multi-user Domains (MUDs) or Multi-user Object Oriented Environments (MOOs).

8.5.1 Self-Directed Learning

Self-directed learning is learning initiated and directed by the learner and can include self-paced, independent, and individualized learning as well as self-instruction. Whatever terminology is used, self-directed learning places the responsibility for learning directly on the learner. Learners who take the initiative in learning and are proactive learners learn more and better than passive learners (reactive learners). Proactive learners enter into learning more purposefully and with greater motivation. They also tend to retain and make use of what they learn better and longer than reactive learners. The independent learner is one who is more involved and active within the learning process.

Online learning supports the self-directed learner in pursuing individualized, self-paced learning activities. The learner, working at a computer at a convenient time and pace, is able to search and utilize the vast resources of the Internet research nearly any topic imaginable. Students can visit libraries, museums and various institutes world-wide, talk to professionals, access recent research, and read newspapers and peer reviewed scholarly journals online. Students can write collaboratively with peers and even publish written and multimedia products on web pages.

8.5.2 Mentorship

The aim of mentorship is to promote learner development drawing out and giving form to what the student already knows. A mentor serves as a guide rather than a provider of knowledge and serves the function of introducing students to the new world, interpreting it for them, and helping them to learn what they need to know to function in it. Mentors in education teach by interpreting the environment and modeling expected behaviors. They also support, challenge, and provide vision for their students.

A major benefit to online mentorship is the opportunity for frequent, convenient communication between mentor and student. Weekly or even daily journals and communications can be sent between mentor and student via e-mail, providing an ongoing "dialogue" which supports the development of the mentor relationship and offers numerous opportunities for timely feedback on student questions, concerns and issues.

8.5.3 Small Group Work

In small groups learners can discuss content, share ideas, and solve problems. They present their own ideas as well as consider ideas put forth by others. In this way, they can be exposed to a variety of viewpoints on a given subject. There are many small group formats that encourage and provide opportunities for interaction:

The discussion group allows learners to reflect on a subject under discussion and present their views. Discussion within the small group is often on high intellectual levels - specifically analysis, synthesis, and evaluation.

Guided design encourages interaction in small groups. Here the focus is on developing learners' decision-making skills as well as on teaching specific concepts and principles. Participants work to solve open-ended problems which require outside class work to gather information. This format encourages learners to think logically, communicate ideas, and apply steps in a decision-making process. Learners are also required to apply the information they have learned, exchange ideas, and reflect on suggested solutions. The instructor's role is to act as a consultant to the groups.

Role playing is another format available for use with small groups and involves recreating a situation relating to a real-world problem in which participants act out various roles. This promotes an understanding of other people's positions and their attitudes as well as the procedures that might be used for diagnosing and solving problems. Role playing can be used to simulate real-life group work situations and can help learners gain a fuller understanding of a problem or situation.

Games requiring two or more groups to compete while attempting to meet a set of objectives is another form of small group learning. The game follows a set of rules and procedures and information is provided which requires decision making. Most instructional games reflect typical real-life situations. The rules, procedures, and objectives of the game should be clear and concise.

Online learning environments offer several distinct benefits for small group work. First, they allow small groups to work independently while still having access to the instructor. In some cases where it is difficult for all members of an online class to meet synchronously, small groups can be organized according to their time zones, making it possible to find a convenient time to meet synchronously. Larger groups can benefit by communicating asynchronously via conferencing programs. A second benefit of online environments for group work is that they equalize control among participants. Factors such as geography, gender, or disabilities do not disadvantage learners in this environment. Finally, the instructor is able to respond directly to questions and needs of particular groups without taking the time of other groups.

8.6 PROJECT

Online projects give students an opportunity to pursue their special interests and can be done individually or within groups. Projects also provide students with practical experience and a sense of accomplishment. Using projects in a learning activity makes the learning more relevant to the learners. Products can be shared with others in the class and critiqued. Many times an individual project is only critiqued by the facilitator, but by sharing individual projects with other participants, the learner has the opportunity to obtain more diverse viewpoints and feedback.

Many of the instructional strategies discussed above can be considered group projects. Group projects can include simulations, role playing, case studies, problem solving exercises, group collaborative work, debates, small group discussion, and brainstorming. As with individual projects, participants in group projects should receive peer feedback to expose them to diverse viewpoints. With independent and group projects learners pursue special interests, write or create for an audience, and publish or present their findings and conclusions via the Internet. The Internet provides the potential of receiving feedback from experts or interested peers outside the course by accessing the project online.

8.6.1 Collaborative Learning

Collaborative learning is the process of getting two or more students to work together to learn. Students often work in small groups composed of participants with differing ability levels and using a variety of learning activities to master material initially developed by an instructor, or construct knowledge on substantive issues. Each member of the team is responsible for learning what is taught and for helping teammates learn.

Collaborative learning methods are now used in over a third of higher education courses, and their use has increased in the past six years more than any other learning method, according to a recent survey conducted by UCLA's Higher Education Research Institute. Employers want workers with collaborative skills and are looking for graduates of educational programs that teach these skills. Collaborative learning can be more effective than interpersonal competitive and individualistic efforts in promoting cognitive development, self-esteem, and positive student-student relationships.

Online learning models are natural environments for collaborative learning, but they are not collaborative learning environments by definition. Learners may interact with other participants without collaborating, for example when receiving on-line tutorial help. Learning activities have to be specifically and somewhat carefully designed to work effectively.

8.6.2 Case Study

The case study is a teaching strategy which requires learners to draw upon their past experiences, is participatory and has action components which are links to future experience. The key to a successful case study is the selection of an appropriate problem situation which is relevant both to the interests and experience level of learners and to the concepts being taught. The case report should include facts regarding the problem, the environmental context, and the characters of the people involved in the case. It should be factual, but also contain the opinions and views of the people involved. Learners should have access to the problem solution, but not until they have reached their own conclusions and can then compare their results with the actual decision taken to resolve the problem.

The case analysis can be carried out with the learners working independently or in groups One advantage of using the case method is that it emphasizes practical thinking and it assists learners in identifying principles after examining the facts of the case and then applying those principles to new situations Case analysis is equally effective when used in combination with other instructional strategies.

In the online environment case studies can be presented on web pages and discussed in conferencing groups. Cases can be developed by class groups as collaborative projects. In addition, the vast resources of the Internet can be tapped by students and educators to contribute data, information and expert advice to case development and analysis.

8.6.3 Forum

The forum is an open discussion carried on by one or more resource people and an entire group. The moderator guides the discussion and the audience raises and discusses issues, make comments, offers information, or asks questions of the resource person(s) and each other. There are two variations of the forum: the panel and the symposium.

The panel is usually a group of three to six people who sit in the presence of an audience and have a purposeful conversation on a topic in which they have specialized knowledge. Guided by a moderator, the panel is informal in nature, but allows for no audience participation. The symposium is a series of presentations given by two to five people different aspects of the same theme or closely related themes. Although the symposium is formal in nature, questions from the audience are encouraged following the presentations. An obvious benefit of the symposium is that it gives learners exposure to a variety of experts' viewpoints and offers an opportunity for the audience to ask questions.

Because the online environment facilitates group communication, it is ideal for the types of information exchange typical in forums. In fact, the forum can be more convenient and effective in the online environment than in the traditional classroom because speakers, experts and moderator can participate without having to travel or even be available at a particular time. Both synchronous and asynchronous communication can be utilized to support online learning forums.

8.7 STRATEGIES FOR EFFECTIVE ONLINE TEACHING

Many of us are having to move teaching quickly online (tips here if you are still setting up your course). Once you have your technology in place, take a deep breath. Teaching online requires different types of interactions with students. We've simplified what works into nine strategies based on research that will help set you and your students up for success in your newly online course.

8.7.1 Know the Technology

- This is new to everyone, so be prepared to troubleshoot and let your students know you are working on it. Take an hour to familiarize yourself with the technology. Most companies are offering additional training right now.
- Be very clear to students about where they should go for technical support (good digital technologies will have support services). Make the contact information readily available, and be prepared to direct students there if they come to you.

8.7.2 Expect the Unexpected and Remain Flexible

- At some point technology will fail, whether it is a video chat not connecting or assignment and/or resource links not working properly.
- Have a backup plan for all assignments and assessments that rely on technology.
- Be transparent in your communication to students about technology failure. For example, put a policy in place that outlines the actions students should take if they are unable to submit assignments due to technical issues.
- Don't be afraid to solve technical challenges in real time, such as during synchronous discussions or collaborative real-time activities, to save time.

8.7.3 Create and Maintain a Strong Presence

- Send a message to all students, by video if possible, to welcome them to online learning and reassure them.
- Use video chat rather than basic instant message when interacting with students.
- Get the students talking by beginning discussions in the discussion board, and then contributing rapid, regular, and open responses to questions.
- Use non-verbal communication such as emojis.
- Complete your profile with professional and personal traits.

8.7.4 Set Clear Expectations for the Course

- Online learning is new to the students as well. Make it clear to students how their grade in the course will be determined now.
- Set expectations for response time. For example, make it clear that you will respond to emails within one business day, otherwise students may expect you to answer an email within a few hours, and disengage if you don't.
- Share resources for students on how to be an online learner. We have one from college students and from professors.

8.7.5 Establish a Sense of Comfort and Develop a Community of Learners

- Students are looking to you to set the tone. Demonstrate enthusiasm and excitement about teaching the course to alleviate fear, anxiety, and isolation.
- Humanize yourself by posting a welcome video, a biography, photos that tell stories about what you are doing to keep busy during social isolation, links to news articles or video clips.
- Encourage each student to personalize their homepage and spend time going around the class asking students to share information about what they have posted.
- Incorporate instant messaging, web cameras, blogs and vlogs.
- Ask questions that empower participants to question each other, and elicit rich discussion.
- Respond to the community as a whole rather than directing all responses to individual participants outside of the community.

8.7.6 Promote Reflection and Communication Through Quality Asynchronous Discussion

- Return to posted topics that have not been fully discussed and promote contribution and reflection.

- Monitor participation and contact students individually if they are either not participating, or are taking over conversations and not permitting contributions from other individuals.

8.7.7 Have a Good Balance of Active Leader and Active Observer

You will begin the course as the manager of the learning community. As the course progresses, slowly transfer the responsibility to the community of learners. The online community building steps in point 4 will help with this. You should also gradually retract further out of communal discussions.

8.7.8 Request Regular Feedback and be Mindful of Misinterpretation

- Check in with your students to see how things are going. You can do formal or informal surveys to assess attitudes, workload and challenges. Make course correction as necessary — we're all learning.
- Use ad hoc quizzes to assess learner comprehension of material.
- 9. Regularly check content resources and applications
- Regularly check all links, resources, modules, and activities. Online content can move or change, which can lead to disengagement.
- Assist students who are having difficulty navigating course links or managing the material spanning across various web pages.
- Model the process of navigating to websites that are not embedded in the course, and demonstrate how to appropriately manage keeping track of navigation when jumping from site to site.

The online learning environment allows educators and students to exchange ideas and information, work together on projects, around the clock, from anywhere in the world, using multiple communication modes. Given the advantages and resources of this rich learning environment, how can multiple instructional strategies best be utilized for online learning? Just as in the traditional classroom, instructional strategies are most effective when employed specifically to meet particular learning goals and objectives. Effective course design can begin with asking and answering the key question: what are the major learning goals and objectives for this course? Once these goals and objectives have been identified and clearly articulated, the question of which learning strategies, activities, and experiences to employ can be addressed.

Online learning can employ any of the strategies discussed here. Much of the power of learning via the Internet lies in its capacity to support multiple modes of communication including any combination of student-student, student-faculty, faculty-student, faculty-faculty, student-others, others-students, etc. Taking into account the varied learning styles of learners and providing opportunities for self-directed and collaborative learning, educators can facilitate powerful, effective courses geared to achieve specific learning goals and outcomes using the vast resources and capacities of online learning.

The online learning environment is, after all, just another learning environment, in some ways similar to and in some ways different from more traditional environments such as conventional classrooms, seminar rooms, or labs. When we move our class onto the Internet, we should plan for and make the best use of the online environment. The various instructional strategies we use to meet the goals and objectives of our courses are likely to be similar in each environment. However, the ways in which we utilize the strategies will differ as we make the best use of the characteristics and capacities of each environment.

CHAPTER

ONLINE LEARNING IN EDUCATIONAL TECHNOLOGY 9

9.1 INTRODUCTION

The concept of traditional education has changed radically within the last couple of years. Being physically present in a classroom isn't the only learning option anymore — not with the rise of the internet and new technologies, at least. Nowadays, you have access to a quality education whenever and wherever you want, as long as you can get online. We are now entering a new era — the revolution of online education.

There's no need to discount the skepticism surrounding education through the internet. It's hard to understand the notion of leaving behind the conventional classroom, especially if it's to face this vast space called The Internet.

However, that's not reason enough to shy away from this alternative, which has proven to be valid and useful for many students. According to the most recent survey from Babson Survey Research Group, over 30 percent of higher education students in the United States are taking at least one distance course. Online education is a sensible choice whether you're a teenager or an adult. As a student, this can be a useful learning method for sharpening your skills in a difficult subject, or learning a new skill.

Many people can recognize that EdTech is devoting technology to promote education. It's true, but not sufficient. The Association for Educational Communications and Technology (AECT) has defined EdTech as "facilitating learning and improving performance by creating, using, and managing appropriate technological processes and resources." On the other hand, educators who actually use EdTech have a much simpler definition of the term. They say that it is a concept of transforming traditional book teaching and learning to digital form. For them, the main difference lies in the way knowledge is delivered (thanks to technology innovation) to make teaching more effective.

In short, EdTech is simply the is a process of integrating technology into education to build better teaching/learning experiences that result in higher learning outcomes.

9.2 REASONS: WHY EDUCATORS SHIFTED TO EDTECH

There are lots of reasons why educators shifted to EdTech, replacing the traditional paper-and-pen teaching method. Particularly, we list some common advantages of EdTech that you can easily see here:

9.2.1 Innovative Teaching Methods

Technology is an innovation of humans, so when an educator can apply technology to teaching, it is also innovative. EdTech allows teachers to provide multimedia to address diverse learning styles, such as animation, live video, etc. Besides, EdTech enables teachers to create online courses where students can learn in their own space and at their own pace.

9.2.2 Improve Collaborative Teaching

Technology has made it possible for everyone to stay connected. Students and teachers connect, discuss, share their opinions, and act upon situations collaboratively.

For example, eLearning is an educational tool that features collaboration by enabling students to share and discuss. Instead of being in a classroom and listening to teachers speak for 30 minutes, eLearning students can join an online group/platform and learn together by interacting with their peers. In this case, teachers are more accessible and act as mentors to help students develop themselves. This collaborative learning approach has bridged the gap between teachers and students and also helps students strengthen their interpersonal skills.

Teaching and Learning Process

Firstly, EdTech benefits how teachers teach, both online and offline. Not always having to go to a specific class at a specific time, students can learn whenever and wherever. Secondly, EdTech changes the way students approach learning. EdTech makes learning more fun and exciting for students. When we feel engaged in learning, we learn better, remember better, and also apply knowledge better to real life. Lastly, technology makes education smarter, more effective, thus, satisfying learners' needs more. True educators bring valuable knowledge to learners, both in theory and in real life. But smart educators are those who can create teaching from what learners want to learn.

To sum up, EdTech doesn't mean teachers have to become IT experts. But it's true that teachers can do these fascinating things only with technology, and that's why we need EdTech in life.

9.3 DISTANCE EDUCATION

Technology can also allow learners living in remote areas to access education. The evidence on these initiatives is encouraging. For example, Johnston and Ksoll (2017) evaluated a program that broadcasted live instruction via satellite to rural primary school students in the Volta and Greater Accra regions of Ghana. For this purpose, the program also equipped classrooms with the technology needed to connect to a studio in Accra, including solar panels, a satellite modem, a projector, a webcam, microphones, and a computer with interactive software. After two years, the intervention improved the numeracy scores of students in grades 2 through 4, and some foundational literacy tasks, but it had no effect on attendance or classroom time devoted to instruction, as captured by school visits. The authors interpreted these results as suggesting that the gains in achievement may be due to improving the quality of instruction that children received (as opposed to increased instructional time). Naik, Chitre, Bhalla, and Rajan (2019) evaluated a similar program in the Indian state of Karnataka and also found positive effects on learning outcomes, but it is not clear whether those effects are due to the program or due to differences in the groups of students they compared to estimate the impact of the initiative.

In one context (Mexico), this type of distance education had positive long-term effects. Navarro-Sola (2019) took advantage of the staggered rollout of the telesecundarias (i.e., middle schools with lessons broadcasted through satellite TV) in 1968 to estimate its impact. The policy had short-term effects on students' enrollment in school: For every telesecundaria per 50 children, 10 students enrolled in middle school and two pursued further education. It also had a long-term influence on the educational and employment trajectory of its graduates. Each additional year of education induced by the policy increased average income by nearly 18 percent. This effect was attributable to more graduates entering the labor force and shifting from agriculture and the informal sector. Similarly, Fabregas (2019) leveraged a later expansion of this policy in 1993 and found that each additional telesecundaria per 1,000 adolescents led to an average increase of 0.2 years of education, and a decline in fertility for women, but no conclusive evidence of long-term effects on labor market outcomes.

It is crucial to interpret these results keeping in mind the settings where the interventions were implemented. As we mention above, part of the reason why they have proven effective is that the "counterfactual" conditions for learning was either to not have access to schooling or to be exposed to low-quality instruction. School systems interested in taking up similar interventions should assess the extent to which their learners find themselves in similar conditions to the subjects of the studies above. This illustrates the importance of assessing the needs of a system before reviewing the evidence.

9.3.1 Preloaded Hardware

Technology also seems well positioned to disseminate educational materials. Specifically, hardware could also help deliver educational software. In theory, these materials could not only undergo a quality assurance review, but also draw on the interactions with learners for adjustments (e.g., identifying areas needing reinforcement) and enable interactions between learners and educators.

In practice, however, most initiatives that have provided learners with free computers, laptops, and netbooks do not leverage any of the opportunities mentioned above. Instead, they install a standard set of educational materials and hope that learners find them helpful enough to take them up on their own. Students rarely do so, and instead use the laptops for recreational purposes—often, to the detriment of their learning. In fact, free netbook initiatives have not only consistently failed to improve academic achievement in math or language, but they have had no impact on learners' general computer skills. Some of these initiatives have had small impacts on cognitive skills, but the mechanisms through which those effects occurred remains unclear.

To our knowledge, the only successful deployment of a free laptop initiative was one in which a team of researchers equipped the computers with remedial software. Mo et al. (2013) evaluated a version of the One Laptop per Child (OLPC) program for grade 3 students in migrant schools in Beijing, China in which the laptops were loaded with a remedial software mapped onto the national curriculum for math. After nine months, the program improved math achievement by 0.17 SDs and computer skills by 0.33 SDs. If a school system decides to invest in free laptops, this study suggests that the quality of the software on the laptops is crucial.

To date, however, the evidence suggests that children do not learn more from interacting with laptops than they do from textbooks. For example, Bando, Gallego, Gertler, and Romero (2016) compared the effect of free laptop and textbook provision in 271 elementary schools in disadvantaged areas of Honduras. After seven months, students in grades 3 and 6 who had received the laptops performed on par with those who had received the textbooks in math and language. Further, even if textbooks essentially become obsolete at the end of each school year, whereas laptops can be reloaded with new materials for each year, the costs of laptop provision (not just the hardware, but also the technical assistance, Internet, and training associated with it) are not yet low enough to make them a more cost-effective way of delivering content to learners.

Evidence on the provision of tablets equipped with software is encouraging but limited. For example, de Hoop et al. (2020) evaluated a composite intervention for first grade students in Zambia's Eastern Province that combined infrastructure (electricity via solar power), hardware (projectors and tablets), and educational materials (lesson plans for educators and interactive lessons for learners, both loaded onto the tablets and mapped onto the official Zambian curriculum). After 14 months, the intervention had improved student early-grade reading by 0.4 SDs, oral vocabulary scores by 0.25 SDs, and early-grade math by 0.22 SDs. It also improved students' achievement by 0.16 on a locally developed assessment. The multifaceted nature of the program, however, makes it challenging to identify the components that are driving the positive effects. Pitchford (2015) evaluated an intervention that provided tablets equipped with educational "apps," to be used for 30 minutes per day for two months to develop early math skills among students in grades 1 through 3 in Lilongwe, Malawi. The evaluation found positive impacts in math achievement, but the main study limitation is that it was conducted in a single school.

9.3.2 Facilitating Differentiated Instruction

Another way in which technology may improve educational outcomes is by facilitating the delivery of differentiated or individualized instruction. Most developing countries massively expanded access to schooling in recent decades by building new schools and making education more affordable, both by defraying direct costs, as well as compensating for opportunity costs. These initiatives have not only rapidly increased the number of learners enrolled in school, but have also increased the variability in learner' preparation for schooling. Consequently, a large number of learners perform well below grade-based curricular expectations. These learners are unlikely to get much from "one-size-fits-all" instruction, in which a single educator delivers instruction deemed appropriate for the middle (or top) of the achievement distribution. Technology could potentially help these learners by providing them with: (a) instruction and opportunities for practice that adjust to the level and pace of preparation of each individual (known as "computer-adaptive learning" (CAL)); or (b) live, one-on-one tutoring.

Computer-Adaptive Learning

One of the main comparative advantages of technology is its ability to diagnose students' initial learning levels and assign students to instruction and exercises of appropriate difficulty. No individual educator—no matter how talented—can be expected to provide individualized instruction to all learners in his/her class simultaneously. In this respect, technology is uniquely positioned to complement traditional teaching. This use of technology could help learners master basic skills and help them get more out of schooling.

Although many software products evaluated in recent years have been categorized as CAL, many rely on a relatively coarse level of differentiation at an initial stage without further differentiation. We discuss these initiatives under the category of "increasing opportunities for practice" below. CAL initiatives complement an initial diagnostic with dynamic adaptation to adjust both the initial level of difficulty and rate at which it increases or decreases, depending on whether learners' responses are correct or incorrect.

Existing evidence on this specific type of programs is highly promising. Most famously, Banerjee et al. (2007) evaluated CAL software in Vadodara, in the Indian state of Gujarat, in which grade 4 students were offered two hours of shared computer time per week before and after school, during which they played games that involved solving math problems. The level of difficulty of such problems adjusted based on students' answers.

This program improved math achievement by 0.35 and 0.47 SDs after one and two years of implementation, respectively. Consistent with the promise of personalized learning, the software improved achievement for all students. In fact, one year after the end of the program, students assigned to the program still performed 0.1 SDs better than those assigned to a business as usual condition. More recently, Muralidharan, et al. (2019) evaluated a "blended learning" initiative in which students in grades 4 through 9 in Delhi, India received 45 minutes of interaction with CAL software for math and language, and 45 minutes of small group instruction before or after going to school. After only 4.5 months, the program improved achievement by 0.37 SDs in math and 0.23 SDs in Hindi. While all learners benefited from the program in absolute terms, the lowest performing learners benefited the most in relative terms, since they were learning very little in school.

We see two important limitations from this body of research. First, to our knowledge, none of these initiatives has been evaluated when implemented during the school day. Therefore, it is not possible to distinguish the effect of the adaptive software from that of additional instructional time. Second, given that most of these programs were facilitated by local instructors, attempts to distinguish the effect of the software from that of the instructors has been mostly based on noncausal evidence. A frontier challenge in this body of research is to understand whether CAL software can increase the effectiveness of school-based instruction by substituting part of the regularly scheduled time for math and language instruction.

Live One-On-One Tutoring

Recent improvements in the speed and quality of Video conferencing, as well as in the connectivity of remote areas, have enabled yet another way in which technology can help personalization: live one-on-one tutoring. While the evidence on in-person tutoring is scarce in developing countries, existing studies suggest that this approach works best when it is used to personalize instruction.

There are almost no studies on the impact of online tutoring—possibly, due to the lack of hardware and Internet connectivity in low- and middle-income countries. One exception is Chemin and Oledan (2020)'s recent evaluation of an online tutoring program for grade 6 students in Kianyaga, Kenya to learn English from volunteers from a Canadian university via Skype (Video conferencing software) for one hour per week after school. After 10 months, program beneficiaries performed 0.22 SDs better in a test of oral comprehension, improved their comfort using technology for learning, and became more willing to engage in cross-cultural communication. Importantly, while the tutoring sessions used the official English textbooks and sought in part to help learners with their homework, tutors were trained on several strategies to teach to each learner's individual level of preparation, focusing on basic skills if necessary. To our knowledge, similar initiatives within a country have not yet been rigorously evaluated.

9.3.3 Methods

Because of the ability to provide information from a large number and wide variety of respondents, the survey technique was chosen over other typical needs assessment data gathering methods, such as interviews, focus groups, and on- site observations. A survey instrument was developed consistent with the five typical stages of needs assessment survey development noted by McClelland (1995): content definition, composing the survey, pilot testing, revision, and gaining approval to distribute the survey. Some of the instrument's content was developed based on the technological literacy standards released by the International Technology Education Association only weeks before the survey. A preliminary questionnaire was then developed, following recommendations by Gupta (1999) on the writing of training needs assessment instruments.

During the development of the instruments, content and survey specialists were consulted. Content consultants included technology teachers, undergraduate and graduate technology education students, and professors in technology education. Two technology education professors from universities other than the hosting university were consulted specifically because they had recently conducted national surveys in technology education. Two instructional technologists were also consulted, one of whom had recently used the survey software for dissertation research. Finally, two survey specialists from the hosting university's assessment office were consulted regarding the format of the instruments and coding of the results. Pilot testing occurred throughout the development period. Subjects included one undergraduate technology education student, one graduate technology education student, and five technology teachers. During the final round of pilot testing, all subjects seemed to interpret the meaning of the questionnaire's items and the formatting of their response as intended.

After pilot testing, a revised instrument was prepared for delivery by mail and online. In May, 2000, following human subjects protocol approval, 3,203 questionnaires were mailed with a cover letter and a postage-paid return envelop to all professional and student members of the International Technology Education Association (ITEA). A parallel online version of the questionnaire was available as an alternative, and cited in the mailing. The questionnaire included items on demographics, computer use, learning needs, and the educational appeal of online instruction.

9.4 RESULTS AND DISCUSSION

9.4.1 Respondent Characteristics

As of July 20, 2000, 923 usable questionnaires were received (including 111 submitted online) for a response rate of 29%. This was nearly double the response rate from a needs assessment survey of engineering educators. Most of the respondents (88%) indicated they were professional members of ITEA, with only 8% indicating they were student members.

The most typical occupations of respondents were high school technology teacher (38%) and middle school or junior high school technology teacher (29%); ten percent noted they were university technology teacher educators, and 5% and 2% were undergraduate and graduate technology education students, respectively. Most respondents (57%) indicated that the master's was their highest degree completed; 25% indicated the bachelor's, and 12% indicated the doctorate. Only 145 respondents (16%) had ever taken a course online. Thus, the results of this survey must be seen as describing the perception of online education, rather than experience with online education.

When asked about their use of the Internet, 829 respondents (90%) noted that they personally used the Internet to learn about some aspect of technology. This indicated a high level of readiness to engage in non-formal distance learning.

Computer Resources. Developers of online offerings should be aware of the computer resources available to their distance education students. Many more respondents reported using a PC regularly both at work and at home, than a Macintosh (though some reported using both computer platforms). Many respondents reported using Microsoft Office and using the Internet. The use of digital still and video technology was not as common, and was greater at work than at home, probably due to the cost of the equipment and its presence in many technology education laboratories. Most respondents (63%) indicated that they used a 56K modem at home and most (57%) used T1 Internet connection at work.

These responses may seem to indicate that the majority of respondents have access to typical computer resources, including at least a 56K modem. However, online educators are cautioned against developing online instruction that is only appropriate for a fraction of potential students, even if that fraction does constitute a majority. Instead, accommodations for students with lesser technological resources should be devised.

9.4.2 Perceived Learning Needs

Future Coursework Required. Is there a job-related need for future coursework? Sixty-five percent of the respondents indicated such a need. The greatest need (36%, n = 336) was for continuing education credits. Such credits are not necessarily graduate or undergraduate college credits but typically include approved workshops and other training opportunities. Ten percent of the respondents indicated a requirement of one course or less per year, and seven percent indicated the need to finish another degree.

Provision was made on the instrument for respondents to write their requirements for continuing education. A wide variety of required coursework was indicated, due largely to the variability in state requirements. Examples included, "100 workshop credits every 3 years minimum;" "2-4 courses / 5 yr for MA recertification;" and "1 class every 5 years." This variety can be seen as an opportunity for online education that spans geographic boundaries.

Content Areas of Interest. Several questions were included on the survey to determine the respondents' interests in different content areas.

However, this level of interest varied by the educational level of the respondent. For example, "Teaching methods and student management" ranked the lowest of the five, but for respondents whose highest degree was an associate's, (n = 17), it ranked third; for respondents indicating high school as their highest level (n = 29), it ranked first. Is there a need to provide education on teaching methods and student management? Yes, but with the current survey sample this need is more acute with pre-baccalaureate teachers, as might be expected.

The questionnaire also assessed respondents' interests in educational enrichment in regard to the newly released ITEA content standards (ITEA, 2000). The newly identified content areas within technology education such as medical technologies and technology assessment were expected to spark much interest since there have been few educational opportunities in these areas. Interest in these areas were expected to be higher than manufacturing and construction which have long been a part of the curriculum. To assess this interest, some of the twenty areas identified by the ITEA standards document were combined, resulting in a sixteen-part survey question. A seventeenth content area related to usability was added to this list.

As indicated in Table 1, the areas related to ITEA content standards that received the most interest were "information and communication" (3.52) and "technological design" (3.50). Those ranking the lowest were "agricultural and biotechnologies" and "medical technologies," with means of 2.84 and 2.74, respectively. This indicates an interest among the respondents between "little" and "moderate." The overall mean for all seventeen items related to ITEA content standards, indicate a moderate interest in all content areas, warranting attention by those providing courses and workshops. Technology education professionals who are potential students would be well served if ITEA coordinated and facilitated access to education in these areas. This would also serve the needs of this association in ensuring that the content standards are understood and applied.

Some of the more traditional areas received greater interest than some of the newer areas, as seen by comparing means for "manufacturing technologies" and "construction technologies" with those of "agricultural and biotechnologies" and "medical technologies." However, there are multiple reasons why a respondent might indicate a relatively low need. If an area is thought to be important, but the individual is well versed in the area, there might be little perceived need. Likewise, if an area is thought to be unimportant or irrelevant, whether or not the individual has studied the area, there might be little perceived need. Furthermore, although survey research assumes that respondents reply honestly, it is possible that regardless of a respondent's expertise or need, this list of seventeen items was seen as an opportunity to "cast a vote" regarding the importance of certain content areas in technology education.

A rather large number of respondents seemed to recognize no personal learning need that could be met by taking a course or workshop. This is surprising considering that the respondents were professionally involved in education. This view, which was most prevalent in respondents with doctorates, those that have fulfilled job requirements for education, and those near retirement, is contrary to the notion of life-long learning and continued professional development.

Need for Online Technology Education: Two Likert-type questions asked respondents for their general opinion on the need for online technology education. The first question in this area asked: "How much of a need do you think there is for online education in technology education?" The points on the scale were coded with numbers 1 representing "no need" to 5 representing "great need." From the responses to this item, a mean of 3.81 resulted. Sixty-three percent chose the top two levels, and 30% chose "great need," whereas only 1% chose "no need."

Table 1: Mean interest levels for courses or workshops based on content areas included in the ITEA standards. (n = 869 to 891.)

Content Area of Interest	Mean
Information and communication	3.52
Technological design	3.50
Manufacturing technologies	3.40
Construction technologies	3.34
Transportation technologies	3.30
Learning to use technology	3.28
Energy and power technologies	3.25
Technological connections and integration	3.24
Technology and the environment	3.20
Technology assessment	3.15
Technology and history	3.02
The core concepts of technology	3.00
Technology and culture	3.00
Learning about usability	2.95
The characteristics and scope of technology	2.90
Agricultural and biotechnologies	2.84
Medical technologies	2.74

Note: 1 = none, 2 = little, 3 = moderate, 4 = much, 5 = great

This level of perceived need is noteworthy and indicates an opportunity for universities considering offering online education. Possibly contributing to this perceived need is the current shortage of technology teachers and the perception that distance education can overcome previous obstacles.

A similar question asked respondents, "How much of a need is there for online technology education for students in grades K-12?" The mean of 891 responses was 3.49, based on the same 5-point scale. This could indicate further opportunities for online curriculum developers interested in reaching K-12 students.

Likelihood of Taking a College Course. When asked, "How likely are you to take college courses over the next 3 years?", 37% (339 of 916) of the respondents indicated they were "certain" to take a college course, and 19% indicated this was "likely." Although these figures (from this self-selected survey sample) may not be generalizable to a larger population, there is a distinct indication of the need for college courses, whether online or not.

9.5 CONCLUSION AND RECOMMENDATIONS

9.5.1 Perceived Online Learning Needs

A variety of views emerged concerning online learning needs. While some people indicated a need for individual courses, others preferred continuing education credits, or entire degree programs. Although the greatest job-related educational need was for continuing education credit, a higher level of interest was expressed for online programs in technology education and at the master's level than in other alternatives.

Interest was evident in courses and workshops covering a variety of topics, including activities to teach about technology, new and emerging technologies, technology education curriculum, and using the Internet to teach about technology. Teaching methods and student management were also of interest, but more among those who had not yet completed a bachelor's degree. Furthermore, interest was expressed in topics related to the ITEA content standards. Of these areas, the most interest was expressed for "information and communication" and for "technological design." "Medical technologies" and "agricultural and biotechnologies" were of least interest.

Several barriers to meeting online learning needs emerged. Among these were a lack of perception of need, a lack of awareness of online opportunities, a perception that online education is too impersonal, and a perception that online education is of inferior quality. Yet, universities can help overcome some of these barriers if they advertise online offerings that have been designed to ensure both high quality and personal interaction.

A number of preconceptions emerged that may not accurately describe online education. For example, a perceived lack of inter-student contact in online courses seems to be contrary to the use of collaborative online strategies and technologies Other preconceptions that should be scrutinized include a perceived lack of contact with the instructor, a self-paced calendar for an online class, and lower quality of online education compared to traditional education.

9.5.2 Recommendations for Educational Providers

The following recommendations are made to potential providers of online technology education:

1. Take advantage of the perceived need for online education in technology education by offering more online courses and workshops. Areas such as "information and communication" and "technological design" may meet a greater need than other areas and may yield greater enrollments. Courses that are part of complete online degree programs, especially at the master's level, may be useful to those seeking credit only and to those seeking degrees.
2. Ensure high quality in the online learning experience. This concerns the depth of content, accommodations for significant interpersonal interaction, and the facilitation of a wide variety of learner needs and capabilities.
3. Advertise and promote online opportunities using a variety of techniques to reach near and distant technology education professionals. Where possible, note where online courses and workshops meet individual re-certification requirements for teachers from a variety of geographic locations. Help dispel misconceptions about what it is like to take an online course.

Finally, future needs assessments should be performed to gain information on the changing needs of a changing population. Stabb (1995) noted that "there is near universal recognition of needs assessment as an ongoing, dynamic process that responds to shifts in the local context".

9.6 BLINDING TECHNOLOGY OF ONLINE LEARNING

Online learning is often heralded as a way to make college an option for people who would not otherwise have the money or mobility to access it. But for blind students, online learning can present more obstacles than opportunities — especially as e-learning materials become more technologically sophisticated.

"When faculty or course developers hear about a new tool being introduced at a distance education conference, they want to bring it home and try it out," says Kelly Hermann, chair of the Online Education Special Interest Group at the Association on Higher Education and Disability, or AHEAD. "But what they fail to recognize is where that new tool might create barriers to accessibility."

That new types of course content being developed for online learning might create accessibility problems is not a new revelation. But the courts have made little progress toward defining and enforcing accessibility standards for online education in the last decade, even as online degree programs have proliferated and been adopted into mainstream higher education. Only in the last few months has the federal government hinted that online education, and technological innovations associated with it, might soon face legal scrutiny.

In the meantime, advocates for the blind are worried that it is becoming harder for the assistive technology used by blind students to keep pace with advances in educational technology. "Dynamic" e-learning content — e.g., graphics that change as a user rolls over or clicks on different parts — could present huge challenges to blind students, says Chris Danielsen, a spokesman for the National Federation for the Blind, or NFB. Figuring out how translate static tables and diagrams for blind students was trouble enough, he says; it is not yet clear how to deal with newer, more interactive e-learning objects that may soon pervade online education.

"Assistive technology does the best it can to keep up with changes in [educational] technology, but a lot of times you have a university that is using the latest, cutting-edge Web technology... screen-reader technology tries to keep up, but more often than not it's behind," says Danielsen. For example, screen-readers rely on a screen having to reload every time new content appears on a page — a step dynamic content eliminates. Advocacy groups do not believe online classrooms should deploy such materials until they can be made accessible to blind students.

The news is not all bad. The NFB last week gave Blackboard — the e-learning industry leader whose learning-management platform is used by many online programs — a pat on the back for setting a new standard for accessibility with its the latest version of its online learning portal. Moodle, the open-source learning-management platform that has been making modest gains against Blackboard for several years, allows individual campuses to customize their portals such that they are accessible to blind students. The accessibility of learning-management systems is especially germane to the accessibility of online courses, since in online learning the learning-management platform is not just a supplement to the classroom — it is the classroom.

Unfortunately, making the learning-management system accessible is only part of the battle to make online education accessible. "Even though Moodle itself is accessible, courses and imported content might not be," says Brad Schleicher, a spokesperson for Moodlerooms, the company that provides support to users of the Moodle platform. Imported content is becoming as much a part of online course delivery as the discussion forums and other features governed by the accessibility practices of the learning-management system.

At Blackboard's user conference in July, Michael Chasen, the company's CEO, demonstrated how the company was creating more dynamic, seamless ways to integrate outside content into course pages. In the latest version of the platform, "we've taken steps to ensure that content from third-party sources like YouTube and others is fully accessible once it is brought into the course, but as a platform solution, there are infinite types of content that could be used within the system," says Stephanie Cupp, a senior director of user experience at Blackboard.

"Third-party content is a problem," says Anne Taylor, director of access technology at the National Federation for the Blind. As learning-management systems have made it easier to do so, some professors have drawn increasingly from disparate sources — online video sites, blogs, other nonacademic websites — for course material. The more professors "do their own thing," drawing from nontraditional sources, the less likely it is that everything students need to succeed in an online course is accessible, says Pratik Patel, chair of the information access committee at the American Council of the Blind.

9.6.1 Legal Recourse

None of the advocacy groups contacted by Inside Higher Ed could pinpoint the exact number of blind students currently enrolled in U.S. colleges, but Hermann, of AHEAD, says the proportion is very, very small. Only three to five percent of college students report having any disability at all, Hermann says, and that includes learning and mental disorders. Blindness is, she says, a "low-incidence disability."

This means that advocates for the blind often need to use federal anti-discrimination laws to keep from being left in the dust on new technologies. Last summer, the NFB and the American Council of the Blind sued Arizona State University under the Americans with Disabilities Act and other laws, forcing it to end a pilot program designed to assess the educational uses of Amazon's Kindle DX, which had an inaccessible menu feature. The U.S. Justice Department subsequently forced three other institutions to shut down their Kindle pilots.

So if online education presents so many obstacles to accessibility, why has no one filed a similar lawsuit against any of the institutions that offer it?

"It's a good question," says Hermann. "It's the colleges' obligation under federal law to make every program of their institution accessible."

"Obviously, we're cautious about talking about our legal strategies," says Danielsen, the NFB spokesman. However, the spokesman did note that litigation is an "expensive, time consuming process, and outcomes are by no means guaranteed." In other words, you do not sue unless you know you can win. "From our perspective, it's a last resort," Danielsen says.

Eric Bridges, the government affairs director at the American Council of the Blind, noted that advocacy groups have had little success with litigation dealing with a similar topic: the accessibility of college websites. "Some of the litigation that's been done over website access has not always been the greatest as far as settlements and outcomes, so I think some organizations have been hesitant," he says.

The chances of a successful lawsuit might become clearer sometime in the next year or two. The Department of Justice has suggested that it might soon articulate exactly what kind of legal recourse blind and otherwise disabled students have with respect to the accessibility of online courses. Last month, the department issued several notices, saying it is collecting public comment on a number of topics related to accessibility and the Web in preparation to lay out the specific obligations of various institutions under federal law.

While online education is not explicitly mentioned, Bridges says his group is planning to lobby that it be included on the rulemaking agenda. "What they're doing is putting out feelers," he says. "They want to see... how the industry feels about even broaching this subject." The department will probably release a more specific agenda within a year or so, Bridges says, adding that he would be surprised if online learning does not make the cut.

In June, the Justice Department and the Education Department jointly released a "dear colleague" letter to colleges, warning them that the government plans to crack down on institutions that require disabled students to use emerging technology that does not comply with federal accessibility laws. This, again, did not explicitly mention online education, but Bridges says it was a shot across the bow.

John Wodatch, chief of the disability rights section of the Justice Department, did not respond to repeated requests for comment. However, at a June meeting of the National Association of College and University Attorneys, Wodatch urged college officials to think about the accessibility of their online courses to blind students and those with limited manual dexterity, indicating that the government may indeed be preparing to address the issue.

Until then, the innovators will presumably continue to populate online learning environments with new tools, while assistive technology providers and their blind students try to keep up.

9.6.2 Current Educational Technology Trends

If you are an innovative educator, following the trends in education is probably not something new but rather essential. Even with this list, however, it is still up to you to choose the most suitable "trendy" aid for your teaching and training. Here we select the 10 latest educational technology trends that are must-know when diving into this industry.

e-Learning

Distance learning became the top educational technology trend overnight because of the rapid spread of COVID-19 and school closures. This led to a rising demand for online educational platforms. eLearning is education or training delivered electronically. It can be slide-based online activities, or it can also be an online course that helps a business train employees in necessary skills.

With eLearning, educational content is delivered to learners through computers, laptops, tablets, or smartphones. Not only saving time but opening many doors for interactive learning. Rather than being in a passive experience, learners can choose what they need to learn quickly and easily, wherever they are. They also learn through interacting directly with on-screen information through, for instance, dragging content from one place to the next. Moreover, the decision-making scenarios in eLearning also encourage learners to make their own choices on what they will learn next.

In eLearning, learners just soak in knowledge through reading or viewing content, it changes the way education is delivered. Also, many eLearning courses include animation, podcasts, and videos that create a multimodal and practical learning experience.

The last point is, although eLearning has been around for a long time, it is staying green and continuously developing. Educators are using the advantages of technology to make learning more effective. That's why more and more online and blended learning courses are produced nowadays.

Variety is the outstanding feature of online learning platforms. You can teach your students in real time (synchronous) via live stream or group meetings using Zoom or Microsoft Teams, or you can use recorded methodologies with a wide range of media and digital functions available to enrich lessons. A good online learning platform can also be combined with a Learning Management System (LMS) so you can keep track of your students' learning outcomes.

Video-Assisted Learning

In recent years, video-assisted learning has become more and more popular as classroom displays. The "video day" is no longer a television on a trolley being wheeled into a class. With the internet and digital devices, every day can be a "video day."

This trend is also booming in distance learning conditions, which students learn through computer screens. Videos, especially animated videos, are extremely beneficial to enrich lessons and make content comprehensible. It improves students' outcomes and reduces teachers' workload.

Blockchain Technology

The Distributed Ledger Technology (DLT) from blockchain brings so many benefits to education, especially data storage. Every time new data is added, it adds another "block" to the system, so the storage is technically limitless. Simultaneously, the data will be encrypted and distributed across multiple computers in the system. It makes transacting data decentralized and transparent.

Blockchain technology is used in Massive Open Online Courses (MOOCs) and ePortfolios to verify skills and knowledge. The DLT systems will answer the problems of authentication, scale, and cost for eLearning agencies. Moreover, it can help student applicants publish their accomplishments during the job-seeking phase.

Big Data will Get Bigger

To cater to learners' needs, the learning experience needs to be personalized. And with COVID-19 and online learning booming, we now have bigger data than ever before. Instructional Designers have relevant information about learners' experiences to customize and present the course in a suitable format. Some information you should look for is the course's topic, learner enrollment, learner performance, and learner feedback.

Artificial Intelligence (AI)

AI now is the "in thing" in the US EdTech market. People have predicted that through 2021, AI could become the primary trend and grow by more than 45%. So why is the trend booming in one of the world's largest markets for EdTech? First and foremost, AI can automate basic activities in education, like grading. It's now possible for teachers to automate grading of the multiple-choice and fill-in-the-blank questions. Thus, automated grading of students' writing may not be far behind.

Furthermore, both learners and educators could benefit from AI. For example, students could get help from AI tutors when teachers are too busy to take care of everyone. Also, AI-driven programs can give both learners and educators helpful feedback. That's why some schools use AI systems to monitor student progress and to alert teachers when there might be an issue with students' performances. Therefore, it's not too far fetched that AI is a powerful assistant for in-class teaching.

Learning Analytics

The current landscape of learning analytics has dramatically expanded, especially for higher education. Learning analytics allows educators to measure and report student learning just by the web. From that, it's possible for them to better understand and optimize learning.

When teachers read insights from students' learning processes, they can improve the knowledge and skill acquisition of their students accordingly. For instance, teachers are able to see what type of information (text, images, infographics, or videos) that students enjoy most and use it more in their following lessons. Also, teachers are able to notice what pieces of knowledge weren't effectively delivered and enhance them next time. Moreover, learning analytics helps educators identify blocks of students who may have academic or behavioral challenges. From that, teachers could develop a way to help students reach their full potential.

Gamification

If you are looking for a way to turn learning into a more fun and engaging process, gamification is the most suitable educational technology trend. There is no reason for students not to be actively involved in classroom games. Students can learn and practice while they are joining in on exciting game activities. Gaming elements help create a funny and positive learning environment for learners.

The adoption of gamification is most popular in the education sector. It's because kids are quickly engaged in gaming videos or getting higher scores in a game. However, it doesn't mean that higher education or corporate training doesn't need fun elements to improve the engagement level of learners.

Immersive Learning with VR And AR

The class learning experience has undergone a tremendous change since Virtual Reality (VR) and Augmented Reality (AR) came to education. The rise in demand for experiential learning pushes forward the development of learning with VR and AR.

Learning has become much more interactive than traditional methods. While VR provides a constructed reality, AR gives an enhanced view of a real image. Thus, they help explain complex concepts that plain images or even a lab's hands-on experiments couldn't show students. For example, VR is pretty helpful when you are attending a medical training course. In detail, VR creates a chance for students to experience real-world surgeries in a low-risk environment.

Steam

STEAM-based programs are the new EdTech improvement over the STEM programs. This new trend of EdTech applies meaningful Science, Technology, Engineering, Art (the new element), and Math content to solve real-world problems through hands-on learning activities and creative design.

Concerning the advantages of STEAM, the first thing is that it helps students become increasingly curious about the world around them. Moreover, it also creates a safe environment for the learners to express and experience their ideas while thinking outside the box. The comfort of hands-on learning also helps students collaborate better with others.

Social Media in Learning

Have you ever thought that social media would be a part of the learning process? When every student, both young and mature, spends so much time on social media, why don't we turn it into a powerful tool to enhance learning?

It's how the idea to use social media for teaching came about. Many educational institutes have started using social media as a communication tool in which students can interact with others easily. Students can share study materials, discuss with others in a group, or easily comment on someone else's post. Even an animated learning video could go viral on social media. And TedEd is the typical example of this trend! This organization creates lessons worth sharing and posts them on YouTube where people can easily access, find, and share the educational videos with their friends.

Social media is here to stay and build a culture of collaboration and sharing, leading to an improved learning experience.

In the end, we know that there is a lot to digest when we talk about educational technology trends. However, keep in mind that technology has seeped into education and renewed its whole teaching and learning process. Especially eLearning, an educational tool that not only increases the accessibility and convenience of education but also changes the learning behaviors and learners' desires for learning.

But here is good news, you don't need to go alone on this EdTech ship because you have us who will join you in bringing forth the true value of learning, inspiring learners, and making education more relevant and empowering.

CHAPTER

INFRASTRUCTURE SUPPORT FOR ONLINE PROGRAMS 10

10.1 INTRODUCTION

Enrollment in online courses in the United States has outgrown the pace of enrollment in traditional classroom courses. Redpath noted in 2009 that "almost one-third of higher education students in the United States were enrolled in at least one online course." This enrollment trend has continued to increase, even during the recent economic downturn.

The majority of current students are heavy technology users. The acceptance and popularity of online communication and social networking is driving this trend. In turn, higher education institutions need to be responsive to both internal and external changes influenced by technological advances However, the procurement of leading-edge technology is merely the beginning of a journey toward the delivery of online education. Mere access to technology is insufficient in ensuring project success. Faculty and students require appropriate administrative support before, during, and after the implementation of new technology.

A cohesive support structure begins with leaders promoting a synergistic environment conducive to technology adoption. Bruner found significant deterrents to adoption of technology that he labels the "hassle factor." His studies confirmed that the added workload, lack of release time, lack of training, lack of real incentives, and frequent frustrations with technology all came together to build a barrier that he considered the number one reason faculty avoid online education. His advice to administrators: focus more attention on removing each of the issues and create a less threatening work environment. Underscoring the significance of leadership's impact on the success or failure rate of online education is Frith and Kee's finding that many faculty blame the loss of students on the instability of the infrastructure and the inability of campus support personnel to work through issues that subsequently drive away online students.

Current literature identifies the roles of leadership in technology implementation, but little is provided in terms of models or systematic methods that leaders can adopt to improve the organizational resources, structures, and culture necessary for successful technology adoption. This gap is especially true for technology adoption in the academic setting. In this article the authors expand the available literature by suggesting the use of the Administrative Support Matrix (ASM). The ASM identifies processes and elements essential to developing and sustaining online educational programs.

Table 1: Administrative Support Matrix

Foundation Stage	Development Stage	Maintenance Stage
1. Administration's ability to listen and respond to faculty needs	1. Online program policies	1. Continuously evaluate new online technology
2. A supporting and responsive information technology (IT) team	2. Staff development program	2. Update technology only when new technology adds value
3. Effective and well-supported campus network	3. Faculty incentives	3. Periodically assess and update quality of course content
4. Effective server support	4. Teamwork approach	4. Set limits on intrusion of technology on online faculty personal time
5. Online student registration, billing, and payment system	5. Faculty development program	5. Survey faculty semiannually
6. Online bookstore services	6. Faculty mentoring program	6. Survey students at end of every semester
7. Online library services	7. Course management system	7. Make changes to programs based on faculty and student input
	8. Lecture capture or course online delivery system	
	9. Online test security	

10.2 BACKGROUND

10.2.1 Needs of Administrative Support

Efficient and effective use of technology in an online environment requires administrative support at all levels of the institution. Frith and Kee (2003) found that many faculty blamed the loss of students on the instability of the infrastructure and the inability of campus support personnel to work through issues that often frustrated online students and prevented them from having a successful online experience. Though IT personnel are not faculty and may not have daily or direct contact with the students, in an online teaching environment their actions or inactions can significantly impact the success or failure of academic programs.

Rayn, Hodson-Carlton and Ali (2005) presented an exceptional model that captures many of the facets that should be considered when teaching online. They also developed and tested a Matrix that outlines factors to be considered and the sequence that takes place when nursing faculty develop an online program. The focus in the development of an online program should be to preserve as much of the same qualities that made the face-to-face program an effective product while making improvements for online presentation.

Factors that should be considered include: How can student/student and student/professor relationships be preserved and developed in an online and often isolated environment? How must the teaching strategies change to accommodate technology and the online environment? How is the course content affected when moved from a campus to an online environment? What infrastructure support functions must be modified to accommodate online teaching environment and the online or distant students? Each of these factors provides its own set of needs that should be carefully addressed when developing an online program.

The development of an online program should begin with a careful evaluation of the process involved in such an undertaking and an evaluation of each of the factors affected by such a move. The infrastructure that must be in place before an online program can even begin to be developed includes the support from administration, technology support systems, a Course Management System (CMS) or process, faculty and staff development systems, and policies that will drive the development process. These policies must specifically outline how questions of content ownership will be handled, how faculty will be compensated for their online teaching effort, and how the appropriate course workload will be determined for the online programs. Once these initial steps have been taken, then the process of online program development can begin.

10.2.2 Models of e-Learning

If the infrastructure support is not appropriately designed, equipped and trained, faculty are often burdened with additional roles of instructional designer, technology support specialist, and sometimes even administrative advisor or admissions processor. Restauri (2004) discusses two prevailing models often used by default on campuses for the development of online programs.

The first model, the individual model, seems more prevalent than it should be. It consists of the process whereby individual faculty are left to fend for themselves in gathering of support, learning new technology, and designing an online program from scratch with little or no support from the infrastructure in place. Programs developed under this model often fail due to faculty burnout, poor course design, or a technology infrastructure that is so riddled with problems that students quit the program due to the frustration of frequent disconnects and the inability to get the technology to work as intended.

The second model, the team approach, has proven far more successful and resilient. With this model, campus administration actually develops a teamwork approach where experts from each critical area of the infrastructure are intimately involved in the online course developmental process from beginning to end. In some cases new technology support personnel must be hired to support the online technology needed for the program. Other support personnel such as content developers, instructional designers, and administrative support are either realigned to support the online endeavor or new personnel are hired to provide the support. The second process may seem more expensive at the onset, but in the long run it can save critical faculty from resigning in frustration and encourage more student enrollment. Universities that use the team approach also experience much better buy in from faculty campus wide.

Escoffery et al. (2005) identified what a team structure should look like and the traditional roles of each team member in the process of online course delivery. Faculty are generally expected to develop the course content, interact with students, and provide guidance in an online course environment. The roles of other players include the instructional designers who are expected to provide assistance in developing course materials, provide assistance with integration of technology with the curriculum and provide expertise on the implementation of online courseware. They may also serve as a liaison to the program, provide faculty and staff with guidance and expertise on distance learning, assist faculty in identifying course needs, and help troubleshoot technical or software problems when they arise. Multimedia staff are frequently tasked with the roles of designing and developing web pages, upkeep, maintenance, and support of training software and technologies, assisting faculty in the development of new online technologies, researching, evaluating, testing, recommending, implementing, and supporting new courseware and other online applications, and maintaining security and backup of all educational data. Unfortunately the reality is that these roles are ideal scenarios, and not the norm. The norm is that most faculty fulfill many if not all of the roles mentioned above in addition to their teaching load as part of an online teaching program.

Pauoluccci and Gambescia (2007) reaffirmed earlier research conducted by Laird (2004) where he found that online infrastructure support often can be identified or categorized into one of four general models of e-Learning integration. At some universities the Independence or Distance Education unit is established as its own sub-department within the larger campus but operates independently from the rest of the campus and has no real connection to the traditional academic mission of the campus. The independent or distant education style may have worked in the past, but in the modern university system it is becoming much more efficient and effective to have an integrated system.

In the Lone Wolf Model as Laird (2004) calls it, each faculty member is given exclusive control over how he or she will create and deliver in the online program. The Silo Model is similar to it in that each department in the institution operates independently from any other departments on the campus. These examples can work in a very small organization, but can quickly result in chaos and redundant support systems in a larger organization. Portions of these models still have merit however, since the faculty member is usually the subject matter expert, a limited amount of autonomy should be given within each department to have a certain amount of control over the look, feel, and presence of the online learning experience for students.

The last and final model Laird (2004) discusses is the Integration Model, and is the most progressive and forward thinking model in the group. The process brings together all the campus resources and unifies the traditional instruction with the online instruction, creating a synergistic effect that allows technology, infrastructure, and resources to be shared by all faculty and staff. The online learning and the traditional learning infrastructure are combined and share resources equally. This method maximizes efficient use of administrative and technological resources, minimizes redundant systems and costs, and allows faculty to provide better quality instruction in a more productive atmosphere.

10.2.3 Administration's Perspective

The research focused on the needs of faculty and the value of faculty feedback in administrative decision-making. The administrative perspective may be somewhat different depending on the institution and the varying needs at each level of administration. One unifying objective, however, is accreditation. While one may be able to find differing points of view about how online education should be implemented and supported among administrators at different levels, accreditation sets standards that must be adhered to by all levels of administration.

Accreditation guidelines are the driving force behind the decisions made by administrators concerning the course of action to take when developing an online or distance education program. Every program at the institution must meet accreditation standards in order to be considered an option at all. If administration chooses to implement an online program, the university must consider the appropriate accrediting body guidelines.

Magiuka, et al., (2005) discuss ten critical design and administrative concerns that were a vital part of the decision making process for the careful planning and development of what is now Indiana University's Kelley Direct (KD) online program. In the early stages of the planning process, KD administrators and planners searched the literature to find what other universities had done in similar situations. They found five elements or questions that could be posed for careful consideration by administrators when planning and developing an online teaching program. These elements included a focus on the vision of the university and the plans for the future; (1) how the curriculum would change for the online environment; (2) what was needed to train the faculty and staff and provide for continued support services; (3) how student services need to be modified for online support; (4) what kind of student training and support would be needed; and (5) what policies would be needed to address the question of copyright and intellectual property.

In addition to the five elements there were ten administrative concerns or issues to be considered.

The first was that a decision had to be made on which student group would be served by the online program. Would this program be a substitution for current part-time or residential programs, or would it target new students who could not attend current campus offerings? University administrators decided that the KD program would be a separate entity from the traditional programs offered by the Kelley School of Business at Indiana University. The program would run parallel to the on campus programs and would share the same faculty.

The second issue facing administrators was how the graduates would be treated and whether there would be an online identifier on the diploma. Administrators decided that since the same faculty who taught the program in residence would also be teaching the online program, there would be no need to identify the online program as being any different than the residential program. Both sets of students would receive equivalent instruction.

The third administrative factor to consider dealt with whether to have a residential component to the online program, and if so for how long and how often. Because there was a fear that students may feel isolated from the main campus, a week-long residence component was established as essential to the online program.

The fourth administrative issue is how faculty should be used to provide instruction in the online program. Would they only teach in-load, or would they be allowed to teach overload? Factors to be considered in this issue were: could this be accomplished by using existing faculty, hiring temporary faculty, or developing a plan to use both full-time and adjunct faculty. A faculty committee was formed to help make this decision and it was decided that existing faculty would be allowed to teach overload, but be given additional compensation.

The fifth administrative factor was whether to focus the design effort and funding on developing teaching templates for adjunct faculty to use, or to provide training for existing faculty on the finer aspects of online pedagogy? The development of templates for online courses assists in streamlining course content and course layout so that temporary or adjunct faculty can be used to teach the course, but quality of instruction often suffers with this option. Full-time faculty are more expensive, but provide a higher quality of education. For the KD programs administrators decided to use full-time faculty in order to maintain a more professional culture.

A sixth factor considered by administrators was whether any type of template would be used to streamline or standardize online instruction. Students often prefer a standardized template so that the location of options and features are the same across all courses. Administrators decided to implement a standardized template for the online component so that all courses would have the same look and feel.

The seventh administrative issue was how much interactivity to design into online courses, and how much of the interactivity to leave to the judgment of the individual faculty. This is an issue that deserves careful consideration, because the greater interactivity designed into the course the more work is created for faculty to monitor and participate. Students often expect or demand immediate response from faculty in an online environment, and if that response is delayed students often express extreme dissatisfaction with faculty responsiveness. Ultimately, in the KD program, the decision was left up to faculty to decide how much interactivity to build into a course.

The eighth administrative factor is whether to use commercial off-the-shelf online technology, open source technology or whether the campus should develop its own proprietary teaching tools. There are numerous advantages and disadvantages to consider with any online teaching technology, so this process may take some time. In the end, the KD program decision makers decided to adopt the ANGEL Course Management System (CMS) with the understanding that in-house programmers would make modifications as necessary to meet online teaching goals.

The ninth issue was how to select a CMS that would best fit the goals and design of the curriculum to be placed online. Some universities may start out with one CMS and later decide to change over to another one that best fits the needs of the growing online program.

The tenth and final factor for administrators to consider is the identification of the role corporate partners and alliances with other universities will play in the design and implementation of an online teaching program. This decision will inevitably be different for each university system because it is closely tied to the types of programs that will be offered. Corporate partners may request specific accredited training for their staff and corporate leadership.

The economics of administrative decision-making may be driven more by a desire to expand enrollment. Where expansion once meant costly land purchases and building projects, online education programs may seem like a much less expensive alternative. Other important administrative considerations are collaborative agreements, not only with other institutions, but also with corporations that may become a valuable source of funding. Online education has brought on a new paradigm of cooperation between governmental and private agencies seeking to pool resources and share expertise. Collaborative efforts can spawn a new age of flexibility in curricula implementation.

10.2.4 Methodology

A case study was used to determine what specific administrative support services are already being provided at a premier medical university and whether faculty feel that these services are adequate or need improvement. Surveys may be used to provide valuable information concerning the current and future needs of online teaching faculty, and can be used repeatedly to show trends, update procedures, or revise policies as needed.

10.2.5 Research Methods Employed

A descriptive survey was developed that identifies specific elements outlined in the Matrix (Table 1) to be evaluated for their perceived importance by online teaching faculty. This survey also included questions asking faculty to validate the content of the Matrix as part of the case study to determine what administrative support elements faculty value and consider important to the success of an online teaching program.

The investigation and survey produced a validated Matrix and tool for evaluating support needs of online teaching faculty at various institutions, and showed a detailed analysis of the perceived support needs of the faculty at a premier southern medical university. This detailed analysis delineates valuable information for administrators and decision makers at many institutions to assist them in making future decisions on where and how to allocate resources.

The survey used close-ended questions with five-point Likert-scale responses. The questions were developed to collect data on the perceptions of online teaching faculty along with demographic information. A few open-ended questions were included to allow faculty the opportunity to make additional comments.

The sample size was the total population of full-time online teaching faculty at a premiere medical university, which is approximately 100 faculty. At a premiere medical university the support needs for both full-time and part-time faculty are substantially the same. Part-time faculty have a larger clinical responsibility, so they may only teach one or two classes as compared to the full-time faculty. The survey was sent electronically to 206 full-time faculty at a premiere medical university who potentially teach online classes in various schools on the main campus in Augusta, Georgia and at satellite campuses throughout the state of Georgia. The actual number of faculty who teach online is 100, but surveys were sent to all faculty in departments that have online teaching programs in order to reach all possible eligible participants. The focus of the survey was on those who taught online, hybrid, or some combination of face-to-face and online. Faculty who did not have an online teaching element to their instruction were eliminated from the survey.

The responses were collected and evaluated using the statistical analysis software SPSS® to ascertain whether there is a significant difference with the two questions and compare the importance of a support function with whether that function is adequately provided by the institution. Part a of the question was compared with part b using a paired sample t-test to ascertain whether there was a statistically significant difference between the two questions. A statistically significant difference means that either the support function was important to faculty, but was not adequately supported, or that the support function was not that important to faculty, but was well supported. The descriptive statistics help identify which is the case for each set of questions.

10.2.6 Survey

The survey was developed using a variety of surveys found in literature as models. The survey was designed to take approximately 20 to 30 minutes to complete and consisted of 85 Likert-scale response questions with a few optional fill-in questions allowing faculty to add comments. The Matrix was then presented and faculty were asked three questions that inquire about their view on the overall accuracy of the Matrix. Two of these questions asked faculty to comment on any items they would add to or delete from the Matrix as shown. Four multipart questions follow that ask specific questions about infrastructure support for online students. In order to gather accurate data concerning incentives and disincentives, the final two questions ask faculty to rate a list of incentives or disincentives from most desirable to least desirable. The opportunity is provided to allow faculty to add an incentive or disincentive that may not be listed.

The survey was evaluated and edited by a panel of experts consisting of a statistician, an instructional designer, a program support specialist, a multimedia support specialist, an academic services professional, an information technology network support professional, and two faculty online program directors. The survey was then piloted to a group of five online teaching faculty who provided feedback as to the flow of the survey and the time it took to complete it. Completion times ranged from 15 to 30 minutes. Other feedback was evaluated for incorporation into the survey, and modifications were made based on faculty suggestions.

The Matrix shown in Table 1 was modeled after Ryan, et al., (2005). The major difference is the focus on the infrastructure support needs in the development of online teaching programs vs. Ryan, et al.'s focus on curriculum development. The descriptions and explanations provided in Table 2 review the relevant literature relating to each aspect of the Matrix.

Personal experience, and multiple needs and strategies indicated in the literature were used to design the Matrix. It is divided into threeSupportive Infrastructure Stages to clarify at what stage each particular element should be considered important in the planning process. These include the initial or Foundation stage, the Development stage, and the Maintenance or continuance stage.

The Foundation stage defines the infrastructure and procedural groundwork that should be in place before beginning an online teaching program. The Development stage outlines important elements that should be implemented during the development of an online program, and the Maintenance stage identifies processes and housekeeping elements that should be implemented to encourage a progressive online teaching program.

Table 2: Online Teaching Infrastructure Matrix

Supportive Infrastructure Implementation Stage		
Foundation	**Development**	**Maintenance**
1. Administration in tune with faculty needs	1. Online Program Policies	1. Continuously evaluate
2. IT department with customer oriented support role	2. Staff Development Program	2. Update technology only when value added
3. Effective and well supported campus network	3. Faculty Incentives	3. Periodically assess and content
4. Effective Server Support	4. Teamwork Approach	4. Set limits on online faculty personal time intrusion
5. Online Student Registration, Billing and Payment System	5. Faculty Development Program	5. Survey faculty semiannually
6. Online Bookstore Services	6. Faculty Mentoring Program	6. Survey students at end of every Semester
7. Online Library Services	7. Course Management System	7. Make changes to programs based on faculty and student input
	8. Lecture capture or course online delivery system	
	9. Online test security new online technology	

Table 3: Online Teaching Infrastructure Matrix Description.

Foundation Stage: Defines the infrastructure and procedural groundwork that should be in place before beginning an online teaching program		
Factor	**Description**	**Source(s)**
1. Administration in tune with faculty needs	Far too often administration may take action based on outside recommendations or market influences without first taking time to determine faculty needs and concerns. In an undertaking of this magnitude, it is important that administration develop a teamwork atmosphere with faculty in order to secure buy-in and the full understanding and cooperation of the faculty	McLean, 2006

Foundation Stage: Defines the infrastructure and procedural groundwork that should be in place before beginning an online teaching program		
Factor	**Description**	**Source(s)**
2. Information Technology (IT)department with a customer oriented support role	In order to create an effective and harmonious work environment for faculty who teach online, technology support personnel must learn to be extremely supportive and responsive to immediate needs of the faculty. Little is more frustrating to faculty who teach online than the breakdown of equipment or slow responsiveness of technical support. These issues need to be addressed at the highest levels to ensure the IT department is ready to support the additional demand that will result from the implementation of an online program	Frith & Kee, 2003 Jennings & Bayless, 2003
3. Effective and well supported campus network	It should be obvious that online teaching program success is going to rely heavily on the network infrastructure and campus servers to provide the needed connectivity to online students. These functions should be up and running 100% of the time in order to adequately support an online teaching program	Frith &Kee, 2003
4. Effective Server Support		
5. Online Student Registration, Billing and Payment System	Support and services for students who will enroll online must be in place before an online teaching program can be developed. These services are essential parts of the basic foundation needed to support an online teaching program. If these services are not established well in advance of implementation, online students will have difficulty with registration, counseling advice, purchase of required books, and performing research	Tallen-Runnels et al., 2006

Foundation Stage: Defines the infrastructure and procedural groundwork that should be in place before beginning an online teaching program		
Factor	**Description**	**Source(s)**
6. Online Bookstore Services		
7. Online Library Services		

Development Stage: Designed to identify the processes and elements that are essential during the development of an effective online teaching program		
Factor	Description	Source(s)
1. Online Program Policies	It is important to establish policies before or very early in the development process so that a guide to follow exists. These policies should address issues such as methods to be used in the development process; how the program will be administered; what groups or individuals will handle various aspects; how training will be conducted; what, if any, faculty incentives will be implemented; what hardware and software will be used and how technology will be configured; how the curriculum will be developed and placed in the online format; and finally, how the program will be funded	Compora, 2003
2. Staff Development Program	Staff and faculty development is essential to the strength and effectiveness of any online program. The expense of proper training pales in comparison to losses of time and energy that result from staff and faculty who lack proper training. Several studies show that it is even better if faculty development classes can be offered online, so faculty can get a better feel for what their students will experience. A healthy online training program must be preceded by a healthy development program for both faculty and staff	McQuiggan, 2007

Development Stage: Designed to identify the processes and elements that are essential during the development of an effective online teaching program		
Factor	Description	Source(s)
3. Faculty Incentives	Incentives are often expected or are offered to faculty as an enticement to work in an online program. The reason incentives are often expected or required is that online teaching is more of a strain than normal classroom teaching. Without proper control of time spent online, longer work hours and a higher workload may easily result with an online teaching program. Since students are likely to be studying in the online environment at anytime 24/7, there is often a tendency for students to also want access to the professor 24/7	Dahl, 2003; McKenzie, et al., 2004
4. Teamwork Approach	A well honed Teamwork Approach to the online teaching process can often be enough incentive in itself. If faculty and staff feel they are part of an effective well-organized team, they will often find satisfaction in that fact alone	Dahl, 2003; McKenzie, et al., 2004
5. Faculty Development Program	See #2 above	
6. Faculty Mentoring Program	Faculty mentoring has been lauded as one of the more effective methods of helping faculty retain and apply training session information. Training that takes place without mentoring is quickly forgotten and refresher training is required, but training that is followed by a well organized mentoring program has proven very effective in helping faculty remember what was discussed in the classroom. Mentoring can also be a form of encouragement to faculty who might otherwise not implement certain technology at their disposal	Helton & Helton, 2005; Mandernach, Donnelli, Dailey, & Schulte, 2005

Development Stage: Designed to identify the processes and elements that are essential during the development of an effective online teaching program		
Factor	Description	Source(s)
7. Course Management System	Selection of the proper Course Management System(CMS) is critical to the development of an online teaching program. Some of the more common include WebCT®, Blackboard®, eCollege®, Desire2Learn® ANGEL®, and Moodle™. Each CMS has unique features that may or may not be useful or user-friendly for a given institution. This is why it is critical to evaluate several systems before launching an online teaching program to ensure your institution is getting a product that will adequately meet the needs of the faculty and the students	Ruiz et al., 2006
8. Lecture capture or course online delivery system	This line of online teaching products includes Tegrity™, Impatica®, Camtasia®, Elluminate®, or Wimba®. The author calls these Course Delivery Systems because each of these products has a unique way of managing multimedia for online delivery of course lectures or lessons either synchronously or asynchronously. Most of these products are software-based and can work with or augment the capabilities of a CMS to provide better student comprehension of online course content. The careful selection of these products is also very important to the overall quality of an online teaching program	Kosak et al., 2004; Ryan, et al., 2005

Development Stage: Designed to identify the processes and elements that are essential during the development of an effective online teaching program		
Factor	Description	Source(s)
9. Online test security	Faculty are often, and rightfully, concerned about online test security. How can tests be proctored or students be monitored while taking a test online and at a distance? The answer in many cases is, you can't, but online tests can be designed so that minimal time is given to complete the test in order to restrict a student's ability to find answers they do not already know. Software is available that will restrict a student's ability to exit thetesting software until test completion, but at times this can be cumbersome and difficult to use. This issue is an important consideration in the development of an online teaching program and policies should be developed early to prevent future problems	Tallen-Runnels et al., 2006

Maintenance Stage: Designed to keep a well-developed online teaching program going strong, and to map out changes, updates and improvements that may be needed along the way		
Factor	Description	Source(s)
1. Continuously evaluate new online technology	This process ensures the online teaching program is managed and supported by the best and most up-to-date technology available	Ryan et al., 2005
2. Update technology only when value added	This is closely related to #1 in that decisions to upgrade technology should only be made when it can be proven that there will be value added with the updated technology. Many times technology is updated just because it is the latest and greatest, with no evaluation of the need for the upgrade	Ryan et al., 2005

Maintenance Stage: Designed to keep a well-developed online teaching program going strong, and to map out changes, updates and improvements that may be needed along the way		
Factor	Description	Source(s)
3. Periodically assess and update quality of course content	This process is much more critical in an online environment than with campus courses because technology and online student demands change much more rapidly. Maintaining accreditation is often another factor that requires constant monitoring and updating of online course materials. Many institutions evaluate their online curricula and update it each semester	Cook & Dupras, 2007; Tallen-Runnels et al., 2006
4. Set limits on online faculty personal time		
intrusion	This factor is often overlooked by administrators who are not familiar with the stresses and demands of an online teaching program. Without constraints, faculty could very easily become overwhelmed from the 24/7 demands on their time. Policies should be carefully designed to take this factor into account, and build in faculty release time and downtime to recuperate and regenerate. Poor management in this area can result in the loss of valuable faculty members at a very high cost to the institution	McLean, 2006
5. Survey faculty semiannually	These factors work closely with item #3 because they are an integral part of the update and upkeep process. It is common practice to provide an exit survey to students at the end of each semester, but faculty surveys are much less common. Faculty also need to have a continuous process where they can voice their opinion on what policies are working well and what may need to be changed. Faculty surveys are a good way for administrators to be proactive and keep abreast of trends and changes that may be needed	Ryan et al., 2005

Maintenance Stage: Designed to keep a well-developed online teaching program going strong, and to map out changes, updates and improvements that may be needed along the way		
Factor	Description	Source(s)
6. Survey students at end of every Semester		
7. Make changes to programs based on		
faculty and student input	This is a follow up to items #5 and #6. Surveys are great, but they have little affect if not used to make positive changes to the curriculum, the technology, and the support structure for an online teaching program. Feedback from faculty and students should be carefully evaluated and changes should be made when possible and feasible	Ryan et al., 2005

10.2.7 Results

The purpose of this study was to evaluate the availability and effectiveness of administrative support elements for online teaching faculty. Four main factors were the focus of this study and they include: 1) faculty perceptions of what elements are important to the development of a successful online teaching program; 2) perceptions on which of those elements had been successfully implemented at their specific institution; 3) factors serving to enhance faculty participation in an online teaching program, and which factors impede their involvement; and 4) faculty perceptions of the clarity and expected effectiveness of the Matrix.

The elements outlined in the Matrix were used as the basis for evaluating the infrastructure support of a premier southern medical university. The goal was to provide a means to better understand what specific administrative support services are already being provided and whether faculty feel that these services are adequate or need improvement. The investigation concentrated on identifying gaps in administrative support and training for online educators. Of the 206 survey invitations sent only 51 surveys were completed. This results in a 51% response rate which is based on the 100 full-time online teaching faculty.

Infrastructure support for online teaching faculty needs to be a well organized effort with a never ending process of improvement. At whatever state the current infrastructure is, there is always room for improvement, but the implementation of an online teaching program requires certain considerations not normally an issue in a campus only type of teaching environment. The Matrix created and tested here outlines the processes and functions needed at each stage of the implementation process in order to establish an online teaching program with the infrastructure needed to adequately support it. The contents of the Matrix are summarized below for a better understanding of how this process can be effectively implemented.

In the Foundation stage of the Matrix there are at least seven elements that need attention before an online teaching program is developed. These elements are outlined below.

- Administration in tune with faculty needs
- IT department with customer oriented support role
- Effective and well-supported campus network
- Effective Server Support
- Online Student Registration, Billing and Payment System
- Online Bookstore Services
- Online Library Services

In an undertaking of this magnitude it is important that administration develop a teamwork atmosphere between administration and faculty in order to secure buy-in and the full understanding and cooperation of the faculty. In order to create an effective and harmonious work environment for faculty who teach online, technology support personnel must learn to be extremely supportive and responsive to the immediate needs of the faculty.

An online teaching program is going to rely heavily on the network infrastructure and campus servers to provide the needed connectivity to online students. These functions should enjoy a 100% uptime, or very nearly 100% uptime in order to adequately support an online teaching program. Online student Registration, Billing and Payment System, Online Bookstore, and Online Library Services are essential parts of the basic foundation needed to support an online teaching program. These online services should be well established in advance of implementation of an online teaching program.

In the Development stage of the Matrix there are at least nine elements that need to be included as part of the development process for an online teaching program. These elements are outlined below.

- Online Program Policies
- Staff Development Program
- Faculty Incentives
- Teamwork Approach
- Faculty Development Program
- Faculty Mentoring Program
- Course Management System

- Lecture capture or online course delivery system
- Online test security

It is very important to establish clear online program policies before or very early in the development process so that everyone has a guide to follow. These policies should address issues such as methods to be used in the development process; how the program will be administered; what groups or individuals will handle various aspects; how training will be conducted; what, if any, faculty incentives will be implemented; what hardware and software will be used and how technology will be configured; how the curriculum will be developed and placed in the online format; and finally, how the program will be funded.

Staff and faculty development is essential to the health, wellbeing, and effectiveness of any online program. Several studies show that it is even better if faculty development classes can be offered online, so faculty can get a better feel for what their students will experience. A healthy online training program must be preceded by a healthy development program for both faculty and staff.

Faculty Incentives are often expected or offered to faculty as an enticement to work in an online program because online teaching is often much more of a strain than normal classroom teaching. Incentives are helpful, but a well honed Teamwork Approach to the online teaching process can often be enough incentive in itself. Teamwork is vital to the effective implementation of an online training program.

Faculty Mentoring has been lauded as one of the more effective methods of helping faculty remember and put into practice what was learned in training sessions. Training that takes place without mentoring is quickly forgotten and refresher training is required, but training that is followed by a well organized mentoring program has proven very effective in helping faculty remember what was discussed in the classroom.

Selection of the proper Course Management System (CMS) is critical to the development of an online teaching program. Some of the more common include WebCT, Blackboard, eCollege, Desire2Learn, ANGEL, and Moodle. Each CMS has unique features that may or may not be useful or user friendly for a given institution. This is why it is critical to evaluate several CMS before launching a online teaching program to ensure your institution is getting a product that will adequately meet the needs of the faculty and the students.

A lecture capture or course online delivery system may include Tegrity, Impatica, Camtasia, Elluminate, or Wimba. These products can augment the capabilities of a CMS to provide better student comprehension of online course content. Online test security should also be a consideration in the development stage. How can tests be proctored or students be monitored while taking a test online and at a distance? The answer in many cases is, you can't, but online tests can be designed so that minimal time is given to complete the test in order to restrict a student's ability to find answers they do not already know. There is software available that will restrict a student's ability to exit the testing software until this test is completed, but at times this can be cumbersome and difficult to use. This issue is an important consideration in the development of an online teaching program and policies should be developed early to head off future problems.

The Maintenance stage of the Matrix is designed to keep a well developed online teaching program going strong, and map out changes, updates and improvements that may be needed along the way. The elements of this stage are outlined below.

- Continuously evaluate new online technology
- Update technology only when value added
- Periodically assess and update quality of course content
- Set limits on online faculty personal time intrusion
- Survey faculty semiannually
- Survey students at end of every Semester

The process of continuously evaluating new online technology is important to ensuring the online teaching program is managed and supported by the best and most up-to-date technology available. Updating technology only when there is value added ensures that decisions to upgrade technology are only made when it can be proven that there will be value added with the updated technology.

Periodically assessing and updating the quality of course content is a process that is much more critical in an online environment than with campus courses because technology and online student demands change much more rapidly. Many institutions evaluate their online curriculum and update it following each semester.

Limiting intrusions into faculty personal time is critical to ensuring faculty do not become overwhelmed and burnout from the 24/7 demands on their time. Policies should be carefully designed to take this factor into account, and build in faculty release time. The result of poor management in this area can be the loss of valuable faculty members at a very high cost to the institution.

Surveying faculty and students at predetermined intervals is essential in maintaining a flow of information between administration, faculty and students. Faculty and student surveys are a good way for administrators to stay ahead of the game and keep abreast of trends and changes that may be needed. Along with frequent surveys it is important that administration stay aware of the information provided by the surveys and make changes to programs based on faculty and student input. Surveys are great, but they have little affect if they are not used to make positive changes to the curriculum, the technology, and the support structure for an online teaching program. The feedback from faculty and students should be carefully evaluated and changes should be made when possible and feasible.

The research highlighted the processes necessary for effective implementation of an online teaching program. The Matrix provides an outline for administration to follow in the implementation process. The data collected from the survey of faculty at a premier southern medical university provides invaluable insight into the specific needs of online teaching faculty at this institution, but this survey can also be used at any institution so administrators can gain a better understanding of their faculty needs with regard to online teaching.

CHAPTER

THE IMPACT OF E-LEARNING DURING COVID-19 PANDEMIC

11

11.1 INTRODUCTION: AN OVERVIEW

During the present pandemic crisis when the entire globe is sailing amid the storm, technology has played a pivotal role. Technological development and the internet have changed the lives of people immensely and have also brought a huge change in various fields. Especially in the education system E-learning has been found to be a significant tool for effectively continuing the teaching-learning process during the lockdown. The web has become one of the important mediums of learning that opens the door for people around the world to access education easily at free or lesser cost. E-learning has fixed it's root specially in the field of modern education. The need of modern learners is quite different and E- learning has been found beneficial for fulfilling their needs. The mediums of E-learning and principles of artificial intelligence are gradually gaining

Different countries though-out the globe have introduced several solutions in this pandemic to carry forward the education system. TV broadcast, Online libraries, resources, guidelines, online channels, video lectures, are highly introduced at around 96 countries. The quality of E-learning needs much improvement. Due to the sudden out-break of COVID-19 there was insufficient time to assure the quality of the E-learning or online teaching-learning process because the focus was to save and continue the education process at any cost and in all possible format during the global crisis. UNESCO portal on COVID-19 has provided immediate support to many countries across the globe to facilitate the learning-continuity and minimize the disruption of education, especially for the sake of the vulnerable class (Under National Learning Platforms and tools by UNESCO 2020). Though there are few challenges related to E-learning, it has actually emerged as a benefit to learners and educators around the world. The global crisis has specially manifested the immense importance of e-learning in today's modern world. Without the means of e-learning platforms education would have come to a sudden halt since the outbreak of the virus.

popularity in the world It is providing a solution to the learners who are unable to access the traditional means of education due to the present pandemic situation.

11.2 IMPORTANCE OF E-LEARNING IN COVID-19 CRISIS

Education is one of the key factors in building a good nation. The outbreak of the COVID-19 virus has caused a sudden suspension of schools, colleges, universities and other government institutions. Amid these hard times, teachers have been utilising e-learning platforms to impart education to the students. E-learning refers to a learning system that is conducted via electronic media. It was first used in 1999 at a CBT systems seminar. It is also described as virtual or online learning. It offers a way to share reading materials using internet through emails, documents, presentations or webinars. IT has become an important part of modern education and it shows huge involvement of ICT in the present teaching-learning process. Educators can share study materials and lectures in the form of PPT, PDF or Word document by uploading them on their respective university webpages, on whatsapp or through e-mails to maximum students during this lockdown. Lectures have been also taken through WeChat, by sharing audio-visual videos through e-mails, by different online teaching apps like Voov, Zoom, Superstar, g-suite cloud meeting and so on. The development in technologies has offered a favourable domain for teaching-learning processes. It offers teachers to change their pedagogical approaches. It enhances the teaching and learning procedures. The teachers can motivate students to enhance their learning skills through innovative ways. E-learning has brought a huge change in the traditional methods of teaching and learning. Due to ongoing of COVID-19 an increased number of students are found to use the learning platform and apps. Some of the platforms are already established like ED-TECH and cloud computing as they are available in reasonable prices and are easy to access.

11.3 TRANSITION TO ONLINE-EDUCATION IN EDUCATIONAL INSTITUTES DURING THE COVID PANDEMIC CRISIS

Since the outbreak of the COVID-19 virus, educational institutions from all around the world have migrated from the traditional methods of learning to imparting education through online means. The education system has been suddenly shifted from the conventional classroom environment to electronic devices and online applications Most universities in India have asked the Professors and students to opt for e-learning platforms for educational purposes and to motivate students to study from their respective residents. The faculty members were urged to provide study materials in the form of PPT, PDFs or Word documents and other forms such as audio, videos to upload on online platforms. Chinese universities have implemented online education since the starting of the 21st century. With the widespread of the virus, educational procedures have been accomplished via apps like Zoom and Voov. Various undergraduate and graduate courses have been provided to students through online means. In Iraq, students have been using online platforms and applications since the global lockdown. Mostly apps like Google classroom, Teams and Zoom have been used to fulfil the academic needs. The Education Ministry of Georgia has provided the application of Microsoft Teams for all the public schools.

The Association of African Universities have created an online resource page to aid educational institutions in proper planning of class lessons and to easily shift to E-learning methods. The outbreak of the Pandemic has caused the association to offer efficient learning through online mode of education. The Association of American Colleges and Universities are providing a wide range of webinars to support educators and learners. Virtual seminars and discussions are been conducted to help the students to cope with the ongoing tough times.

11.4 MOST UNIVERSITIES ARE UPLOADING STUDY MATERIALS ON THEIR RESPECTIVE UNIVERSITY WEBSITES

In this pandemic situation, well-known companies like Google, Microsoft, Zoom and Slack have offered many features of their products that could be beneficial in the field of education for free to the educational institutes. According to the recorded report Microsoft team users were 750 as of 10th March but by 24th March it has risen up to 138698 which is indeed a significant growth. Zoom has elevated the video calling time limits in Italy, Japan, US and China on request. The world still demands much more access to Zoom and Google Meet communication solution facilities. Thus, globally there has been a huge and sudden change in the field of academia with the spread of the deadly COVID-19 virus. There has been a global transition to online methods of teaching and learning. The conventional classroom atmosphere has been replaced by digital means to stop the spread of the virus and to ensure safety of the educators and learners.

11.5 ADVANTAGES OF E-LEARNING

E-learning fulfils the needs of today's learners at their own comfort and requirements. Thus it has proven to be fruitful because of various reasons. It can be availed at any time at the learner's own convenience by purchasing the subscriptions of different platforms or logging in to access the courses (Colchester et al., 2017). It can share and offer teaching-learning materials in diverse formats such as slideshows, audios, videos, PDFs, e-mails, word documents and so on. Webinars and direct communications with teachers via various chat forums or messaging is also an open option in E-learning process. It offers free access to certain e-manuals like PDFs. It provides clear, easy, gradual instructions for better understanding of the learners. It is often regarded as the most suitable way for self-learning. It provides a wide range of materials for the learners that covers almost all topics and doubts (Bajaj and Sharma, 2018).

11.6 CHALLENGES OF E-LEARNING

Due to the pandemic crisis, there has been a huge, disruptive shift from existing educational system to online education system. An online course requires detailed lesson plans to design good study materials. Certain challenges of online education include, lack of online teaching skills in educators, online preparation of lesson plans as it is very time-consuming, lack of appropriate support from the technical teams, and traffic overload in online educational platforms. Not only the teachers but the students are also facing challenges due to their deficiency of proper learning attitude, lack of suitable materials for learning, more involvement in classroom learning, incapability of self- discipline, and the inadequate learning environment at some of their homes during self-isolation.

11.7 BENEFICIAL ROLE OF E-LEARNING PLATFORMS DURING THE PANDEMIC

E-learning has specially proven to be beneficial during this COVID-19 crisis. More students have opted to Ed-tech and other online platforms for education during this ongoing pandemic. Online platforms have been offering free access to live classes to help students learn comfortably from homes and a significant elevation in students have been recorded for using these educational apps. Educators of the online platforms have also started to take more live classes. Furthermore, it has been also offering free access to live classes to students. The app includes features like curriculum management, attendance control, time-table automation, homework assigning, messaging features and grading.

11.8 INSTRUCTIONAL STRATEGIES TO IMPROVE STUDENT'S ENGAGEMENT DURING E- LEARNING

The following instructional strategies can improve the E-learning efficiencies of the students when educators implement them efficiently. For the accomplishment of large-scale online education, it is very essential to generate advance contingency plans to overcome the technical problems like traffic overload in the online educational platforms. Educators have divided the teaching material into several smaller modules to enhance the focus of students and to ensure their better understanding. Faculty members have appropriately dropped the speed of their speech to drag their attention, allow them to note down the key points from the lectures and the jot down the necessary information from the board in an audio-visual lecture. Inexperienced faculty members consulted online teaching assistants to ensure the objectives and needs of each and every class that has to be taken by them. Educators have modified their various teaching techniques by providing creative and skilful assignments that can fulfill the learning requirements of the students for engaging them during the online classes. The faculty incorporated online teaching methods and offline self-studying. Professors can engage students in discussion to encourage their perspectives and can provide feedbacks on their assignments. Through this mode of teaching student will not learn surface, ambiguous and fragmented knowledge. Instead, the students would experience thorough learning through diverse discussions. Insufficient pre-class study preparation, limited participation in class discussions, and inadequate discussion depth are common phenomena in traditional in-class teaching, similarly, those issue should not be overlooked in online teaching. The difficulty, length and quality of teaching material should match the student's online learning behavioural characteristics and academic readiness. Timely feedback should be shared by the educators with their students to motivate them Educators should provide email guidance within and after class as well as online audio-visual tutoring. It is always advisable to adopt few measures for the improvement of student's in-depth participation in online classes. This would help in generation high-quality participation of students. Student's mental health should be taken into consideration and various suitable measures should be taken by the educators to relieve their mental stress and anxieties during the COVID-19 crisis, to ensure that the students could regularly, effectively and actively participate in their online learning sessions.

11.9 INEQUALITIES FACED BY LEARNERS AND EDUCATORS IN THE PRESENT SCENARIO

Educators are experiencing huge weight on their mental health as they have to endure the load of the education system during these difficult times. They have to follow administrative and ministerial directives. Teaching through online mediums has become a challenging task for most of the educators. Lack of resources is also becoming a great hurdle for the teaching-learning process. Sometimes the unhealthy environments and technical issues are reasons behind discontinued process of teaching-learning. Learners sometimes do not have proper means to learn from the online medium. As most of the learners and educators are habituated with the traditional way of teaching-learning processes the outcome on E-learning is obtained comparatively low. Students are also facing difficulties with poor internet connection majorly in few places of the world like India, Iraq, Iran, Syria, Africa etc. Due to lack of motivation and shaky mental health issue E-learning is not providing expected success in the global education system.

11.10 IMPACT OF COVID-19 ON LIBRARIES

Lockdown has closed the physical access of library. The day to day work of library is hampered during this pandemic situation. Housekeeping activities (such as acquisition, processing, classification, cataloguing, and periodicals subscription) of Library and services had a great impact specially circulation and reading room facility. Some observations on impact of Covid-19 on libraries are notes as below:

- ***Restricted access to the Library for students*:** Reading hall and stack room access was not available for students.
- ***Circulation of books*:** Issuing of books and current reading resources access such as periodicals, newspapers also restricted.

- ***Reaching to users became challenging*:** Students are connected to the college through online mode and hence face to face connectivity is disconnected. Reaching to each and every user of each class become challenging for library.
- ***Adverse effect on library resources Utilization*:** As students were connected through online mode, hence visitors' record of the library, use of various sections (*e.g.* Reading Room, Stack Room, Internet section) were restricted and affected adversely on physical utilization of library.
- Library Facilities such as open access restricted
- Sanitization has become an essential part.
- ***Effects of printed academic resources*:** Supply of books, periodicals, newspapers was not available for some period. Most of the books recommended in the syllabus became out of stock with publishers during this Covid-19 pandemic situation, some of the periodicals were available and some of them were not printed for some period.

11.11 CHALLENGES AND OPPORTUNITIES

Challenges: Online working system requires technical support to run and execute. In this pandemic situation, everyone is connected through this online mode.

- **Internet Connectivity:** The most important aspect is internet connectivity unless and until you have net connection then only you can survive in this online mode.
- **Digital Literacy:** Effective services can only be delivered and utilized when there is a digital literacy. Digital literacy is essential factor and need training for users
- **Technical Barriers:** Online services are dependent upon various technical aspects and with the strong technical support system these services can be delivered
- **No Physical Connectivity:** This situation has hampered the physical connectivity. This online mode has broken down the personal touch among library and users which impacted on library services.

Opportunities: Challenges always make opportunities. This pandemic situation also created new opportunities for libraries.

- **Transformation of Traditional Library to Digital Library:** Traditional Library is transformed into Digital Library. The current situation has given wider exposure to Digital Library. Digital Library is full-fledged working in a virtual domain for library users.
- **Online Services:** Every service is available in an online mode. Various social media and social networking sites are used effectively in the current scenario. Facebook, WhatsApp are the most effective mode of communication among users. Library Webpage has become mirror of library.

- **Online Connectivity:** Various online social networking tools, library website, Online Catalogue, Library Blog, many others online tools are made available 24*7 connectivity for users
- **Remote Access:** Access to library resources are available through various domain through remotely. E-resources are available through VPN as well as User Name and password basis. Doorstep Services are made available for users.

11.12 BARRIERS/OBSTACLES TO PROVIDE SMART LIBRARY SERVICES

- Even though, library and information centers restructured with modern technologies and converted traditional to modern form, there are various obstacles specifically in rural area.
- Various barriers are still there for libraries to reach user. Every user does not have smart phones and internet connectivity.

11.13 NEW HORIZONS/DIMENSIONS OF LIBRARY IN COVID-19

- ***Information Literacy Sessions*:** Every year library conducts orientation program for freshers. Library can conduct online induction program, Orientation to the online e-resources and accessibility for teachers as well as students. Information Literacy sessions, training programs can be conducted online.
- ***Web based Library Services*:** Access to the library webpage, WebOPAC (Online Catalogue), Display all the information on the website and guide for the access to the e-resources to be upload, Library Blog: to give current information and updates,
- ***QR Codes*:** can be used for the access of library services and facilities
- ***Digital Library*:** Digital Library is one of the important aspects where all the access such as online resources, Institutional Repository made available to the library users.
- ***Digital Connectivity*:** Library can connect to its users through various social networking tools such as Whats App, Facebook, twitter, Instagram, *etc.* Various online meeting apps are available such as ZOOM, Webex, Google Meet, Microsoft team where online connection can be set up and library can approach users.
- ***Library Activity and Events*:** Online activities can be conducted such as library day celebration, Vachan Prerana din. Exhibitions can be held digitally. Digital Exhibitions can be conducted and link could be shared among teachers and students.

- ***Access to e-resources***: Online User guide Links, You tube Videos, Access from the Library webpage or Digital library access is useful for the use of e-resources.
- **Conventional Services into Digital Form such as:**
  - **Online I-card system:** Every year library prepares I-Cards due to this Covid 19: the system can work with the help of google form. Google form link can be sent to students and i-card forms are filled by the students through this system and I -Cards can be prepared.
  - **Reference Service:** Library can use Ask a Librarian Service where students can sent request and library can make available and provide requisite information
  - **Circulation Desk:** Issuing of books with open access has become a difficult task. To overcome the problem students can approach online to library and send a request. Library can issue requisite material with precaution to make in advance with time and date.
  - **Current Awareness and SDI:** These both service are effectively work in an online mode. Email Alert, Document delivery, SMS alert are the effective mode of communication to provide CAS and SDI.

Although all these services are available in the present scenario, these are effectively used in COVID 19 pandemic. This situation and digital work culture reflected the adoption of digital literacy and technology among library staff.

11.14 MEANS TO BRIDGE THE UNEQUAL GAP BETWEEN LEARNERS AND EDUCATORS

The pandemic had undeniably made clear that countries throughout the globe need to allocate funds for proper training of educators and to create innovative learning domain that could provide education to the learners in the easiest way. This situation of crisis shows the urgency to consider the needs of the learners. Education materials and pedagogical provisions should be greatly introduced in all emergency curricula which could keep educators and learners safe and mentally healthy in the present pandemic crisis. Education ministers or the government should provide funds for the disadvantaged children and focus on the educational needs of marginalized learners. Most significantly National authorities in their respective countries should provide efficient measures to convey the vital significance of wellbeing for both students and educators.

11.15 AT A GLANCE

It has been recommended by Google that the Google classroom platform can be integrated to Google meet system for creating laboratory practices for STEM courses (Google. 2020). Other suitable educational platforms can also be integrated to Google meet system for lab practices. Educators and students should be provided suitable trainings to become efficient users of educational apps that are widely used globally such as Voov, Zoom, Google classroom, Teams etc during the COVID-19 crisis. The pandemic situation demands tech-savvy and highly skilled educators. Thus, educators should enhance their knowledge and skills that is required for the maximum usage of technological devices, E-learning tools, educational apps and other online platforms like TV School, Online portals, Google Meet, Slack, Zoom, Edu-Page etc. Students should be encouraged to use different educational apps and should be provided with easy, effective and interesting study materials by the educators to drag student's attention towards eLearning. Various online-learning types can be also promoted to the students and educators. They could get appropriate online-training to use various learning methods such as knowledge-based training, hybrid training, synchronous training and asynchronous trainings.

BIBLIOGRAPHY

- Ardichvilli, Alexander; Page, Vaughn; Wentling, Tim (2003). "Motivation and barriers to participation in virtual knowledge sharing in communities of practice". Journal of Knowledge Management. 7 (1): 64–77. doi:10.1108/13673270310463626. S2CID 14849211.
- Barton, T; Tusting, K (2005). Beyond Communities of Practice: Language Power and Social Context. Cambridge University Press. ISBN 978-0-521-83643-2.
- Bourdieu, P. (1991). Language and symbolic power. Cambridge, Massachusetts: Harvard University Press. ISBN 9780674510401.
- Bourdieu, P. (1991). Language and symbolic power. Cambridge, Massachusetts: Harvard University Press.
- Brown, John Seely; Duguid, Paul (2000). "Balancing act: How to capture knowledge without killing it". Harvard Business Review.
- Bukowitz, Wendi R.; Williams, Ruth L. (1999). The Knowledge Management Fieldbook. FT Press. ISBN 978-0273638827.
- Cabrera, A.; Cabrera, E. F. (2002). "Knowledge-sharing Dilemmas". Organization Studies. 23 (5): 687–710. CiteSeerX 10.1.1.192.4368. doi:10.1177/0170840602235001. S2CID 14998234.
- Chohan, Usman (2013). "Fostering a Community of Practice Among the Parliamentary Budget Offices of the Commonwealth". Commonwealth Parliamentary Review, "The Parliamentarian". 31 (3): 198–201 (40–43).
- Chua, Alton (October 2002). "Book Review: Cultivating Communities of Practice". Journal of Knowledge Management Practice.
- Corder, S. P. (1967). The significance of learners' errors. International Review of Applied Linguistics in Language Teaching, 5, 161–170.
- Cox, Andrew (2005). "What are communities of practice? A comparative review of four seminal works" (PDF). Journal of Information Science. 31 (6): 527–540. doi:10.1177/0165551505057016. S2CID 206453933.

- Dalkir, K. (2005). Knowledge Management in Theory and Practice. Burlington: Elsevier Butterworth-Heinemann. ISBN 978-0-7506-7864-3.
- Dalkir, Kimiz (2005). Knowledge management in theory and practice. Cambridge, Massachusetts: MIT Press. ISBN 9780262036870.
- Dalton, R.A (2011). Knowledge Transfer for the Military Leader. pp. Chapter 5. Archived from the original on 2018-11-09. Retrieved 2018-12-11.
- Davenport, Thomas H.; Prusak, Lawrence (2000). Working knowledge. How organizations manage what they know, 2nd Edition. Cambridge, Massachusetts: Harvard Business School Press. ISBN 978-1-57851-301-7.
- Dubé, L.; Bourhis, A.; Jacob, R. (2005). "The impact of structuring characteristics on the launching of virtual communities of practice". Journal of Organizational Change Management. 18 (2): 145–166. doi:10.1108/09534810510589570.
- Duguid, Paul (2005). """The Art of Knowing": Social and Tacit Dimensions of Knowledge and the Limits of the Community of Practice". The Information Society. 21 (2): 109–118. doi:10.1080/01972240590925311. S2CID 6881436.
- Duguid, Paul (2005). "The Art of Knowing: Social and Tacit Dimensions of Knowledge and the Limits of the Community of Practice". The Information Society. 21 (2): 109–118. doi:10.1080/01972240590925311. S2CID 6881436.
- Gannon-Leary, P.M. & Fontainha, E. "Communities of Practice and virtual learning communities: benefits, barriers and success factors" ELearning Papers 26 Sept 2007 [Accessed Nov 2007]
- Grossman, P. (2001). Toward a theory of teacher community. 103, 942–1012.: Teachers College Record. ISBN 978-0-7506-7864-3.
- Ipe, M. (2003), "Knowledge sharing on organizations: a conceptual framework", Human Resource Development Review, Vol. 2 No. 4, p.341
- Kietzmann, Jan; Plangger, Kirk; Eaton, Ben; Heilgenberg, Kerstin; Pitt, Leyland; Berthon, Pierre (2013). "Mobility at work: A typology of mobile communities of practice and contextual ambidexterity" (PDF). Journal of Strategic Information Systems. 3 (4): 282–297. doi:10.1016/j.jsis.2013.03.003. S2CID 3714450. Archived from the original (PDF) on 2013-11-10. Retrieved 2013-11-22.
- Kimble, Chris; Hildreth, Paul; Bourdon, Isabelle (2008). Communities of Practice: Creating Learning Environments for Educators. Information Age Publishing. ISBN 978-1-59311-863-1.
- Lave, Jean; Wenger, Etienne (1991). Situated Learning: Legitimate Peripheral Participation. Cambridge: Cambridge University Press. ISBN 978-0-521-42374-8.; first published in 1990 as Institute for Research on Learning report 90-0013

- Lesser, E.L., Fontaine, M.A. & Slusher J.A., Knowledge and Communities, Butterworth-Heinemann, 2000
- Lesser, L.E.; Storck, J. (2001). "Communities of Practice and organizational performance" (PDF). 40 (4). IBM Systems Journal. Archived from the original (PDF) on 2011-04-09.
- McDermott, Richard; Archibald, Douglas (2010). "Harnessing Your Staff's Informal Networks". Harvard Business Review. Vol. 88, no. 3.
- Miller, D.; Shamsie, J. (1996). "The resource-based view of the firm in two environments: The Hollywood film studios from 1936 to 1965". Academy of Management Journal. 39 (5): 519–543. CiteSeerX 10.1.1.598.9250. doi:10.2307/256654. JSTOR 256654.
- Nonaka, Ikujiro (1991). "The knowledge creating company". Harvard Business Review. 69 (6 Nov–Dec): 96–104. Archived from the original on 2009-11-25.
- Perkins, D. N., & Salomon, G. (1992). Transfer of learning. International Encyclopedia of Education (2nd ed.). Oxford, UK: Pergamon Press.
- Polyani, Michael; Sen, Amartya (2009). The Tacit Dimension. University Of Chicago Press; Reissue edition. ISBN 978-0-226-67298-4.
- Putnam, Robert (2001). "Social Capital: Measurement and Consequences". ISUMA (spring): 41–51.
- Roberts, Joanne (2006). "Limits to Communities of Practice". Journal of Management Studies. 43 (3): 623–639. doi:10.1111/j.1467-6486.2006.00618.x. S2CID 153340083.
- Saint-Onge, H & Wallace, D, Leveraging Communities of Practice, Butterworth Heinemann, 2003.
- Salomon, G., & Perkins, D. N. (1989). Rocky roads to transfer: rethinking mechanisms of a neglected phenomenon. Educational Psychologist, 24, 113–142.
- Seely Brown, John; Duguid, Paul (1991). "Organizational learning and communities-of-practice: Toward a unified view of working, learning and innovation". Organization Science. 2 (1): 40–57. doi:10.1287/orsc.2.1.40. JSTOR 2634938. S2CID 16012075.
- Serban, Andreea M.; Luan, Jing (2002). "An Overview of Knowledge Management" (PDF). University of Kentucky. Retrieved 17 April 2013.
- Sheridan, Molly (2015). "Got a Question? Get Answers on Twitter #musochat". New Music Box. Retrieved 2020-04-19.
- Shields, Patricia M. (2003). "The Community of Inquiry: Classical Pragmatism and Public Administration". Administration & Society. 35 (5): 510–538. CiteSeerX 10.1.1.1008.9702. doi:10.1177/0095399703256160. ISSN 0095-3997. S2CID 146759673.

- Smith, M.K. (2003). "Communities of practice". The Encyclopedia of Informal Education.
- Sveiby, Karl-Erik; Simon, Roland (2002). "Collaborative climate and effectiveness of knowledge work - an empirical study". Journal of Knowledge Management. 6 (5): 420–433. CiteSeerX 10.1.1.323.9870. doi:10.1108/13673270210450388. ISSN 1367-3270.
- Thomas, J.C.; Kellogg, W.A; Erickson, T. (2001). "The knowledge management puzzle: Human and social factors in knowledge management" (PDF). IBM Systems Journal. 40 (4): 863–884. doi:10.1147/sj.404.0863.
- Tinberg, H. (2017). Teaching for Transfer: A passport for writing in new contexts. Peer Review, 19, 17-20.
- Tu, Chih-Hsiung (2002). "The measurement of social presence in an online learning environment". International Journal on E-learning. April–June: 34–45.
- van Winkelen, Christine. "Inter-Organizational Communities of Practice". Archived from the original on 2004-02-08.
- Vignati R.(2009) Il transfer cognitivo nei processi di apprendimento: un paradifma del cambiamento e della creatività?
- Wallace, Danny P. (2007). Knowledge management: Historical and cross-disciplinary themes. Westport, Connecticut: Libraries Unlimited. ISBN 978-1-59158-502-2.
- Wasko, M.; Faraj, S. (2000). ""It is what one does": why people participate and help others in electronic communities of practice". Journal of Strategic Information Systems. 9 (2–3): 155–173. doi:10.1016/S0963-8687(00)00045-7.
- Wenger, Etienne (1998). Communities of Practice: Learning, Meaning, and Identity. Cambridge: Cambridge University Press. ISBN 978-0-521-66363-2.
- Wenger, Etienne; McDermott, Richard; Snyder, William M. (2002). Cultivating Communities of Practice (Hardcover). Harvard Business Press; 1 edition. ISBN 978-1-57851-330-7.
- Yao et al (2021) Construction Safety Knowledge Sharing on Twitter: A Social Network Analysis, Safety Science, 143, 105411, https://www.researchgate.net/publication/353546913_Safety_knowledge_sharing_on_Twitter_A_social_network_analysis.

INDEX